D-DAY

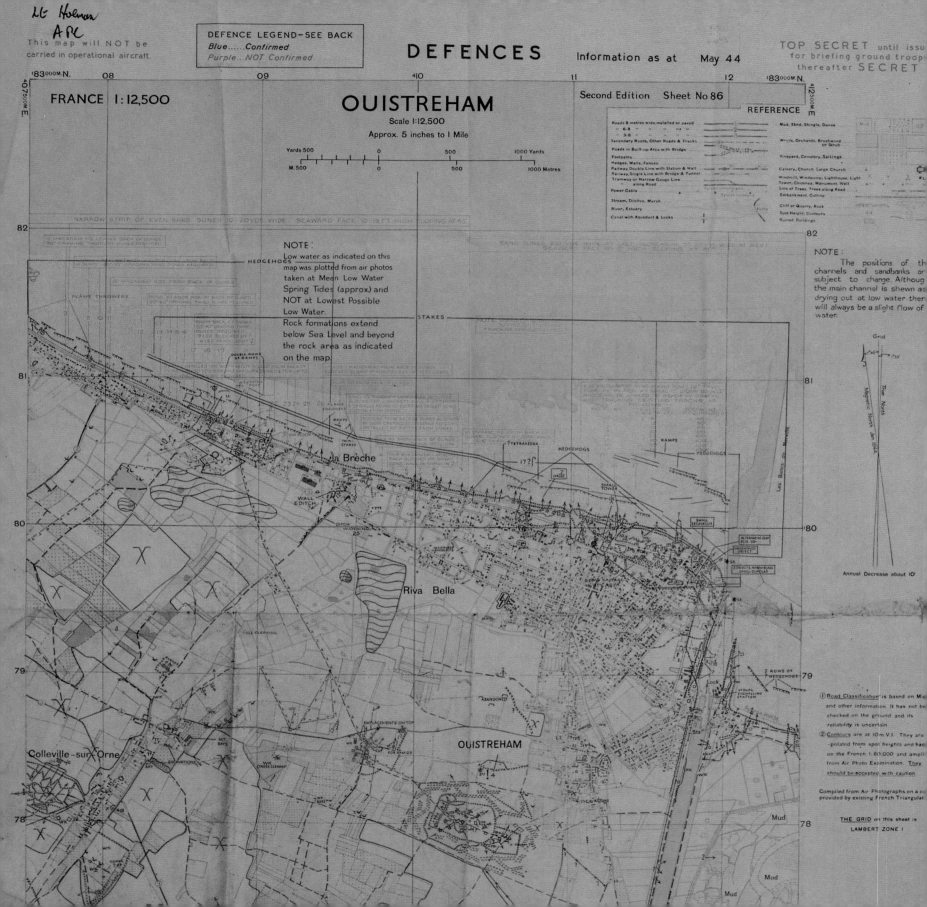

Lt Holman
APC

This map will NOT be
carried in operational aircraft.

DEFENCE LEGEND—SEE BACK
Blue......Confirmed
Purple..NOT Confirmed

DEFENCES

Information as at   May 44

TOP SECRET until issu
for briefing ground troop
thereafter SECRET

FRANCE 1:12,500

OUISTREHAM

Scale 1:12,500

Approx. 5 inches to 1 Mile

Second Edition   Sheet No 86

REFERENCE

Yards 500   0   500   1000 Yards
M. 500   0   500   1000 Metres

NOTE:
Low water as indicated on this
map was plotted from air photos
taken at Mean Low Water
Spring Tides (approx) and
NOT at Lowest Possible
Low Water.
Rock formations extend
below Sea Level and beyond
the rock area as indicated
on the map.

NOTE:
The positions of th
channels and sandbanks ar
subject to change. Althoug
the main channel is shewn as
drying out at low water ther
will always be a slight flow of
water.

la Brèche

Riva Bella

Colleville-sur-Orne

OUISTREHAM

Grid

Annual Decrease about 10'

① Road Classification is based on Mi
and other information. It has not be
checked on the ground and its
reliability is uncertain
② Contours are at 10m.V.I. They are
-polated from spot heights and had
on the French 1:80,000 and ampli
from Air Photo Examination. They
should be accepted with caution

Compiled from Air Photographs on a c
provided by existing French Triangulat

THE GRID on this sheet is
LAMBERT ZONE I

Mud

Mud

Mud

D-DAY

6 JUNE 1944

THE NORMANDY LANDINGS

RICHARD COLLIER

SPECIAL PHOTOGRAPHY BY JOHN KALBIAN

THE ABBEVILLE PUBLISHING GROUP
NEW YORK · LONDON · PARIS

TO THE MEN AND WOMEN OF D–DAY

Went the day well?
We died and never knew.
But, well or ill,
Freedom, we died for you.
ANON.

First published in the United States of America in 1992 by
Canopy Books, a division of Abbeville Publishing Group,
488 Madison Avenue, New York, NY 10022.

First published in the United Kingdom in 1992 by Cassell,
Villiers House, 41/47 Strand, London

Library of Congress Cataloging-in-Publication Data
A catalog record for this book is available from the
Library of Congress.

Printed and bound in Singapore.

ISBN 1-55859-396-9

CONTENTS

AT FIRST THE demands were muted, no more than graffiti chalked on factory walls in the misty English autumn of 1941: SECOND FRONT NOW. But by the spring of 1942 the appeals had grown insistent, daubed in paint on bridges and railway arches: SECOND FRONT NOW! It was suddenly an issue bannered in newspaper headlines, stridently proclaimed at Saturday afternoon rallies in London's Trafalgar Square and at Speaker's Corner in Hyde Park: SECOND FRONT NOW!!

The anger was understandable. Since June 22, 1941, when Adolf Hitler launched 186 divisions against his erstwhile ally, Josef Stalin, the brunt of World War Two had been borne by the Russians. From September, Leningrad, "the White City" of Peter the Great, faced its historic 932-day siege. December saw a momentary respite: the pitiless Russian winter and a fierce counter-offensive by Marshal Georgi Zhukov witnessed fifty-one German divisions in retreat from Moscow. But on May 16 Korch, the heart of Crimean industry, was to fall, followed by Sevastopol on July 2. Soon Stalingrad, too, would be a front-line city.

The belief, widely held by the British public and shared, since Pearl Harbor, by the American Chiefs of Staff, was that the Allies must measure up to these sacrifices and open a second front.

It was a concept that the Russians had urged from the first. As early as June 23, Ivan Maisky, the Russian Ambassador, had broached the creation of a Second Front with the Foreign Secretary, Anthony Eden—and on July 18 Stalin in turn took up the cudgels. What he sought was primarily a British offensive in

Without Moscow's sanction I could not undertake negotiations for the conclusion of an Anglo-Soviet military alliance . . . But what about creating a Second Front in France? . . . The Germans were always afraid of a Second Front . . . Churchill, as I had supposed, was unfavourable to this idea. . . . Three years of stubborn struggle by the Soviet Union were required before the Second Front in France was at last opened, and then only because the western powers were afraid that the Red Army might come to Berlin before they did.

(from *Memoirs of a Soviet Ambassador* by Ivan Maisky)

Trafalgar Square, London, in wartime trim. Yet even in the grimmest years of war, this people's arena saw political meetings and rallies (See page 9). (Hulton Picture Library)

R.O.F. WORKERS NEED

ODO-RO-NO

cream DEODORANT

Checks perspiration instantly.
Gives 1-3 days' protection.
Dries at once.
Does not irritate the skin.
Protects clothes from perspiration stain and perspiration rot, even if dress shields are unobtainable.

Keeps the armpits cool and fresh.
Keeps uniforms fresh and sweet as cotton frocks.
Can be used before or after shaving.

WARNING! *Keep lid tightly screwed down when not in use*

SAVINGS STAMPS HAVE GOT ME IN A STICKY MESS

northern France to divert Hitler's armies from the east—or, failing this, twenty-five to thirty British divisions to fight on the Russian front.

In vain, Winston Churchill strove to convey the reality. "The Germans have forty divisions in France alone," he replied, with truth, on July 20, "and the whole coast . . . bristles with cannons, wire, pillboxes and beach-mines . . . To attempt a landing in force would be to encounter a bloody repulse. . . ."

The fact that 400,000 British troops were then engaged against the Afrika Korps in the Western Desert did nothing to appease Stalin or,

indeed, President Franklin Roosevelt; both men saw these Middle East campaigns as little more than "Mediterranean ventures." And to Churchill's dismay, the Russian cause now loomed larger on the home front than that of his cherished British Empire. Stalin's appearance on a cinema newsreel prompted warm applause. "They worship the very thought of Stalin," noted the poet Stephen Spender, then an officer in the Auxiliary Fire Service, "Russia is their only religion"; for on blitz-free nights Spender's firemen were foremost in scrawling up second front slogans. Sales of the *Soviet War News* had climbed to 50,000 weekly, British Communist Party membership neared an all-time level of 65,000, and at Birmingham, where tank workers painted "Marx," "Lenin" and "Another for Joe" on each completed chassis, Ambassador Maisky was hoisted high on to a tank by shift workers who sang the *Internationale*.

Thus, on March 9, 1942, when Roosevelt hinted broadly, "I am becoming more and more interested in the establishment of a new front this summer on the European continent. . . .," Churchill was goaded to act.

The answer, given the limited nature of Britain's resources, was an uneasy compromise—known variously as a "dress rehearsal" for the invasion of Europe or "a reconnaissance in force"—but one which would test the amphibious techniques of Vice-Admiral Lord Mountbatten's Combined Operations Headquarters to the full. Their task would be to seize and temporarily hold a port on the English Channel, a port, above all, that was well within the range of RAF fighter cover.

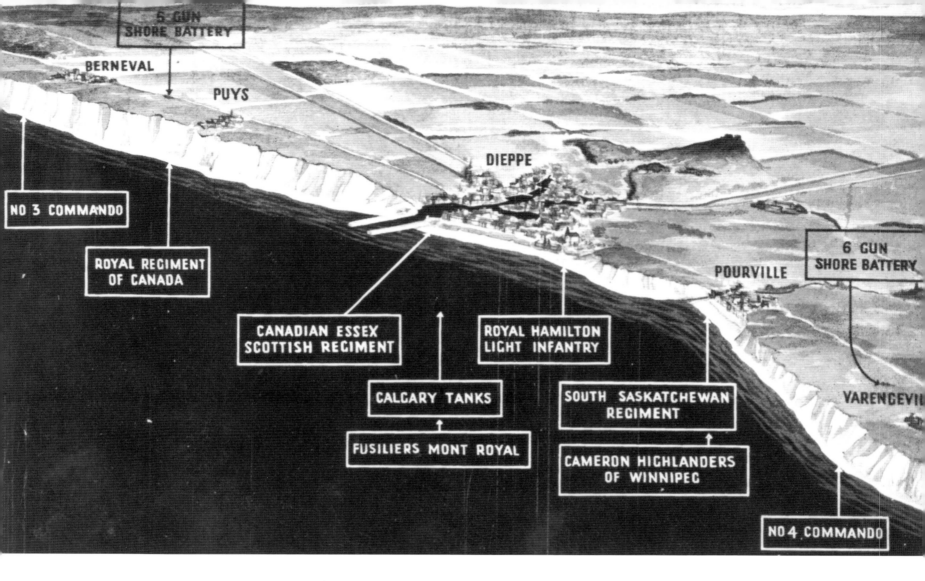

5 GUN SHORE BATTERY

BERNEVAL

PUYS

DIEPPE

NO 3 COMMANDO

ROYAL REGIMENT OF CANADA

6 GUN SHORE BATTERY

POURVILLE

CANADIAN ESSEX SCOTTISH REGIMENT

ROYAL HAMILTON LIGHT INFANTRY

VARENGEVIL

CALGARY TANKS

SOUTH SASKATCHEWAN REGIMENT

FUSILIERS MONT ROYAL

CAMERON HIGHLANDERS OF WINNIPEG

NO 4 COMMANDO

Dieppe: the Attack Plan.
(Author's Collection)

By a process of elimination, Dieppe, sixty-seven miles distant from Newhaven, Sussex, on the old peacetime cross-Channel route, known, from its white wedding-cake Casino, as "the poor man's Monte Carlo," became the subject of an attack-plan code-named "Operation Rutter" on Saturday April 4.

Although this was the first-ever Combined Operation, its objectives were strictly limited. No permanent beachhead was envisaged at Dieppe. It was to be a nine-hour one-tide oper-ation, allowing for five hours ashore and four for withdrawal. The 10,000 raiders involved would carry food, medical supplies and ammunition for one day only. In assaulting six separate beaches along a ten-mile front they had three primary missions: following the neutralization of two powerful coastal batteries, they were to capture the port in something close to working order, destroy the aerodrome at St Aubin, and examine, perhaps destroy, the radar station at Pourville.

It would be the first time the Allies had set foot on French soil since the 1940 débâcle of Dunkirk, and it was also, noted the doomsayers, the first massed amphibious Allied landing since the disaster of Gallipoli in 1915.

At the same time Churchill faced another political pressure — this time from William Lyon Mackenzie King, the Canadian Premier. "I don't know how long I can go on leading my country while our troops remain inactive," he had confided on a visit to London in September 1941, for the Canadian 2nd Division, quartered round Horsham, Sussex, since December 1939 had thus far seen no action in the field. The result was bitter disillusion on the Canadian home front; a recent recruiting drive had failed to take fire, and military commentators sniped constantly at "our army of noble idlers" or "the taxpayers' army of remittance men."

Although the Canadian Army Commander, Lieutenant-General Andrew McNaughton, spoke of them proudly as "a dagger pointed at the heart of Berlin," the 2nd Division, through no fault of their own, had tangled more frequently with the Sussex police than with their Axis foes. Thus they became the ideal choice to fill the breach.

Even so, at 10 a.m. on Tuesday August 18, as the long convoys of trucks groaned from market towns like Lewes and Billingshurst towards their main embarkation ports, hearts were high. At last the British were giving them the chance to prove their worth — and after five weeks' intensive training at Freshwater, on the Isle of Wight, the Canadians felt a quiet confidence. One chaplain, Father Major Armand Sabourin, of the Fusiliers Mont-Royal of Quebec, would afterwards remember how his battalion embarked at Shoreham "with such enthusiasm as I had never witnessed before and never will again."

Survivors of that day recall this mood as universal. At 11.30 p.m., as the massed flotilla of infantry landing ships, "Hunt" class destroyers and tank landing craft headed from Newhaven and Shoreham and Portsmouth towards the swept channels through the mine-fields, few were beset by doubts. Lieutenant Jerry Wood, of the Royal Canadian Engineers, commanding a beach assault group detailed to help more than 100 Churchill tanks gain the main promenade, remembered it as "a beautiful, moony, balmy night, so peaceful that it was hard to believe that we'd be working at our trade in the morning." Aboard the head-quarters ship, the destroyer HMS *Calpe*, the Canadian commander, Major-General J. H. "Ham" Roberts, a tall, tough gunner from Vancouver, assured the American war corres-pondent, Quentin Reynolds, "The plan is good, the men are keen and they know what to do." Captain Roy Murray, commanding six officers and forty-five men of the newly formed US Rangers, who were there to furnish back-up support, marvelled, "Never realized before how quiet a combined operation can be."

Only Major Brian McCool, of the Royal Regiment of Canada, the Principal Military Landing Officer, had cause to wonder. Two days later, following McCool's capture by the Germans, his interrogator was to put the question point-blank, "Look, McCool, it was too big for a raid and too small for an invasion. What was it?" To this McCool could only reply,

Let's have less nonsense from the friends of Joe:/We laud — we love him, but this nonsense: NO,/In 1940, when we bore the brunt,/We could have done, boys, with a Second Front.

(—A. P. Herbert, June 1942)

Jubilee, meaning a year celebrating release of slaves, cancellation of debts, and a return of property to former owners, usually proclaimed by the sound of trumpets, was an unfortunate code name. It implied that the raiders would sound a blast on the trumpets, the West Wall would crumble, and France would be handed back to Frenchmen — something that in 1942 could be little else than wishful thinking.

(from *Dieppe: The Shame and The Glory* by Terence Robertson)

It started early, the
attacking trek/by sea and
sky. Early/and quietly,
like a well-told lie.

His hair was very crisp
and curly./I ran my
fingers through his hair
while he/expressed his
views/on this and that
and my new hat and the
length of movie
queues./Nothing
dramatic. And now
he's—there. And I/
tune-in to the News.

The barge-like boats,
packed panting-tight,/eat
up the narrow strip of
water,/and in the sky the
grey wings wait/poised on
the edge of a well-planned
slaughter.

Lieutenant-Colonel the
Lord Lovat. (The
Weidenfeld Archive)

"If you can tell *me* the answer, I would be very grateful."

Of the 6100 Canadians cramped aboard 237 ships heading for Dieppe—"a pea-shooter armada," one man scoffed—few knew the tortuous history of the raid to date. As "Operation Rutter" it had been timed for Friday July 3, then, when the British 1st Airborne Division raised the objection of a heightening wind, cancelled—only to be resurrected, within a week and without airborne backing, as "Operation Jubilee." But whatever its code-name, the assault had found few adherents in high places. From the first, Mountbatten and his Naval Adviser, Captain John Hughes-Hallett, RN, had insisted on a heavy pre-assault bombardment, but the First Sea Lord, Admiral Sir Dudley Pound, had flatly declined to risk a battleship in the Channel narrows. Air Vice-Marshal Arthur Harris had equally refused to provide 300 bombers—"I have neither planes nor crews to spare for useless side-shows."

Thus the troops would be zeroed in on heavily manned beaches, with no more than a few bombers and cannon-firing Hurricanes to divert the German defenders. Even Lieutenant-General Bernard Montgomery, who had temporarily overseen the attack before departing for the Middle East, had only approved a frontal assault if heavy bombardment was available. The prophecy of Air Vice-Marshal Trafford Leigh-Mallory, the air commander, now seemed all too likely: "The troops will be pinned down on the beaches at the very beginning. They'll never get going again, you mark my words."

That spring, the 302nd Infantry Division, 6000 men under *Generalmajor* Conrad Haase, had turned the East Headland of the harbour—the target of the Royal Regiment of Canada—into a fortified strongpoint, transforming the cliff face into a warren of machine-gun nests and anti-tank guns. Following this, they had wrought the same transformation on the West Headland, the objective of the South Saskatchewan Regiment. But these had been only routine precautions, since *Feldmarschall* Gerd von Rundstedt, Commander-in-Chief, West, had told his staff, "Dieppe is a most unsuitable place for invasion." The task force could still count on the element of surprise.

At 3.47 a.m. on Wednesday August 19, that element was abruptly lost. At Berneval, four miles east of the main harbour, E-boats escorting a German tanker sighted British landing barges moving in and opened fire. Aboard the ships at that moment, hundreds of men, faces clammy with sweat under their netted steel helmets, were poised on one knee "like sprinters ready for the hundred yard dash"; suddenly the sleeping night came alive "in a riot of dazzling green and bright red sparks." Aboard SGB (Steam Gunboat) No. 5, which was shepherding twenty-five Landing Craft Personnel (LCPs) of No. 3 Commando towards Berneval beach, Commander David Wyburd, RN, yelled, "My God, we're in for it—better get below quick!" Colonel John Durnford-Slater, No. 3 Commando's CO, reached the bridge to find it "piled up with dead and wounded like a collapsed rugger scrum," and a naval officer, his mind unhinged, shouting hysterically, "This is it! This is the end!"

But Major Peter Young, Durnford-Slater's No. 2, saw it as only the beginning. As a glittering paper-chain of tracer engulfed SGB 5, all but four of the frail wooden LCPs had gone hopelessly adrift; Young, in LCP 15, now had only twenty men as against the 250 scheduled for this sortie. Still he saw no alternative. Unless the Berneval battery—composed of five powerful 150-mm guns with a twelve-mile range—was neutralized, the main carrier force assembling off Dieppe would be annihilated.

In what Captain Hughes-Hallett later acclaimed as "the most outstanding incident of the operation," Young deployed his men in a classic Foreign Legion manoeuvre. Following their landfall, and a forty-five-minute scramble up a narow gulley, his team at length reached a cornfield 200 yards from the Berneval battery. Then, splitting them into three groups, with orders to keep moving and keep firing, Young organized a deadly sporadic fire from all sides, until the 200-strong artillery force, convinced they were under attack from the rear, traversed their heavy guns inland. The battery was never captured—but the Dieppe task force was unharmed. By 8.20 a.m., LCP 15, cocooned inside a self-laid smokescreen, was heading home across the Channel.

Seven miles to the west, at Varengeville, the success had been even greater: 250 men of No. 4 Commando, under 31-year-old Lieutenant-Colonel the Lord Lovat, had scaled the same 400-ft cliffs where Claude Monet had peacefully painted forty-five years earlier, to knock out a six-gun 150-mm battery 1100 yards inland. "Screams, smoke, the smell of burning cordite—mad moments soon over," recalled

Lieutenant Donald Gilchrist, later a pillar of the Royal Bank of Scotland, and the survivors were to treasure many such. Corporal Frank Koons, of the US Rangers, became the first American soldier to kill a German gunner; not to be outdone, a British sniper toppled another German from a flak tower 200 yards distant, then hailed his troop leader, "Now do I get back my bloody proficiency pay, sir?" (It had been docked by sixpence a few weeks earlier.) A French allotment-holder, startled from sleep in an ankle-length nightshirt, hastily changed into a ceremonial black coat and striped trousers to offer Major Derek Mills-Roberts, a former Liverpool solicitor, a glass of wine.

At 7.30 a.m., back on the beach according to timetable, Lord Lovat sent off a nonchalant signal to his fellow peer, Lord Mountbatten: "Everyone of the gun crews finished with the bayonet. OK by you?"

All this would have been news to both General "Ham" Roberts and Captain Hughes-Hallett, Mountbatten's observer, aboard HMS *Calpe*; despite the profusion of wireless sets, walkie-talkies and inter-ship systems, only garbled and imperfect shore-based messages were reaching the concourse of shipping off Dieppe. The commanders knew nothing of these early successes—or that the men of the 302nd Division, now fully alerted, were picking off both wireless operators and their aerials. *Generalmajor* Haase's Order of the Day— "THEM or US must be the watchword of every man"—left them no alternative.

At Puys, two miles east of the main harbour, the guns of the East Headland looked down on a beach fifty yards deep, massed with

I wait as well and see it right/in my mind's eye.

Then suddenly a white/smoky curtain covers the beach where the/forsaken promenade winds its course,/and men charge up from the sea, hoarse/with excitement, afraid to swallow lest they/miss a sound.

Then everywhere/the carefully planned attacks mass in their place/and hundreds, hundreds falling in the race/for shelter from the stuttering guns; falling face-/downwards, just a mile or two of sea between/them and us and all that might have been,/the trampled sand blinding already sightless eyes.

Yet, when all's said and done, who'd have/it otherwise?/Not they./Women wait long enough for paradise/and if it's now—or in a million years—/it makes no odds. Their blood flows, and/my tears/if I could shed them.

There's the pips./And news again of men and planes and ships./But I already know and feel my lips/grow cold, and my heart a hot, hard ball/wedged in my throat. I know they could not all/come back.

(from *Dieppe* by Joyce Rowe)

Lieutenant-Colonel
Cecil Merritt, South
Saskatchewan
Regiment, Canada's first
V. C. (Canadian War
Museum)

painful 6-in. pebbles, and beyond these were layers of heavy concertina wire which Intelligence had quite overlooked. Ross Munro, a Canada Press war correspondent, was one witness of the Royal Regiment of Canada's mad plunging dash ashore from the bows of landing craft like the *Queen Emma*, a converted cross-Channel steamer — "Machine-gun bullets laced into them. Bodies piled up on the ramp . . . there must have been sixty or seventy of them . . . cut down before they had the chance to fire a shot." Six feet away from Munro, a crouching youngster lunged vainly for the ramp, then "collapsed on the blood-soaked deck" as "a streak of red-white tracer slashed through his stomach." "Christ, we gotta beat them; we gotta beat them," he was crying as he died.

As the landing craft commanders watched, a beach which Intelligence had reported as "only lightly defended" became a cemetery. Of

14

Dieppe: some of the
2000 Canadian prisoners
line up near the
Boulevard Verdun.
(Bundesarchiv-Koblenz)

the 554 men of the Royals who went to Puys, only 65 came back. The East Headland was never secured.

At Pourville, two miles west of the harbour, the picture was marginally brighter, thanks primarily to the valour of Lieutenant-Colonel Cecil Merritt, of the South Saskatchewan Regiment, a 33-year old Vancouver barrister, who was to win Canada's first Victoria Cross in World War Two. "Don't try and win medals,

Cec. You just come home," his wife, Grace, had cautioned him before his departure overseas, but Merritt's men knew him better—"You've got to put a drag-rope on the Colonel to keep up with him." On August 19, Merritt lived up to this verdict; six times that morning he led isolated groups of his men across a threatened bridge towards a white concrete fortress on the West Headland. To his adjutant, Captain G. B. Buchanan, Merritt at times seemed close to euphoria: "I've just bombed out a pillbox. Try it some time before breakfast."

But when Merritt and the remaining Saskatchewans surrendered towards noon, the West Headland, too, was unsecured. Dieppe's main beach lay naked to Haase's gunners.

It was a mile long, and fifty yards deep, ending in a 12-ft-high sea wall. Beyond, on the Boulevard Verdun, lay the genteel hotels of the pre-war era, and, at the western end, Dieppe's one concession to frivolity, the Casino. But it was from the Casino's upper windows, from those staid hotels, from concrete pillboxes and from both Headlands that an enveloping fire met the men of the Essex Scottish, the Royal Hamilton Light Infantry, the Calgary Tanks and the Fusiliers Mont-Royal, all of them storming the beach in the greying daylight at 5.20 a.m.: machine-gun fire, mortar fire, anti-tank gun fire, infantry rifle fire. "Every German weapon turned on us," remembered Lieutenant-Colonel Robert Labatt, of the RHLI. "The sea was littered with the wreckage of assault boats and dotted with bobbing heads and waving arms."

Sergeant Jack Nissenthal, an RAF technician, who had no chance of reaching the radar

Dieppe was one of the most vital operations of the Second World War. It gave to the Allies the priceless secret of victory . . . if I had the same decisions to make again I would do as I did before.

(—Earl Mountbatten of Burma)

Was Dieppe a worthwhile effort? It is difficult to think so . . . I hold the raid itself was a disaster, and the changed plan nothing short of suicidal.

(—Lord Lovat, OC No. 4 Commando)

station at Pourville, escaped only after swimming a quarter of a mile to a departing boat. Behind him he left the unforgettable sight of Canadians who had built a rampart from their own dead, to support one still-defiant machine-gun.

The second assault wave had no illusions as to the carnage they were approaching. "I realized that this landing was to be a sea parallel to the Charge of the Light Brigade," Lieutenant Marcel Buist, commanding the assault boats of the Free French Chasseurs, recalled later, and as crew after crew struggled ashore "with courage terrible to see," even a hardened professional like Lieutenant-Colonel J. B. Phillipps, CO of No. 40 (Royal Marine) Commando, was

stopped in his tracks. Pulling on a pair of white signal gauntlets, he was gesturing frantically from the shoreline—"For God's sake, go back"—when a sniper's bullet cut him down; but 200 of his Marines had been saved from disaster.

The end was very near. Already scores of wounded men, in a spirit of self-preservation, were wading chest-high towards those landing craft still afloat; such was the chaos at the water's edge that almost 1000 Canadians had never got ashore. At 10.22 a.m. Captain Hughes-Hallett ordered the withdrawal of the fleet with the one-word signal: "Vanquish." Aboard HMS *Calpe*, the last ship to leave the port, Major-General Roberts had to admit the truth to Quentin Reynolds: "It was tougher than we figured."

It was certainly arguable that Combined Operations had learned many lessons for a future assault on Fortress Europe: the need for capital ships, for rocket ships, for saturation bombing, for a personal naval assault force, for up-to-date intelligence, even, in the last resort, for a portable harbour. But the lessons had been learned at an appalling cost of Canadian lives: 2000 prisoners, nearly 1000 dead. Had it, in the end, been worth it?

At least one man, the commander of the day's most successful assault, did not think so. It was after midnight when Lord Lovat reached the Guards Club, on London's Brook Street, and at that hour, no beds were available; the CO of No. 4 Commando had to make do with a shakedown in the library, wrapped in warm towels, while an old servant took away his clothes to clean and dry. But sleep did not come easily; he shivered in a waking nightmare where

"tracer bullets probed the darkness, and leaden feet pounded desperately on slopes of slippery shingle, like shifting walnut shells."

With dawn, came a bleaker realization: the knowledge that it was he who must break the news to the families of the forty Commandos wounded or missing, the sixteen who had died at Varengeville.

Dieppe: the aftermath. An LCT burns in the background; a Churchill tank, one of 27 to reach shore, is grounded at left of picture. (Bibliothek fur Zeitesgeschichte)

2 THE FAR SHORE

WEST OF PICCADILLY, the streets were silent. A yellow-grey fog, rolling in from the Thames, blanketed the glistening miles of London's rooftops. Only the footsteps of a few late revellers, shuffling in search of bus-stops, broke the unnatural quiet. It was Friday January 15, 1944.

At Addison Road Station, West London, a private military train, code-named "Bayonet," slid to a halt at a siding. Through wraiths of fog a group of gangers, huddled round a coal brazier, saw four men duck from the train to exchange salutes with a WAC driver waiting beside an American Packard staff car. Then the car moved forward down the long dank Kensington Road, heading for a more salubrious destination: Hayes' Lodge, in Chesterfield Street, off Berkeley Square.

General Dwight David Eisenhower, the newly appointed Supreme Allied Commander, had arrived to master-mind the invasion of Europe, henceforth known as D-Day.

Few commanders had ever received more concise instructions. Eisenhower's directive from the Combined Chiefs of Staff in Washington had left no room for equivocation: "You

England resembles a ship in its shape; and if it were one, its best Admiral could not have worked or anchored it in a more judicious or effective position.

(from *English Traits* by Ralph Waldo Emerson)

Unheeding now through summer days they give/Their drilled attention to the killers' art/Rehearsing in their minds the life they'll live/When some day soon their second life they'll start./And ripping, every time they thrust, the drab./Embittered present with a bayonet jab.

(from *Home Front* by Robert Chaloner)

Norfolk House, St James's Square, London – Eisenhower's first London HQ.

Memorial plaque, Norfolk House.

Lieutenant-General
Sir Frederick Morgan,
COSSAC – architect of
D-Day. (US National
Archives)

will enter the continent of Europe and, in conjunction with the other United Nations, undertake operations aimed at the heart of Germany and the destruction of her armed forces . . . ."

It was a daunting task, and one for which history offered few precedents. That much was plain as early as March 12, 1943, when Lieutenant-General Frederick Morgan, an urbane 49-year-old British artilleryman, mysteriously titled COSSAC—Chief of Staff to the Supreme Allied Commander (designate)—had set up shop in a former Lloyds Bank boardroom on the sixth floor of Norfolk House, St James's Square. For long months thereafter, Morgan, with a small Anglo-American staff group, *was*, "Operation Overlord," the code-name for an ultimate cross-Channel invasion, plucked from a list of available symbols by Winston Churchill. Yet at this time, no Supreme Allied Commander existed, and there was no hint as to available resources. The Chief of the Imperial General Staff, Lieutenant-General Sir Alan Brooke, offered cold comfort: "It won't work, but you must bloody well make it."

There was a multitude of questions, and few could be answered with precision. Where should the Allies invade and when? How many men would be needed and, more cogently, how many would be available? How many landing craft, planes and warships did such a plan call for? Above all, the lessons of Dieppe loomed large: the need for overwhelming naval gunfire support to neutralize German batteries, the need to drench the invasion beaches with many tons of bombs.

Long before "Ike" Eisenhower's appointment as SAC, one factor had worked in the Allies' favour: time. Once Adolf Hitler had seemed omnipotent: the supreme arbiter of 250 million Europeans. "Armed as never before we stand at the door of the New Year," he had rallied his *Wehrmacht* in January 1941, and this was no empty boast: for six months his troops had manned the ramparts unchallenged from the North Cape to Sicily. Behind him stretched a whole succession of conquests: Austria and Czechoslovakia, annexed as part of his Third Reich before war even began in September 1939, Poland, overrun within twenty-six days, Norway within six weeks, Denmark and Luxembourg within a day. Holland, Belgium and France had lasted little longer before the British were driven into the sea at Dunkirk.

By contrast, in January 1944, Hitler faced the blackest New Year since Versailles. Since December 1941, when the United States entered the war, his luck was irreversibly running out. Implacable Soviet attacks were decimating division after German division on a 2000-mile front. After the July 1943 invasion of Sicily, Italy had come over to the Allied side; her dictator, Benito Mussolini, was now an impotent German puppet on Lake Garda. As recently as October 1942, the German armies had been virtually within sight of Suez—until the British Eighth Army, under General Sir Bernard Montgomery, had won a crushing victory over *Feldmarschall* Erwin Rommel, at the desert whistlestop of El Alamein. By May 1943, Axis-held North Africa had crumbled. These lessons were not lost on the small nations of Europe, whether Axis satellites—Hungary, Romania—or uneasy neutrals like Spain and Turkey. All were seeking closer accommodation with the Allies.

An assault on The Far Shore—the planners' name for any final target—at last seemed feasible. But which Far Shore?

For Morgan and his American deputy, Brigadier General Ray W. Barker, their ultimate choice was a process of elimination. If Calais, closest to Europe and to Europe's first port, Antwerp, was obvious to the Allies, it was obvious to the Germans, too; since Dieppe, defences in the Pas de Calais had been formidable. North of Calais, the coastal sites were pockmarked with sand-dunes; south of Normandy, the Brittany peninsula was almost beyond fighter cover and vulnerable to Atlantic storms. Thus Normandy, with a serviceable port, Cherbourg, close to Portsmouth, and the city of Caen, with its road and rail networks linked to Paris, seemed the soundest choice.

It was a project on which Churchill, despite his lone stance against Hitler in 1940, remained distinctly cool. As a battalion commander of the Royal Scots Fusiliers in World War One, he had never forgotten the human devastation he had seen around Ploegsteert Wood and Armentières. "Let us take care that the waves do not become red with the blood of American and British youth," he was to caution Eisenhower, and to General Henry "Hap" Arnold, Chief of the US Army Air Forces, he confided, "I think dolefully of 300,000 dead British soldiers floating in the Channel."

It was thus with reason that Roosevelt's Secretary of War, Henry Stimson, had warned the President, "The shadow of Passchendaele and Dunkerque still hang too heavily over the imagination of these leaders," and equally, with reason, that Churchill's scientific adviser, Pro-

...then the Americans came. They arrived in jeeps and trucks, parking in long khaki lines behind our terraced house. They changed the atmosphere literally as well as metaphorically, driving everywhere and overlaying the smell of horse dung with the stench of gas fumes, blotting out the clang of the canalside smithy with the roar of internal combustion engines. They were tough rangy men with twanging accents familiar from the movies and weird western expletives never heard before. They were open, amiable, gregarious, and above all generous. 'Got any gum, chum?' became the first slogan my lips uttered and, like thousands of contemporaries, my jaws soon ached with chewing. From their fantastic abundance the Americans lavished a cornucopia of coffee, candy, Camels, corned beef (not to mention contraceptives) on the pinched people of Northern Cornwall. It was as though a dozen Liberty ships . . . had spilled their cargoes on the shore.

(from *Ike: The Life and Times of Dwight D. Eisenhower* by Piers Brendon)

fessor Frederick Lindemann (later Lord Cherwell) warned the Army Chief of Staff, General George Marshall, "You must remember you are fighting our losses on the Somme." What Churchill sought instead was a slow war of attrition against the "soft underbelly" of Europe: a drive towards Germany from the south through Italy and Yugoslavia with Vienna, Budapest and Trieste falling to the Allies alone. Failing this, he saw with foresight, it would be the Red Army which "liberated" eastern Europe. To Churchill, any Far Shore would be one that was washed by the waves of the Mediterranean.

For Roosevelt and his Chiefs of Staff, this was mere political foot-dragging, and Morgan, to his credit, saw why. "Their eyes were firmly fixed on the German target," he explained later. "Their main idea was to hit it quick, switch rapidly to deal with Japan and get back to business." Crisply he summed up the alternatives: "We went to Normandy or we stayed at home."

Only the Tehran Conference, held in the Iranian capital between November 28 and December 1, 1943, saw the issue finally resolved. With Stalin's guarantee to aid America against Japan following Germany's defeat, Fleet Admiral Ernest King now agreed to divert landing craft from the Pacific War, which to King had always been priority. Of more than 19,000 landing craft built by American shipyards, some 2500 of all kinds were now available for D-Day.

This was the situation as Eisenhower found it on the eve of the greatest amphibious operation in history.

He arrived in an England now increasingly weary after fifty-three months of war. For most civilians, it was a land of tired shift-workers queuing in the blackout for overcrowded buses, of forty-deep lines outside Lyons teashops for one rasher of bacon and one off-the-ration egg, a nation now supremely bored by exhortations to beware "The Squander Bug" or to sample the Ministry of Food's latest unappetizing recipe. For the troops of fourteen British divisions, crammed into tents or Nissen and Quonset huts, the long weeks of repetitive training was fast palling: bayonet practice, tommy-gun practice, endless mock attacks or deployments in tanks. Lieutenant Arthur Heal, of the 1st Suffolks, remembers being "simply eager to see the end of it all and go home." Corporal Chris Portway, of the 4th Dorsets, thought that any invasion, anywhere, would be a relief "from all those ghastly exercises." The occasional weekend leave or SOP (sleeping-out pass), the cue to head for home and the arms of a wife or girlfriend, was now the most sought-after prize.

But if Eisenhower's "great crusade" was to succeed, the final answer lay in logistics. More materiel, above all, more men, would be called for than in any battle ever known, and indeed for eighteen months before his arrival a floodtide of both had been engulfing England—bringing what Lieutenant John Mason Brown, USNR, called "a man-made Mississippi of strength and arms, of steel and gasoline, of concrete and woollens, of foodstuffs and homesickness." The man hailed as "the first GI"—actually the first the BBC could corral for an interview—Private First Class (Pfc) Milburn H. Henke of Hutchinson, Minnesota, had stepped off the

boat on to Dufferin Quay, Belfast, on Saturday January 26 1942, but within months a million more Americans would follow him. By D-Day, two million of them had crowded into a country only slightly larger than Colorado.

To the bemused British, the GI invasion was akin to a dawn takeover bid. Their needs were insatiable: billets, training grounds, firing ranges, storage depots, hospitals. "When there were no towns we built them," John Mason

"The First GI": Pfc Milburn H. Henke, of Hutchinson, Minn., reaches Belfast, January 26, 1942. (Imperial War Museum)

Brown related. "We built them in the rubble left
by air raids . . . we built them in the coast towns
and in parks far inland. Hut camps mush-
roomed over England." Airfields were needed
for the 185,000 officers and enlisted men of the
Eighth Air Force, and 163 of them were built
from the Wash to High Wycombe—"concrete
was poured and levelled round the clock,"
recalls one camouflage specialist, Robert Arbib.

In time the GIs came to occupy 100,000
buildings in 1100 locations, notably, from
December 20, 1943, 30,000 acres of South
Devon, involving the temporary eviction of
3000 people from 750 farms. Two months
before this, twenty-five square miles of North
Devon had been hived off at Appledore, on

With a B17-F Flying Fortress as background, GIs on an English airfield turn over a 40-acre site as part of the ''Dig for Victory'' campaign. (USAF)

Notice To Quit: this eviction order to 3000 people turned 30,000 acres of South Devon into American territory. (Torquay Central Library)

Those three or four thousand men of one machine-like movement, some of them swashbucklers by nature; others doubtless of a quiet shop-keeping disposition who had inadvertently got into uniform—all of them had arrived from nobody knew where, and hence were matter of—great curiosity. They seemed to the mere eye to belong to a different order of beings from those who inhabited the valleys below.

(from *The Trumpet-Major* by Thomas Hardy)

Bideford Bay, where Colonel Paul Thompson, US Engineers, set up a full-scale replica of a German strongpoint area one-and-a-half miles square, studded with concrete bunkers 6 ft thick. Beyond lay four miles of beaches where landing craft made endless dummy runs.

The impact on the British way of life was long remembered. In pubs, clubs, cinemas and dance halls, the GIs were an ever-present horde. The same phrases were heard on thousands of lips: "That grass is so green it hurts the eyes"—"What's that in American money?" —"Doesn't it ever stop raining?"— "What's for chow? Not lamb stew and brussels sprouts *again*!" From the PX (Post Exchange) came rationed goodies whose existence the British had almost forgotten: razor blades, chocolate Hershey bars, Lucky Strike cigarettes at threepence for twenty, and nylon stockings. One Bournemouth belle of that time, Brenda Devereux, saw a GI's typical approach as irresistible: "Come on, babe. How about you and me steppin' out, huh? Gee, you look cute, babe. No kiddin'." This, above all, was the era of the wolf-whistle, the pin-up, the big band sounds of Glenn Miller and Tommy Dorsey, when propriety vied with promiscuity as the Number One priority and sometimes prevailed.

With seemingly unlimited gasoline, the GIs drove everywhere, and the traffic congestion, as Eisenhower soon found, was appalling: in the punishing schedule he set himself, he was to visit twenty-six divisions, twenty-four airfields, five ships of war and countless workshops, depots and hospitals. West of Winchester, the narrow lanes had become one-way, to facilitate the tireless flow of staff-cars and fast-weaving Jeeps;

for office workers in Andover and points west, an extra fifteen minutes for lunch just to cross the street became mandatory. One Dorchester, Dorset, school teacher, Doris Meech, remembers that at intervals she simply suspended dictation; when Sherman tank or dispatch riders hit the town, her pupils stopped their ears and studied their notes. But darkness brought no respite. "Our nights echoed to the ceaseless clatter of heavy tanks," remembered the writer, Vera Brittain, from her cottage in the New Forest, "lumbering down the Bournemouth—Southampton road."

At times the logistics were almost frightening. D-Day had become an inventory of 700,000 separate items, ordered in quantities running into millions, from Trousers, Wool, Protective (in the quartermaster's jargon) to Bags, Vomit, Soldiers, For The Use Of: the seasick traveller on the choppy English Channel, long a staple item for *Punch* cartoonists, would become a nightmare reality for the men of the first wave. Any chance demand would unleash a flood of new needs as in Dukas's *The Sorcerer's Apprentice*. Enthused by the planners' panoramic photographs of the landing zones, Eisenhower had called for "forty sets"— meaning 40,000 prints—but British resources could not cope. Until the job was done, American bombers flew in 730 miles of paper and ten tons of chemicals every other day.

Whether on land or sea, the problems were of the same magnitude. Admiral Sir Bertram Ramsay, the brilliant, aloof architect of the Dunkirk evacuation, called from retirement to oversee "Operation Neptune"—the naval side of "Overlord"—found himself in overall command of more than 6000 ships, including 4126 landing ships, split into five separate assault forces, all of them distributed evenly through twelve different ports from the Humber to the Bristol Channel.

Thus among the people closest to "Ike" —his naval aide, Captain Harry C. Butcher, his WAC driver, Lieutenant Kay Summersby—one concern predominated: how soon would the pressures begin to tell?

"If I could give you an exact diary account of the past week," he wrote to his wife, Mamie, in White Sulphur Springs, West Virginia, "you'd get some idea of what a flea on a hot griddle really does!" That was on January 23, but by April "Ike" was smoking more than three packs of cigarettes a day; his hand was so crippled by pressing the flesh and drafting memos that he wrote home in soft lead pencil. Frantic with fatigue, he complained of a constant ringing in his right ear.

At 54, "Ike" Eisenhower's fame rested chiefly on his command of the successful 1942 North African landings. An open-minded Kansan, who enjoyed dialect jokes and singalongs, his prime asset was his likeability rather than his active service: until the RAF flew him over the Mareth battle line in April 1943, he had never before seen a soldier killed in action. To his chief weatherman, Group Captain James M. Stagg, his ebullience recalled "a gymnastic instructor about to give his first lesson." His ready grin and self-effacing approach—"Good morning, my name's Eisenhower"—were a palpable hit with GIs and browned-off Tommies alike, and though senior British officers like Sir Alan Brooke snootily dismissed him as "just a

co-ordinator, a good mixer," Eisenhower's own definition of leadership was revealing. It was, he maintained, "pulling a piece of spaghetti across a plate rather than trying to push it."

Thanks to his tact and diplomacy as leader of a coalition unique in war, many vexed issues had now been decided. Five divisions, not three, as first mooted, would initially bear the brunt, and the front had been extended for sixty-five miles from the Cotentin Peninsula on the west to the line of the Orne River on the east—avoiding the heavy shore batteries at Le Havre. It would now be a one-day landing, no longer an assault spread out over two days.

Many of these conditions had been formulated by Montgomery, who would command the ground forces; and as the victor of El Alamein, and an idol of the British public, the prickly, didactic Montgomery was in a position to lay it on the line—"Give me five divisions or get someone else to command." But apart from Montgomery, whom the Canadian 3rd Division called "God Almonty," Eisenhower had also to mediate between his own Chief of Staff, Major-General Walter Bedell-Smith, a short-tempered man racked by ulcer pains, his air commander, Air Chief Marshal Sir Trafford Leigh Mallory, who could prove both pompous and obstructive, and the Third Army's General George S. Patton—"a foul-mouthed bully who looked like a rural deacon," in one man's memory.

Only Eisenhower's immediate deputy, Air Chief Marshal Sir Arthur Tedder, a taut, confident man, and the US Army's General Omar N. Bradley, a relaxed Missourian, made no part of what Eisenhower in despair called "that bunch of prima donnas."

In their major ways of life the British and American people are much alike. . . . But each country has minor national characteristics which differ—for instance: the British are more often reserved in conduct than we. On a small crowded island where forty-five million people live, each man learns to guard his privacy carefully . . . if Britons sit in trains or buses without striking up conversation with you, it doesn't mean they are being haughty or unfriendly . . . they don't speak to you because they don't want to appear intrusive or rude.

Another difference. The British have phrases and colloquialisms of their own that may sound funny to you. You can make just as many boners in their eyes. It isn't a good idea, for instance to say 'bloody' in mixed company in Britain—it is one of their worst swear words. To say: 'I look like a bum' is offensive to their ears, for to the British this means that you look like your own backside; it isn't important—just a tip if you are trying to shine in polite society . . . .

(from *A Short Guide to Great Britain for All Members of the Allied Expeditionary Forces*)

But if much had been decided, areas of grave doubt remained. The choice of time was still a complex issue. D-Day must be an assault at low tide — so that Allied engineers could neutralize any obstacles sited to rip out the bellies of landing craft. It must be a near-dawn attack, so that men and ships could cross under cover of night. A full moon was too risky — yet some moonlight was needed by the air arm. The attack must come late enough for troops to complete their training — yet early enough to give the Allies four months of good weather after landing. In the late spring and early summer of 1944, these conditions for tide, moon and weather pertained only three times — in the first few days of May, and during the first and third weeks of June.

It was in full awareness of the enormity of these decisions that Eisenhower had written to an old friend, Lieutenant General Brehon Somervell, Chief of Supply Services in Washington: "We are not merely risking a tactical defeat; we are putting the whole works on one number . . . ."

Americans in and out of uniform, on every kind of mission, and in every branch of the services must have appeared as inexhaustible to Londoners as England's supply of Brussels sprouts did to Americans.

(from *Many a Watchful Night* by John Mason Brown)

. . . If I must choose I prefer to sing/The tommy-gun, the clean, functional thing,/The single-hander, deadly to rigid line,/Good at a job it doesn't attempt to conceal./Give me time only to teach this hate of mine/The patience and integrity of the steel.

(from *Camouflage* by John Manifold)

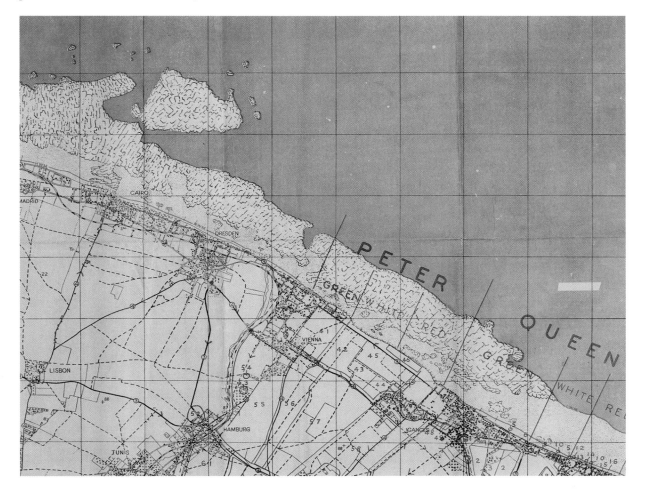

The D-Day Commanders. Standing at rear: Bradley, Ramsay, Leigh-Mallory and Bedell Smith. Seated L to R: Tedder, Eisenhower and Montgomery. (US National Archives)

29

3 BIG WEEK

P-38 Lockheed
Lightnings: an integral
part of the USAF's ''Big
Week.'' (RAF Museum)

The fliers had been given full details, including altitudes, routes, timings, manoeuvres for each group between the initial point and the target, directions on reassembly of the force — everything but the date and time of departure. Then they'd been . . . shown something only British patience could have constructed — a sand model of a big piece of a city, with the projected target at the centre. And what was the target? Schweinfurt. 'It means in German "In a Pig's Arse". Honest. . . . It's clear the other side of Germany. . . . God-damn near to Czechoslovakia . . . .'

(from *The War Lover* by John Hersey)

General Carl A. Spaatz, US Air Forces commander. (Imperial War Museum)

MONTHS BEFORE TAKING over 21st Army Group, and command of D-Day ground forces, General Montgomery liked to propound a riddle to the young aides grouped outside his caravan, south of Italy's Sangro River. "What is the first principle of war?" he would demand, then, more often than not, come up with the answer himself. "Win the air battle first!"

Early in January 1944, Lieutenant General Carl A. Spaatz, the overall commander of US Air Forces in England and the Mediterranean, knew that his own battle against the Luftwaffe was far from won. Even so, Spaatz, a wry, freckled Pennsylvania Dutchman, who relished late-night poker sessions over bourbon high-balls, had not lost heart. A World War One fighter veteran, he was charting the Luftwaffe's defeat on a long-term basis.

To command the sky above the beaches, Spaatz saw little merit in the RAF's unswerving policy of "leaning forward into France" — mass fighter sweeps of Spitfires, Hurricanes and Hawker Typhoons that struck at radar stations, shipping and airfields, in the hope of luring the Messerschmitt 109s into combat. Nor did he place much faith in the RAF Bomber Command's concept of carpet-bombing German cities by night.

Spaatz's eyes were fixed instead on the German economy — above all, its aircraft industry — and thus his Eighth Air Force bombed always by day, viewing their industrial targets whenever possible through Norden bomb sights, which in clear weather guaranteed accuracy up to 33,000 feet.

That was the ideal; the reality was a terrifying rate of attrition. Each crewman was committed to sweat out twenty-five missions, but as Lieutenant Lou Bober, a navigator of the 467th Bombardment Group, who had trained as an insurance actuary, calculated, "There just ain't any way we're gonna live through this thing." An average life was fifteen missions, for at least a quarter of Spaatz's formidable Boeing B-17s, the Flying Fortresses, stepped up in their massive boxes across twenty miles of sky, would be hit by flak on their first sortie. Every 1000 tons of bombs dropped equalled the loss of sixty-seven men and thirteen planes, and by October 1943 the daily count of NYRs (Not Yet Returned) was spiralling.

"Where were they all coming from, these offhand cowboys looking so like the offhand cowboys who had gone before them?" wondered Lieutenant Elmer Bendiner, a navigator of the 379th Bombardment Group at Kimbolton, but the crunch question was: Where were they going? Three October missions — to Bremen, Anklam and Marienburg — saw 580 men lost. On October 14, a second attack on the aircraft ball-bearing plants at Schweinfurt, Bavaria, proved as disastrous as an earlier attack in August: of 330 planes assigned, exactly 291 made the target, and only 25 bombers returned unscathed. In six days, 1480 men had died or become prisoners of war. As winter drew on, the attacks ground painfully to a halt.

In the small, tight ethos of the "Mighty Eighth," a chequerboard of airfields strung across an area no larger than Vermont, forty miles by eighty miles, north and north-east of London, there was mounting concern. Every man knew the odds; the cockiness that had gripped the Eighth following their first successful

raid on Rouen on August 17, 1942 belonged to the past. The bogey with which they contended now was the Luftwaffe's deadly blue-painted Focke-Wulf 190, a fighter that could zoom into the attack at 416 mph, then break from combat in a quick half-roll. Briefed in their tactics by their new General of the Fighter Arm, the Battle of Britain ace, Adolf Galland, they would bore in from up to five miles ahead of the bombers, then swoop beneath to savage the next formation. When one mess-hall notice board featured a magazine clip of a bomber pilot asking, "Who's afraid of the Focke-Wulf?," every combat officer from the Group Commander downwards promptly signed his name below.

At first glance, as the squadrons rolled down the runways at Framlingham and Alconbury, Ridgewell and Grafton Underwood, the B-17 seemed a plane that could take care of itself. With an operation ceiling of 36,700 feet and a maximum range of 3500 miles, it was literally a flying fortress: aside from the pilot and co-pilot, every one of the ten-strong crew manned one or more guns, each with its own field of fire. Yet survivors still emphasize their sense of instability, with the cold as implacable a foe as the Focke-Wulf 190s. "It was always winter up there," one man recalls of a world where ice two inches thick could form on the windows and the temperature at operational

. . . those who in their lives fought for life./Who wore at their hearts the fire's centre./Born of the sun, they travelled a short while/toward the sun/And left the vivid air signed with their honour.

(from *I think continually of those who were truly great* by Stephen Spender)

From my mother's sleep I fell into the State./And I hunched in its belly till my wet fur froze./Six miles from earth, loosed from its dream of life,/I woke to black flak and the nightmare fighters./When I died they washed me out of the turret with a hose.

(from *The Death of the Ball Turret Gunner* by Randall Jarrell)

The Republic P-47 Thunderbolt – "Big Week" was a field-day for this "tough baby." (RAF Museum)

The plane that made "Big Week" possible: Rolls-Royce Merlin-powered P-51B Mustangs over the River Stour. (USAF)

height could drop to − 50° Fahrenheit. Despite their bright blue electrified flying suits, leather fleece-lined jackets and many layers of sweaters, frost-bite could strike within seconds six miles above the earth. On days like October 14, when Galland's defences numbered 300 day fighters plus 40 fighter-bombers and night fighters, some men were more at risk than others: the pilot, the tenth man, holding the plane steady while others baled out, pinned against the inside of the fuselage by centrifugal force as the Fort went into a spin, the ball turret gunner, freezing in a sea of blood inside the Plexiglass bubble slung beneath the belly of the bomber.

Escort fighters gave of their best, but there were many restrictions. The Lockheed P-38 was

prone to mechanical trouble in the damp English climate, and with a 600-mile range often had to turn back before the real attacks began. The Republic P-47 Thunderbolt was, in one pilot's words, "a tough baby that brought you home for supper," but until 108-gallon drop tanks were fitted, they, too, had to break for home after 640 miles.

Discontent was in the air, and Spaatz knew it. Men like Elmer Bendiner, survivors of both Schweinfurt raids, were haunted by "the landmarks of a nightmare...yellow blazes among the...landscape, like bonfires in a field," which "clocked the fall of Fortresses." "You couldn't help but see them," says Bob Hanson, who soldiered through twenty-five missions as radio operator with the *Memphis Belle* out of Bassingbourn, "and the men who thought about it ended up with the psychiatrists." Sensitive men went "Section 8," which signalled near-derangement, a phrase known to girlfriends at every station hop; don't-give-a-damn men served time in the stockade rather than fly again. Cynical men chose "targets of opportunity," loosing the bomb load anywhere just to gain height and turn for home; others contrived "navigational errors" and set their planes down for the duration of the war in neutral Sweden. On morale-boosting trips to bomber airfields, Spaatz and the new chief of the Eighth, Major General Jimmy Doolittle, turned a deliberately deaf ear to rude and just-audible gibes—"Only one thing hurt our morale...having three-star generals coming around to see what's the matter with it."

In a twist of fate as improbable as a fairy tale, it was a "Cinderella" aircraft that turned

34

the tide: the North American Aviation P-51B Mustang, rejected out of hand since 1941 by the US Air Forces and relegated to low-level Army Co-Operation Command work by the RAF. Tests by Rolls-Royce, who suspected the plane was under-powered, substituted their own Merlin 61 engines for the original Allison 1150 hp. The result was what Ernest Hemingway, then a war correspondent, called "a bad, tough, husky angry plane," a plane, moreover, that with long-range fuel tanks, could cover bombers up to 1500 miles from base, that could achieve 440 mph, even at 35,000 feet, faster than a Focke-Wulf 190 by 70 mph—and easily able to outdive it. This was a plane that could hunt and kill.

The effect on aircrew morale was electric. "You couldn't tell enlisted men from pilots," recalled Lieutenant Grover C. Hall, Jr, when the first Mustangs reached Colonel Don Blakeslee's 4th Fighter Group at Debden, Essex, for both groups were engaged in the same tasks: washing the fuselages, gassing up and "slipping the snaky belts of 50-cal armour-piercing incendiaries into the wing guns." "Sonofabitch, listen to that motor," one noncom exulted. "We've got Seven League Boots."

Inevitably, the Mustang had its detractors. It was "an unforgiving s.o.b.," some pilots claimed, which could stall without warning. In a tight turn, its Browning Mg 53-2 machine-guns might jam unexpectedly. Landing the plane at 75 mph could be tricky, for the torque could flip the plane on its back at the last moment: wise pilots made wheel landings with their tails up. Even so, by December 1943, enough Mustangs had left the production line to break the back of

Galland's defences. No German target was now out of reach.

Yet all would depend on the weather. When Major General Doolittle, who two years earlier had led the first strike on Tokyo, took over the Eighth on January 6, 1944, he was staggered to find that the English climate was as big a stumbling block as German fighters or flak. Out of 365 days, Spaatz's weathermen explained, 240 could be counted on as bad; all weather fronts originated over the Atlantic, then travelled from west to east across the British Isles. Eighth Air Force bombers might take off at 6 a.m. in bright sunlight, then return five hours later to an England invisible beneath fog. The verdict of C.K.M. Douglas, senior guru at the Dunstable Central Forecasting Office, would have struck a chord with generations of British holidaymakers: "A forecast for more than a day or two ahead in this country can be nothing more than speculation."

Late in January, with the English weather at its nadir, Spaatz received a letter amounting to a challenge from General "Hap" Arnold in Washington: "Can't we some day and not too far distant, send out a big number—*and I mean a big number*—of bombers to hit something in the nature of an aircraft factory and lay it flat?"

The stage was thus set for an operation which to Spaatz was "Operation Argument" and to the air correspondents of the day was "Big Week," although the goals were identical: the destruction of the German aircraft industry in the five days stretching from Sunday February 20 to Friday February 25.

As late as February 19, the mission remained in doubt. Over most airfields in eastern England, the weathermen predicted cloud bases of up to 5000 feet, which could critically impede the assembly of formations. Cloud bases, too, meant icing, which could hamper escort fighters. The stakes were high, for if "Big Week" was launched, 1000 bombers were earmarked to attack twelve primary targets on this first day, with an escort of 73 P-51 Mustangs, 94 P-38s, 668 P-47s and a final back-up of 16 RAF fighter squadrons.

In the small hours of Sunday, Spaatz clinched the issue: "Let 'em go." The mightiest strategic air attack in history up to then was under way.

Yet for the men who lived through them, those five days afterwards merged into one, with no single raid standing out above the others. On every day there was the routine 2 a.m. reveille in the Nissen huts where most men were quartered, the hasty shave—it was a point of honour to shave—followed by the routine mess-hall breakfast of mushy powdered eggs and black coffee. In the briefing room, called "the sweat-box," where a cigarette haze "like a Pittsburg smog" hung heavy, the pilots, or "throttle-jockeys" shared with other crewmen an abiding

All men would be brave if only they could leave their stomachs at home.

(Edward R. Murrow, in a CBS broadcast, December 3, 1943, following a raid on Berlin)

In bombers named for girls, we burned/The cities we had learned about in school—/Till our lives wore out; our bodies lay among/The people we had killed and never seen./When we lasted long enough they gave us medals:/When we died they said, 'Our casualties were low'./They said, 'Here are the maps'; we burned the cities.

(from *Losses* by Randall Jarrell)

'Tis not too late to-morrow to be brave.

(from *The Art of Preserving Health*, 1744 by John Armstrong)

Framlingham, Suffolk, base for the 390th Bombardment Group: 500 and 1000lb HE bombs stacked on hardstands for "Big Week." (USAF)

"Big Week": Regensburg-Obertraubling, following raids by the Mighty Eighth on February 22 and 25 targeting ME-109 plants. (USAF)

contempt for all "ground grippers," as base personnel were known. Finally there was the ride in darkness on a weapon carrier round the five-mile perimeter track to dispersal, where the Forts with the sexy names were parked: the *Any Time Annie*, the *Fancy Nancy*, the *Virgin on the Verge*.

The targets, too, were little more than names: Leipzig, Tutlow, Brunswick, Gotha, Regensburg. Only the top brass who shared Spaatz's thinking realized that bombs falling sheer towards the Junkers-88 twin engine factory at Bernberg were an integral part of a programme, with bombs simultaneously striking the fuselage factory at Oschersleben and the wing factory at Halberstadt, since all three were interdependent. What the crews remembered were, first, the harmless images, the contrails of crystalline vapour streaming back from engine exhausts at 41,000 feet, then the ominous sounds, guns shaking the Fort's nose "like a dentist's drill," a last lost cry, "We're going down. Our oxygen's gone," finally the maelstrom, "slogging through a mass of flame and smoke, diving through a rain of steel splinters."

"They [the Luftwaffe] had all their planes up but their trainers," was one gunner's recollection. Another recalled with awe, "Twenty millimetre shells zinging past with our names and rank on them, everything but our serial numbers." By contrast, the Thunderbolts and Mustangs relived these as five field-days. The P-47 ace Robert S. Johnson recalled gliding beneath a cloudbank until his Messerschmitt 110 broke cover, streaming black smoke and spiralling towards the ground. Captain Mike

ABOARD THE LINER *Queen Mary*, outward bound from Greenock, on the Clyde, for Quebec, the mood was one of buoyant expectation. Crowded round the bathtub in a luxury suite, Winston Churchill and his chiefs of staff were as seemingly absorbed in a bathroom game as children postponing their bedtime. As they watched, the master of ceremonies, 41-year-old Professor John Desmond Bernal, one of Mountbatten's chief scientific advisers, was manoeuvring a fleet of twenty paper boats towards the bath's shallow end. This, his audience knew, represented the Normandy shore. But once Lieutenant David Grant RN made turbulent waves with a loofah from the deep end of the bath, the frail fleet shuddered and sank.

Undeterred, Bernal now laid an inflated Mae West lifebelt at the bath's shallow end. Another fleet of twenty ships, made from newspaper, replaced the first. "More waves, please, Lieutenant Grant," Bernal exhorted, so exciting the First Sea Lord, Sir Dudley Pound, that he scrambled on to the lavatory seat for a better view. Again the loofah rotated violently, but sheltered by the Mae West the new fleet remained triumphantly afloat. "That, gentlemen," Bernal concluded, in the manner familiar to scores of London University students, "is what would happen if we had an artificial harbour." It was the late afternoon of Friday August 6, 1943, five months before Eisenhower was even appointed.

Eighteen days later, at the Roosevelt-Churchill Quebec Conference, which reached many decisions on Operation "Overlord," the concept was officially approved. Two artificial

Entrance passages are very draughty places, and the Channel is like the rest. It ruins the tempers of sailors. It has been calculated by philosophers that more damns go up to heaven from the Channel, in the course of a year, than from all the five oceans put together.

(from *A Pair of Blue Eyes* by Thomas Hardy)

Birth of a Mulberry at London's East India Docks, January 1944. (Imperial War Museum)

43

harbours, one British, one American, in a project arbitrarily code-named "Mulberry," should be constructed forthwith, to be fully operational off Normandy two weeks after D-Day.

As Lieutenant-General Frederick Morgan later recalled, the idea of an artificial harbour was the natural outcome of Dieppe. Ever since that disastrous raid, both photographic reconnaissance and Free French intelligence had stressed that Germany was giving top priority to fortifying the Channel ports: Calais, Cherbourg, Le Havre. Yet plainly any successful invasion hinged on port facilities being available within days. At the end of one abortive conference, Morgan remembered, the Naval Adviser to Combined Operations, John Hughes-Hallett, RN, "pencil being rubbed briskly between palms," announced, "Well, all I can say is if we

Rear-Admiral William Tennant RN, commanding Mulberry "B." (Admiral Sir William Tennant)

can't capture a port we must take one with us."

It was a throwaway line concealing a hard grain of truth. With the Far Shore now narrowed down to Normandy, the D-Day planners faced the same problem currently bedevilling General Carl Spaatz: the atrocious English weather. "Sheltered water," noted one desperate Morgan minute, "is the crux of the whole operation." What was needed, the planners now realized, was a harbour area where large coasters, tank landing craft, Liberty ships and amphibious vehicles could discharge their cargoes or unload on to barges for up to ninety days—after which, hopefully, Cherbourg would fall. It must be a harbour impervious to a Force 6 wind, a harbour, moreover, which could handle 10,000 tons of stores and 2500 vehicles a day—a precursor of the famous "Red Ball Highway," whose final frontier was the Rhine.

Already there had been progress of a kind. Once European invasion seemed feasible, a particular thought had nagged at Winston Churchill—who, in turn, nagged at others. "Piers for use on beaches," he had chivvied Mountbatten on May 30, 1942. "They *must* float up and down with the tide. The anchor problem must be mastered . . . . Don't argue the matter." In time, too, it became apparent that the piers must rise and fall 22 ft, in harmony with the tides of Normandy—"to practically breathe with the sea," as one engineer put it. For their model, the War Office's Transportation Branch (Tn 5) looked back to 1923, when the dredger *Lucayan* rode out a Bahamas hurricane anchored firmly on three 89-ft legs, called spuds, embedded in the bottom of the sea. It was spuds that proved the mainstay of the 480-foot floating pier, christened "Winnie" by her builders, that was towed into Wigtown Bay, Scotland, on April 23, 1943, and fifteen floating Spud Piers (code-named Whales) would play a vital role after D-Day.

This was a beginning, but in the autumn of 1943 the artificial harbours called "Mulberry"—which one commentator later dubbed "the Eighth Wonder of the World"—were still in the drawing-board stage. Diverse talents made solid contributions: men like Iorys Hughes, who had designed Wembley's Empire Swimming Pool, Sir Ralph Freeman, renowned for his Sydney Harbour Bridge, and Sir Malcolm McAlpine, whose Dorchester Hotel on London's Park Lane affirmed his faith in reinforced concrete. It was Brigadier Bruce White, of Tn 5, who produced the first designs for the concrete caissons (large watertight containers) code-named Phoenixes: it was Robert Lochner, a naval lieutenant turned back-room boy, who speculated that a floating barrier might successfully repel waves. Experiments on his trout-pond near Haslemere, Surrey, with a rubber inflatable mattress fitted with a metal keel, proved the breakthrough. His wife, Mary, made miniature waves with the aid of a biscuit tin, and before she fell in head-first a principle had been established: confronted by a floating wall, waves would lose much of their energy below a certain depth.

Under the code-name Bombardon, 93 giant inflatables, 200 ft long, and 25 ft high, rendered rigid by steel plating, became another intrinsic piece in the "Mulberry" jigsaw.

But not until December 15, 1943, with D-Day five months distant, did a long and wordy

Professor J. D. Bernal, who sold the Mulberry concept to the Combined Chiefs of Staff. (Henry Grant)

meeting finally clarify who would do what—and when. A US Navy team under Captain Dayton Clark, a gaunt, terrible-tempered disciplinarian, would construct the American "Mulberry A" for installation at St Laurent on the coast north-west of Bayeux. His team would be seasoned professionals of No. 108 Construction Battalion, the "Seabees," many of them tough oil drillers from Texas. The British harbour, "Mulberry B," destined for Arromanches, east of St Laurent, came under the supervision of Rear-Admiral William Tennant, RN, with Captain Harold Hickling as his deputy.

As Senior Naval Officer, Dunkirk, in May 1940, Tennant, backed by an expert team, had seized upon the port's East Mole, a narrow concrete breakwater, as the sure way to

Mankind . . . do not truly believe in anything new until they have had actual experience of it.

(from *The Prince* by Niccolo Machiavelli)

Your science will be valueless, you'll find,/And learning will be sterile, if inviting,/Unless you pledge your intellect to fighting/Against all enemies of mankind.

(from *To The Students of the Workers' and Peasants' Faculty* by Bertolt Brecht)

Sinking the Breakwater, by war artist Dwight Shepler, shows one of the concrete caissons of Mulberry harbour being manoeuvred into position. (US Navy Combat Art Collection)

evacuate the maximum number of British troops—and ultimately almost 200,000 who lined up on the Mole survived to fight again. Thus it seemed likely that the resourceful Tennant, abetted by Hickling, a brash down-to-earth New Zealander, would prove a formidable team of trouble-shooters.

Even so, theirs was an uphill task. "The making of the artificial harbours is ... in the realm of fairyland and may or may not be a practicable proposition," Admiral Ramsay noted in his diary as late as January 15, for, as with so many other facets of D-Day, the "Mulberries" were now a race against time. After four years of attrition, everything was in short supply—"Austerity followed one about like a lean and hungry dog," noted the war correspondent, Alan Moorehead. Labour was pitifully scarce, above all, skilled welders, scaffolders and carpenters: if timber was lacking, so, too, was steel. Where were the dry docks to build the caissons and pierheads? And when they were complete, where were the tugs that would tow them at a sedate four knots to the final assembly points, the Selsey Peninsula, West Sussex, and Dungeness, the southernmost point of Kent? (Even on the eve of D-Day only 132 tugs proved available, and many were rescue tugs stripped from the North Atlantic convoys.)

So the speed of the operation was frenzied. At first, only 20,000 workers were involved, but as production stepped up, 45,000 artificers were drafted in, many of them released from the forces at the eleventh hour and assigned to more than 400 civilian contractors. On the Kent marshes, the WVS (Women's Voluntary Services for Civil Defence) stood by day and

night to provide hot food; at Selsey, the Fire Service was called in to sluice channels with hoses through the soft silt of the foreshore. Almost overnight, it seemed, new sites were appearing like mushrooms at dawn: as far apart as the Morfa River at Conway, North Wales, and Hackney Marshes, East London, where breaches would presently be cut in the banks to float the harbour down the Thames. They were building round the clock at Marchwood, now the site of Southampton power station; they were hammering and welding on Southsea promenade, and even on slipways at Beaulieu, in the New Forest, where shipwrights had worked in Nelson's time.

One naval officer, Lieutenant Lambton Burn, RNVR, never forgot the panorama which greeted him at London's East India Docks: "the improvised basins dug into the mud of the Thames riverside . . . dust-covered workmen in thousands . . . hammering at wooden Noah's Arks, which served as moulds for tons of steel reinforcing and concrete. By night, the unfinished monsters, with steel reinforcing rods projecting like wireless poles above suburban flats, were ferried to . . . assembly points in the south until the protected waters resembled green-blue plains studded with anti-tank blocks."

Fifty years later, the folk memories of "Mulberry" remain indelible. At Conway, where hairdressers, tailors and even flower-sellers had been conscripted as welders, a new ailment was soon puzzling local doctors: an acute form of eyestrain known as "arc eyes." Others recall proudly that a Russian was drafted in to resolve their labour disputes; no one then knew that Oleg Kerensky, an engineer supervising buffer pontoons, was a White, not a Red, Russian, the son of a moderate revolutionary

Partly-completed Phoenix caisson under tow from London River to the final assembly point at Dungeness, Kent. (Imperial War Museum)

ousted by Lenin in 1917. Only long afterwards did the significance of the work in hand dawn on many; on Merseyside, the rumour was current that the caissons would support colossal nets to trap submarines. Naval look-outs at Dover remember wryly the panic reports of a sea-serpent off Shakespeare's Cliff: the spars of a bridge tow, gliding low in the water, en route to Selsey by night.

The Official War Artist, Richard Eurich, called in to make sketches for posterity, still complains: "They wouldn't tell me what it was for . . . it was like a lot of factories standing out of the water," and his bewilderment made sense. To Harold Hickling, the "Mulberries" most resembled "a block of flats being towed by a taxi"; to Tennant it was "for all the world as if some one had picked up Chicago and put it down on the Sussex foreshore." "We know exactly what you intend to do with those concrete units," the Nazi propagandist, "Lord Haw Haw," William Joyce, taunted from Berlin on April 21, but he, too, was wide of the mark. As the German High Command saw it, the "Mulberries" were self-propelled quays, to be brought to existing ports, although some experts identified them as ack-ack gun towers.

The entire enterprise staggered the imagination. Each Phoenix, or caisson, was 200 ft long, 50 ft wide and 60 ft high; placed end to end they would stretch for two-and-a-quarter miles, and this was in addition to the Spud Piers and six miles of floating roadways. Both the British and American "Mulberries" were to enclose two square miles of water, larger than Dover Harbour, which had taken seven years to build. It was, in Hickling's words, two million

tons of harbour, costing in excess of £40 million, and he never forgot one occasion when the Third Sea Lord, Admiral Sir Frederick Wake-Walker, bearded an Admiralty mandarin. The dialogue was succinct:

"We want a million pounds."
"What for?"
"For a floating breakwater called Bombardon."
"That's a lot of money."
"There's a lot of breakwater."
"I'll do my best to fix it with the Treasury."
"And so he did," Hicking related subsequently, "next day."

"We ranged the kingdom far and wide," Hickling would remember. "One day we would be up at the Solway Firth, seeing Bruce White's *Whale* pier-heads, the next down to Tilbury to see . . . *Phoenix* caissons; along to Southampton where a hundred *Bombardons* were under construction . . . followed by a run up the Hamble River to see Commander Hutchings with his *Pluto*."

Although Pluto (Pipe Line Under The Ocean) was no more than a project in embryo, once Cherbourg fell it would become reality: the hopper barge HMS *Persephone* and three cable-laying coasters would bulldoze four separate welded-steel pipes through the mud of the sea-bed, prior to siphoning an intended one million gallons of fuel each day between the Southampton Water terminal and Cherbourg. The advancing army had every intention of advancing farther.

Costs were escalating daily, yet a strange parsimony was in evidence. The entire

We saw them come down the Rivers, the comical secret floats,/Weird shapes like a madman's playthings—and what could the monsters be?/Were they bridges, or docks, or jetties? Were they ferries, or forts, or boats?/We held our peace, and we wondered, and they quietly passed to sea.

But now I have seen the weird shapes made one in a work of art./I have seen the incredible harbour the British have brought to birth:/The puzzle toy is complete now, each mad piece playing a part;/And this, I say, is a Wonder that never was matched on earth.

It was built in the open Channel, it was built on a hostile shore,/It was built in the filthy weather, it was built in a nasty blow:/But it lies as neat as a jig-saw set out on a nursery floor,/It feeds the conquering armies, wherever the armies go.

Give thanks for the wild inventors, give thanks for the fearless wits,/Who set themselves to a riddle that never was put before;/Give thanks to the faultless seamen who ferried the crazy bits,/And fashioned a mighty harbour, in storm, on a hostile shore.

(from *The Harbour* by A. P. Herbert)

"Mulberry" project pivoted on an innermost harbour of sunken blockships—"Gooseberries" to the planners—that would close the gap between the Phoenix caissons and the rocky Calvados reef. If bad weather threatened, almost 4000 smaller craft would need emergency shelter, but Tennant's pleas to the Admiralty were stubbornly rebuffed. "You have the effrontery to come here and calmly ask for sixty-five merchant ships just to take them across the Channel and sink them?" trumpeted Admiral Sir Andrew Cunningham, Pound's successor as First Sea Lord. "Never heard of such damned nonsense."

"We came here to get a gooseberry," Tennant summed up ruefully, "and all we seem to have got is a raspberry."

In the end, it was the Chief of Air Staff, Air Marshal Sir Charles Portal, who saw logic prevail. "Suppose one of those 'infrequent' summer gales blows up," he challenged Cunningham, "and suppose all the landing craft are driven ashore. The army could be driven back into the sea. Are we prepared to face the country and say 'The invasion has failed because we did not give the Navy sixty-five old merchant ships'?"

Cunningham saw the light. On the eve of D-Day, fifty-nine warriors that had seen more than thirty years of maritime service, ships such as the *Empire Bunting* and the *Manchester Spinner*, John Masefield's "dirty British coasters," US veterans like the *Kentuckian* and the *Artemus Ward*, along with the French battleship *Courbet*, presented by General de Gaulle, would set sail from Oban, Scotland, at five knots, little more than walking pace, ultimately

to be sunk with ten tons of ammonal explosive off the Calvados reef.

As late as mid-April, "Mulberry" was in jeopardy. More and more Phoenix caissons on the Selsey foreshore were falling prey to bottom suction—literally stuck in the mud. Yet Tennant's schedule called for eight Phoenixes to be towed across the Channel each day from D-Day onwards if the invasion was to succeed. Salvage experts were hastened to the scene, men like Commodore Edward Ellsberg, USN, who flew in from the Mediterranean, and Commodore Thomas MacKenzie, who had overseen the raising of the German Fleet in 1918, when the crews had scuttled it in Scapa Flow. But only on May 27, with ten naval vessels—two to pump out each Phoenix—and five army vessels in action, was the danger averted. In an operation at all times dependent on the incoming tide, one end of each Phoenix was raised at a time and the mud sent spattering with jets of compressed air—allowing water to seep in and eliminate the suction.

By Sunday June 4, the crews of "Mulberry A" and "Mulberry B" were ready. "The planning was over for better or for worse," Hickling related, so if all went well there were "only some 500 pieces of jigsaw" to be towed across the Channel.

But first it was up to Eisenhower's armies.

Blockships of Gooseberry Four at Courseulles (Juno Beach) prior to sinking. (Author's collection)

STRANGELY, IT WAS Omar N. Bradley, always a quiet and considerate man, who as commander of the US First Army was to provoke the stormiest D-Day controversy of all.

"I, almost alone among the senior commanders, urged the use of airborne troops," he was to go on record almost forty years later. "On my own front I wanted the 82nd and 101st Airborne divisions to drop . . . in darkness before we landed . . . . Nothing could dissuade me from my view that these two superb divisions landing in full strength could be decisive . . . ."

As Bradley saw it, the whole US side of the invasion, focused as it was on the thumb-shaped Cotentin Peninsula and its main port, Cherbourg, stood or fell by an airborne drop. To cut off all enemy reinforcements of Cherbourg, airborne troops must "throw a barricade across the peninsula at its neck." Above all, the two divisions, the 101st, "The Screaming Eagles," and the 82nd, "The All Americans," must early on secure the five causeways lying almost directly behind the American beaches, between St Martin-de-Varreville and the coastal hamlet of Pouppeville. Only then could the men of the 4th US Infantry Division forge their way inland.

To ensure that the paratroopers found their targets, Pathfinder teams of ten men, all hand-picked volunteers, would jump eighty minutes ahead of the main forces, to mark the DZs (drop zones) with five white lights forming a T. Armed with portable radar sets, called Eurekas, they could then home the transport planes in on their drop points. On paper, at least, it seemed a fool-proof plan.

This rosy concept of the paratrooper as a twentieth-century Superman, neither flier nor

Paratroopers go in as dawn breaks over Normandy. When British war artist Albert Richards painted *The Drop - Paratroopers*, he knew what he was doing. A trained paratrooper, he jumped with a group in the early hours of D-Day. (Imperial War Museum)

Preparing for D-Day: 6th Airborne practice drop. (National Airborne Museum)

55

The body can be afraid and tremble, whilst the mind remains calm and brave; the opposite is also true. This accounts for many strange acts of behaviour.

(from *The Black Sheep* by Honoré de Balzac)

Private Donald Burgett, 506th Infantry Regiment, 101st (''Screaming Eagles'') Airborne Division. (Donald R. Burgett)

opposite
Eisenhower rallies US paratroopers on eve of D-Day. (US Army)

foot-soldier, but an amalgam of both, had been born overnight on May 10, 1940. Then an elite force of Germans from *Oberst* Bruno Bräuer's *Fallschirmjäger* (Parachute) Regiment I, had siezed Holland in a single day. One year later, it had taken the Germans only eight days to secure the sizeable Mediterranean island of Crete —along with almost 12,000 British prisoners and the loss of forty-six RAF planes.

Unknown to the Allies, until the war's end, was the fearsome toll of German lives: 4500 paratroopers by some accounts, more than 6000 by others. The loss of aircraft, too, had been phenomenal—with estimates ranging from 271 to close on 400. A man for summary decisions rather than inquests, Hitler had told

Generaloberst Kurt Student, commander of the Seventh Air Division: ''The days of the parachute troops are over.''

Fifteen months later, on August 16, 1942, the 82nd and the 101st Airborne were officially activated at Camp Claiborne, Louisiana, with the goal of raising some 17,650 men who were both ''lean and mean.'' For the Allies, the days of the parachute troops had just begun.

It was not a view that found favour with Eisenhower—and the first mass airborne drop of US troops on July 10, 1943, over Sicily, bore him out. Of the 3400 troopers that had left North Africa under his command, Colonel (later Brigadier General) James M. Gavin, of the 82nd, could muster only 20 four hours after the jump. Some of the troops, he found later, had been dropped sixty miles east of the DZ, and in the British zone things had gone as badly: only 57 out of 156 aircraft dropped their troops near the target. Faced with total casualties of 605 officers and men, including 326 deaths by drowning, Eisenhower, in September 1943, wrote tersely to the Army Chief of Staff, George Marshall: ''I do not believe in the airborne division . . . I seriously doubt that a division commander could regain control and operate the scattered forces as one unit.''

Marshall was unconvinced. As late as February 1944, he had sent aides to London to win ''Ike'' over to the boldest theory to date: why not reconceive the entire invasion as an airborne onslaught, with only a subsidiary operation by sea? This idea Eisenhower had rejected out of hand: only by degrees was he persuaded that Bradley's Cotentin swoop might give the Americans a decisive foothold.

These were, as yet, high-level concerns to almost 13,000 American paratroops, who would form the D-Day spearhead. Their main concern, all through 1943, was to survive each day of training. Most, in the words of the official historian, S. L. A. Marshall, were "born south of the tracks," volunteers because they yearned for "bigger country and a little prestige," men like Private Donald R. Burgett, a 19-year-old from Detroit, Michigan, today a retired roofer in that city. Among the tall green pines of Fort Benning, Georgia, known to generations of recruits as "The Frying Pan," Burgett very soon realized that his instructors were out to break him.

"Don't expect any sympathy from any of us at any time," one "gorilla," or cadre sergeant, told them early on, "because we are going to do everything we can to make you quit the Paratroops," and at Fort Benning he and every other "gorilla" lived up to this promise. At Fort Benning, no recruit ever sat down, leaned, rested or even walked. At best they ran; for the most part they double-timed everywhere. A man might have passed every fitness test—at least 20–40 vision, aged from 18 to 32, under 185 lbs in weight—but to ensure that only the motivated survived, the training was merciless from start to finish. The slightest infraction of rules prompted a bellow of "Gimme twenty-five!"—and the hapless rookie, dropping to a prone position, pumped out the twenty-five push-ups ordered. Nine-mile runs, before a breakfast of cornflakes and black coffee—milk was for wimps—were a daily occurrence, spurred on by the "gorillas'" stentorian cries of "Hubba-Hubba." A day that began at 5 a.m. ended only at 5 p.m.—with more push-ups.

All this, for Burgett, began in April 1943, and for seven months thereafter he, along with recruits like George Koskimaki, a Detroit radioman, and John Urbank, an optical lens grinder from Peninsula, Ohio, stuck it out. Never, they vowed, would they "sign the Quit Slip," as opting out was called. Somehow they would soldier on through the whole gamut of training: the packing and repacking of the T5 parachute assembly, whose "opening shock" could exert a force of up to five G on a man's body, the drops from the 40-ft practice tower, before ascending the lofty pinnacle of the bright red 250-ft central tower. Ahead now lay the final goal of five practice jumps, from 800 ft up to 1200 ft, when yet more skills were hastily absorbed: how to grab the sides of the jump door with your thumbs outside, and thus not block the exit for others, how to perfect the controlled collapsing fall, to right and left, timed at 15 mph once the chute opened, both feet pressed together, with the legs forming a single column. Above all, they learned to rise above the instructors' monotonous gibing: "Most of you will die in combat. You haven't got a chance!"

Some died before combat was even joined. On Burgett's first jump, he sustained a fractured left leg—mercifully, it transpired, for on the next practice jump, which he missed, the C-47 transport plane crashed and twenty-five men died, their chutes tangling in mid-air. They, too, were enrolled in the ruthless training pro-gramme; before the survivors left the field, an instructor passed the dead men's bloodied boots from hand to hand. There was still time to "sign the Quit Slip."

Two months later, when Private Donald Burgett, now a fully fledged paratrooper of the 506th Regiment, 101st Airborne, arrived in England at Aldbourne, Wiltshire, the argument that Bradley's plan had sparked off was at its height. At a meeting presided over by Mont-gomery, the air commander, Air Chief Marshal Sir Trafford Leigh-Mallory, insisted that the risks of an air drop outweighed all advantages. "Your losses will be excessive," he told Bradley derisively. "Certainly far more than the gains are worth. I'm sorry, General Bradley, but I cannot go along . . . with you."

Bradley was courteous but adamant. If the airborne drop was out, so, too, was the Cotentin assault. "I am not going to land on that beach without making sure we've got the exit behind it." Leigh-Mallory, a byword for obstructionism even with the British, became hostile. "Then let me make it clear that if you insist upon this airborne operation, you'll do it in spite of my opposition." With this, he swung round on Montgomery, "If General Bradley insists upon going ahead, he will have to accept full respons-ibility for the operation . . . ."

Until now Montgomery had always left Bradley feeling "like a poor country cousin whom he had to tolerate," but on this day he proved staunch. "That is not at all necessary, gentlemen," he said, rapping the table like a testy schoolmaster. "*I* shall assume full respons-ibility for the operation."

On May 14, to the dismay of Major Robert Low, First Army's Assistant G2 (Intelligence), the German High Command forced a change of plan. Overnight, the Cotentin Peninsula was being substantially reinforced. Agents reported the abrupt diversion of *Generalmajor* Wilhelm Falley's crack 91st Air Landing Division, originally en route from Germany to Nantes, Brittany, to the region of La Haye-du-Puits. This was twelve miles inland from the most easterly American beach. Simultaneously the 101st Regiment, armed with flame-throwers, was split between the east and west coasts, and units like the keen young 17th Machine-Gun Battalion and the 795th Georgian Battalion were included in the switch. Their watchword was said to be, Paratroopers; all of them were now squarely in the path of the airborne landings.

On May 26, Bradley convened a drumhead conference, in the First Army's dingy windowless War Room, at Clifton, outside Bristol—hemmed in by towering piles of wooden crates, for First Army HQ was already on the move. Along with Major General Matthew B. Ridgway, of the 82nd, and Major General Maxwell D. Taylor, he cobbled up a change of plan. Men of the 101st, like Donald Burgett, would stick roughly to their original mission, which was to seize four roads serving as westward exits from the beach area, as well as securing a crossing of the Douve River. But in a move that involved a slide some twenty miles to the east, the 82nd would now drop astride the Merderet River—one regiment to the east, two to the west—to seize the market town of Ste-Mère-Église and battle to protect the beachhead from the west.

Kind-hearted people might of course think there was some ingenious way to disarm or defeat an enemy without too much bloodshed. . . . Pleasant as it sounds this is a fallacy that must be exposed: war is such a dangerous business that the mistakes which come from kindness are the very worst.

(from *On War*, 'Utmost Use of Force' by Carl von Clausewitz)

The parachutist experiences the most exalted feelings of which human beings are capable, namely that of victory over one's self. For us parachutists, the words of the poet, who said that unless you stake you will never win, is no empty phrase.

(—*Generalleutnant* Bruno Brandäuer, OC *Fallschirmjäger* (Parachute) Regiment I)

far left
Major-General Richard Gale, 6th Airborne Division. (Imperial War Museum)

Major General Maxwell D. Taylor, commanding 101st Airborne. (US Airborne)

There was blood upon the risers, there were brains upon the chute;/Intestines were a-dangling from this paratrooper's boots;/They picked him up, still in his chute and poured him from his boots./He ain't gonna jump no more./Gory, Gory, What a Helluva way to die/Gory, Gory, What a Helluva way to die/Gory, Gory, What a Helluva way to die/He ain't gonna jump no more.

(from *Blood Upon the Risers*, the paratrooper's song, as sung on the march at Fort Benning, Ga)

By my troth, I care not; a man can die but once; we owe God a death . . . he that dies this year is quit for the next.

(from *Henry IV* Pt 2, III, ii, by William Shakespeare)

In theory, the line of the Merderet River was well known to every airborne officer. As a tidal tributary to the Douve, it coursed ten miles inland before merging with its parent and flowing on for seven miles to Carentan. Many times Allied reconnaissance planes had braved the German flak to follow the line of the Merderet and their pictures had shown no more than a pastoral valley carpeted with tall grasses. In April 1944, Company B of the 660th US Engineers, publishing their final sheet maps, had ventured to comment: "Ground here probably soft."

This was an understatement. In July 1943, as a wise precaution, the Germans had flooded the entire valley, from the locks at La Barquette—the target of the 501st Parachute Infantry Regiment—to the causeway west of Manoir de la Fière. Beneath the reeds and the tall grasses was a lake measuring 650 yards from shore to shore, 5 ft deep, the height of a man's chest. In this terrain, a paratrooper, weighing 300 lbs when fully equipped, would stand little chance.

Bradley did not know this.

Red Berets of the 6th Airborne in eleventh-hour briefing. (Joan St George Saunders)

American troops manhandle a wrecked British glider to the roadside to clear a way for field ambulances rushing wounded to the beach. (US Army)

Cows graze beneath a Horsa glider used by U S troops in the Cotentin. (USAF)

Oh! I have slipped the surly bonds of earth/And have danced the skies on laughter-silvered wings;/Sunward I've climbed, and joined the tumbling mirth/Of sun-split clouds, and done a hundred things/You have not dreamed of— .../... I've topped the wind-swept heights with easy grace,/Where never lark, or even eagle flew—/And, while with silent, lifting mind I've trod/The high untrespassed sanctity of space,/Put out my hand and touched the face of God.

(from *High Flight* by Flight Officer John Magee, RCAF)

OF ALL THE D-Day strike forces, none, in the last resort, were more vulnerable than the Glider Gang. Over two years, most of their company—the Britons of Brigadier George F. Chatterton's Glider Pilot Regiment, the Americans of the 325th Glider Infantry—came to acknowledge this truth. They were as expendable as the flimsy Horsa, Hamilcar and Waco gliders that they flew.

Like the US paratroops, and their counterparts, the red-bereted British 6th Airborne, the Glider Gang sprang up in the wake of German triumphs. At dawn on May 10, 1940—the day that Holland fell—ten DFS 230 gliders, towed by Junkers 52 transport planes and each carrying nine paratroopers, skidded to a halt on the grassy compound topping Fort Eben Emael. With the capture of Belgium's "impregnable" bastion, the way was clear for Hitler's Panzers to outflank France's Maginot Line. The first glider-borne assault in history was accomplished fact.

It was a coup-de-main of such unrivalled precision that the Allies could only marvel—and even nine months before Pearl Harbor, General "Hap" Arnold, Chief of the US Army Air Forces, decided briskly, "We've got a lot of catching up to do." By May 1942, Arnold's avowed aim was 6000 glider pilots training in thirty-five schools across the United States, men who would "soar to victory with the US Army Air Forces."

After Dunkirk, it was a challenge that the British, too, found hard to resist, and in that twilight of defeat more than 100,000 volunteers stepped forward. Most were men who relished challenges, like Private H. N. "Andy" Andrews, a draughtsman in the Royal Engineers, one of

twelve pilots later chosen for a critical D-Day mission. When his CO refused to release him, on grounds of "indispensability," Andrews saw this as a challenge, too. "I was working on some drawings of a Home Guard headquarters," he recalls, "and I managed to lose one sheet completely, spilt a bottle of ink on another and rub some holes in a third." With that Andrews's CO was only too ready to release him.

Yet of all these volunteers, only one man in twenty-five would finally qualify for the airborne flash of Bellerophon riding the winged Pegasus, with the pale blue wings of glider pilots adorning their jump blouses. Nor was this surprising. Brigadier George Chatterton, the motive force of the Glider Pilot Regiment from 1942, saw his pilots as nothing less than "total soldiers"—men who could not only fly a glider but slip instinctively into a ground combat role after landing. All men who survived the initial weeding next reported to the Regiment's Training Depot at Tilshead, on Salisbury Plain, where Chatterton had cannily secured a posse of Company Sergeant Majors from the Brigade of Guards. "They may not have liked the Guards noncoms," Chatterton mused, in one post-war interview, "but they never forgot them."

In fact, the memory would survive for fifty years. Staff Sergeant Ernest Lamb had just one word to describe his first impression of Tilshead: "Hostile." Reliving this calculated Fort Benning-style harassment, Staff Sergeant John Potts, another D-Day veteran, says, "You had to be fanatical to stay there ... one speck of dust on your boots ... and you were put in the guard room." One fellow trainee, arriving on parade with a small nick on his chin, was at once charged with "idleness while shaving." The slightest error while drilling, remembers Staff Sergeant Tom Pearce, and "you were brought out in front of the squad to face the men and shout at the top of your voice three times, 'I am a bloody idiot.'"

Tilshead was only the beginning. Even at the RAF's EFTS (Elementary Flying Training School), where pilots were broken in on light planes like De Havilland Tiger Moths and schooled in cross-country navigation, aircraft structures and Morse code, the ruthless discipline for glidermen continued. "RAF chaps . . . could go home to study," recalls Staff Sergeant Louis Hagen, later a hero of Arnhem, "but we had to polish our brass and our boots, march up and down and learn how to salute. After four years of war, it was a bit ridiculous." Ernest Lamb views with mixed feelings his gradual transformation to "total soldier." "Once, on parade, a dog barked," he recollects, "and the whole parade jumped to attention!"

Survivors would thus long cherish the memory of how the first American Gliderman, Staff Sergeant William T. Sampson, graduating at Elmira, New York, and asked about the large silver "G" mounted on a shield in the centre of his wings, replied, "That 'G' stands for *guts*!" In that proud boast, Sampson spoke for all of them.

On the surface, the training programmes were poles apart. Not all American pilots were volunteers; fit men could be drafted on to gliders as readily as into combat squads. Until July 1944, they drew neither jump pay nor flight pay. They were not even classed as fighting men, although many had no choice but to battle their way clear after landing in hostile territory; their status was strictly noncom, whether Staff Sergeant or Flight Officer. British glidermen, by contrast, earned all of a shilling a day (five new pence), as against the exalted 6th Airborne's two shillings, and, as "total soldiers," were at all times expected to show initiative.

Months before D-Day, their headquarters at Amesbury, Wiltshire, buzzed with stories of Chatterton's fiendish new "initiative tests". Working in pairs, pilots would be dropped off from a closed truck at any point of the compass, allotted half a crown (twelve-and-a-half new pence) between them and handed an unlooked-for assignment. Two of them had orders to obtain half an hour's dual control on a steam roller. Another team was briefed to ferret out the top secret recipe for Worcester Sauce, then bring back a bottle signed by that city's mayor. One team coaxed a reasoned critique of euthanasia from Professor Julian Huxley, the biologist; another returned with a duck's egg autographed by the singer Elizabeth Welch. But by common consent, the palm went to Sergeants George Biddlecombe and Paddy Ryan, assigned to collect the signature of the Duke of Beaufort, the Master of the Beaufort Hounds.

Although the Duke was away from home, his then house guest, HM Queen Mary, offered herself as a stand-in, and the two noncoms returned to Amesbury with their pay-books solemnly attested: Certified that they came to Badminton House—Mary R.

It was a test of resourcefulness that was to pay off: of the 600 British glider pilots crash-landing in Normandy, 580 would return to base within forty-eight hours.

You're all enthusiasm at the start,/But in the first month we'll break your heart!/You hold up your head and think you can take it—/You don't know just how tough we can make it . . ./ . . . We know all the ways to make you squirm—/Cut out the man and leave the worm . . .

. . . You're wanting to help to win the war—/We'll teach you to wonder what you're fighting for!

(from *Training Depot* by R. N. Currey)

Having to land a glider for the first time in combat is a chastening experience. It gives a man religion.

(—Brigadier General James M. Gavin, 82nd (US) Airborne Division)

Have you noticed . . . how feelings no longer follow their ordinary course, in the times of terror we live in? Everything . . . seems to happen with inexplicable precipitation. People nowadays love or hate one another at sight . . . lately everyone understood all that a handclasp might imply, just as though it were a battlefield.

(from *The Chouans* by Honoré de Balzac)

As into the gliders we crawl,/We're in for a helluva fall./No orchids, no violets/For no-engine pilots,/So cheer up, my lads, bless 'em all!

(from *The Glider Pilot's Song*)

Our business, like any other, is to be learned by constant practice and experience; and our experience is to be had in war, not at reviews.

(—Lieutenant-General Sir John Moore)

Crashed Gliders by the paratrooper artist Albert Richards. (Imperial War Museum)

66

The true bond linking the British and American glidermen was the frail craft they flew—"Flying Matchboxes" or "Airborne Coffins" to the British, "Flakhacks" to the Americans. "They were built like orange crates," says the broadcaster, Andrew A. Rooney, then a staff writer with *Yank* Magazine, "to be used once and abandoned." The British favourite was the Horsa, a high-winged plywood monoplane 67 ft long with an 88-ft wingspan: loaded either with thirty soldiers, or a jeep and ten soldiers, it weighed almost 8 tons on take-off. For more rugged assignments they fell back on the 68-ft Hamilcar, a wooden monstrosity whose 110-ft wingspan dwarfed even the Halifax bomber which towed it; weighing 18 tons when loaded, it could carry up to forty passengers and even a light tank. The Americans all along stuck to the fifteen-place Waco CG-4A (C for Cargo, G for Glider), "the most forgiving ugly beast that ever flew," and the Waco aircraft Co of Troy, Ohio, along with sixteen other factories working to their specification, were to turn out more than 13,000 of them. Not one Waco landing in Normandy survived intact.

Inevitably, there were teething troubles. By February 1944, 2100 crated Wacos had been shipped to England and stored on Cookham Common, Berkshire. But the British civilians set to assemble them had no training for the job; of the first sixty-two gliders put together, fifty-one proved unflyable. Then the Ninth Air Force Command stepped in and semi-skilled US airmen assembled 200—two months before a violent thunderstorm destroyed 100 completed gliders on the ground. Five weeks before D-Day,

Lieutenant-Colonel
Terence Otway. (Imperial
War Museum)

... From the outset there
is a play of possibilities,
probabilities, good and
bad luck, which ... makes
War of all branches of
human activity the most
like a gambling game.

(from *On War* 'What is
War?' by Carl von
Clausewitz)

glider mechanics were rushed from the States to work round the clock: following seven-day weeks of three shifts a day, they put together 910 Wacos. But only a quarter of them had been fitted with the newly devised Griswold Noses—a sturdy bolt-on nose-kit designed as crash protection.

To the very end, the Glider Gang was troubled by shortages. In January, Chatterton was dismayed to find that many pilots had clocked up no more than 150 flying hours in training school; this he could remedy, but not the dearth of co-pilots. Many paratroopers were even now being impressed as second pilots, with the cautionary preamble: "Now if I get shot or killed on the way over...here's what you're going to have to do ... to land this crate in one piece."

Few of the recruits were wholly reassured. A glider was linked to the bomber which towed it by a nylon cable zigzagging from the bomber's tail: all through the take-off, at 120 mph, it must hover above its tow to lessen the huge strain on the four engines. To endure up to six miles of free flight after the cut-off, then land with four tons of men and material, was no task for a novice.

The American glidermen knew the worst that lay ahead early on. The decision on the Cotentin paradrop made that clear. More than 100 of them would have to land in Normandy as early as 4 a.m. on D-Day, two hours after the paratroopers, for theirs was an essential cargo: 57-mm anti-tank guns, the only weapons the airborne could count on if the Germans staged a counter-attack with tanks.

The main British missions were established in April. Six Horsas—one of them piloted by

Staff Sergeant "Andy" Andrews—towed by six Halifax bombers would crash-land in two separate fields beside the bridges spanning the Orne River and the Caen Canal, with the task of capturing both intact. These were a vital link in the D-Day plan, for whoever secured and held them could interdict any flow of German reinforcements from east to west. Once this was assured, the Anglo-Canadian Second Army, landing on the assault's eastern flank, could swing out into open country.

It was an attack deemed so hazardous that every man in the 150-strong task force, the 6th Air Landing Brigade, was there of his own free will. For glidermen like Andrews and his co-pilot, Paddy Senier, it was an operation to be timed in seconds, not minutes, and for days they sat through countless screenings of a film compiled like a training simulator by Squadron Leader Lawrence Wright of the RAF's 38 Group, showing the run-up to the target. Like men under a truth drug they learned to chant as if by rote: "Crossroads...field with a round clump of trees...village with a pond... landing zone coming up now...go in between the two houses!"

Three other British gliders were earmarked for a still riskier task. At Merville, one mile inland from the coast, seven miles north-east of Caen, the Germans were working urgently on a thirty-five-acre site, labouring even by floodlight. Intelligence suggested that the site would house four batteries of 150-mm guns, encased in concrete, more than 6 ft thick, screened by a stockade of barbed wire 15 ft deep, and girdled by an anti-tank ditch. To neutralize these guns was, in the words of

Brigadier James Hill, CO of the 3rd Parachute Brigade, "a grade A stinker of a job," but to do so was imperative, since they menaced the entire eastern flank. This was the goal of the Brigade's 9th Battalion, under Lieutenant-Colonel Terence Otway, a 29-year-old regular.

In April 1944, at Otway's instigation, dummy batteries, made up of hessian, canvas and tubular steel, had been constructed within seven days at West Woodhay, south of Newbury; the urgency was such that seven Ministries involved had given their consent, and £20,000 compensation guaranteed to local farmers, within that period. But even as rehearsals began, Major-General Richard Gale, commanding the 6th Airborne, thought back to Eben Emael. Although Gale had called for a mass bombardment of Merville by Lancaster bombers, prior to the paradrop, the key to success must be

gliders—three of them, to crash-land on the battery at the same time as the bulk of the 9th Battalion moved into attack.

It was then that Major Allen Parry, commander of "A" Company, asked for—and got—100 volunteers to relinquish their roles as paratroopers and function, instead, as glider-borne infantry. As such, they would carry no parachutes but at least, as members of the hitherto-despised "chairborne airborne," they would arrive within inches of their targets. The two main pilots, Staff Sergeants Dave Kerr and Stan Bone, had been briefed to aim so truly that the concrete casemates would shear off their wings and bring the gliders to a standstill.

A few days later Parry reported back to Otway. Of the hundred volunteers he had finally selected seventy—omitting all married men.

Otway was too tactful to ask him why.

The Orne River Bridge – now renamed Pegasus Bridge in honour of the glider-borne patrol under Major John Howard who captured it intact. Two Horsas are seen to the right of the bridge. (World War II Glider Pilots Association)

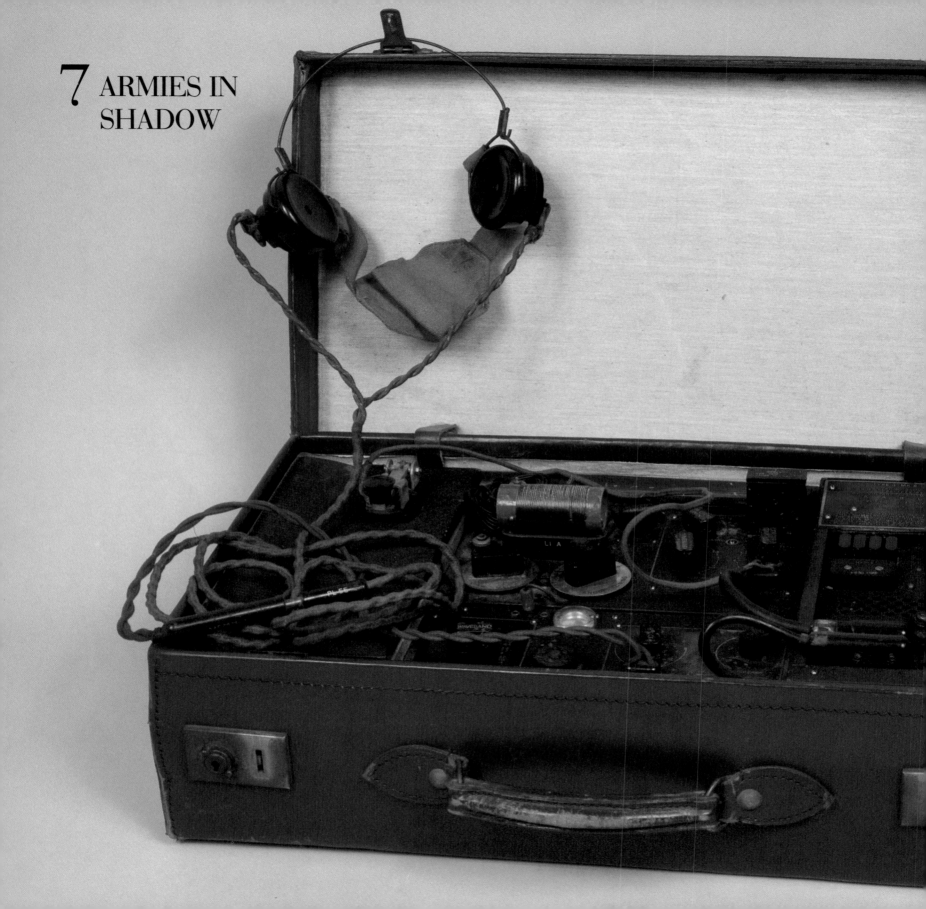

ON JANUARY 15, 1944, while the newly arrived Supreme Commander was sleeping soundly off London's Berkeley Square, *Major* Hermann Sandel of the *Abwehr* (German Military Intelligence) had just reached his office on Hamburg's Sophien Terrasse. There an unsigned ten-word radio message awaited him.

It read: "HOERTE DASS EISEN-HOWER AM 16 JANUAR IN ENGLAND EINTREFFEN WIRD." (Heard that Eisenhower will arrive in England on January 16.)

Sandel was excited, and with good reason. Eisenhower's flight from Washington, DC, to Prestwick, Scotland, on January 13 had been in the approved cloak-and-dagger tradition; the stars had been removed from his overseas cap, and those on his shoulder covered by his overcoat collar. Only on the afternoon of Sunday January 16, did the BBC break the news of his arrival. Yet somehow Sandel's most reliable agent in Britain, A 3725, Wulf Dietrich Schmidt, a young Danish industrial draughtsman, known also as Hans Hansen, had penetrated the web of secrecy. Most remarkable of all, Schmidt had contrived to remain at large since 1940: this was his 935th message.

And a message of special import, for one day earlier the Russians had launched a major offensive on a front stretching more than 100 miles, from the Leningrad sector to Novgorod. After the longest siege ever endured by a modern city, two elite units of the Red Army, the Forty-Second Army and the Second Shock Army, were striking simultaneously to relieve beleaguered Leningrad. To Sandel, Eisenhower's arrival now suggested an imminent diversionary attack on Hitler's Fortress Europe.

Great part of the information obtained in War is contradictory, a still greater part is false, and by far the greater part is of a doubtful character.

(from *On War*, 'Information in War' by Carl von Clausewitz)

Tool of the spy trade. This radio disguised as a suitcase was used by Allied agents – but such clandestine transmitter/receivers were a feature of the Secret War of World War II on both sides.

71

Colonel Thomas Robertson, MI5, who controlled the double agents. (Author's collection)

The Double Agents: Wulf Dietrich Schmidt, aka Harry Williamson, the *Abwehr*'s A 3725, MI5's "Tate." (Express Newspapers)

"Many thanks for excellent No. 935," Sandel replied promptly. "Keep us posted on Eisenhower's movements in context of invasion preparations."

Time was now of the essence. From Sandel, A 3725's message, marked SSD (very very urgent), was swiftly passed to Zossen, the concrete warren of bunkers outside Berlin that housed the Army General Staff. The new recipient was *Oberst* Alexis von Roenne, of the senior intelligence department *Fremde Heere West* (Foreign Armies West).

Roenne, in turn, was encouraged. The crunch questions—when would the invasion come and where?—were still unanswered. Yet here was a pointer that A 3725 was a man with impeccable high-level contacts.

As, in theory, Schmidt undoubtedly was. At 11.15 a.m. on Monday January 3, two of them, Colonel Noël Wild, 11th Hussars, the head of Eisenhower's Anglo-American Deception Unit, along with Lieutenant-Colonel "Johnny" Bevan, head of the London Controlling Section, had passed through the modest entrance of No. 58, St James's Street, London, the headquarters of MI5, ascending to a third-floor conference room. Grouped round a boardroom table, a dozen men were awaiting them—among them the chairman, John Masterman, a don from Christ Church, Oxford, Helenus (later Mr Justice) Milmo, a brilliant barrister, and the art historian, Anthony Blunt, himself revealed in 1979 to have been a Russian agent.

This was the Double-Cross Committee, then celebrating its third anniversary as the co-ordinating body for deception tactics used by all German agents who over four years had been "turned" by Division "B1A" of MI5. Known to all of them, by reputation, if not by sight, was their prize pupil, code-named "Tate," Major Sandel's A 3725. Caught within twenty-four hours of parachuting into England with a transmitter, on September 19, 1940, Wulf Dietrich Schmidt had, for almost four years, radioed his German paymasters exactly what the British wanted them to hear.

On January 3, Schmidt had again featured high on the agenda—for Colonel Wild had outlined a plan as to how twenty-three of the forty-seven tame agents could be employed on an omnibus plan of D-Day deception—a vast web of treachery to be spun from the North Cape to Cairo, from Moscow to Algiers.

"We are in an unique position to feed [the German Intelligence people] with false information," MI5's Colonel Thomas Robertson had enthused to one such agent in the previous November. "We can make them think that we have made our preparations to invade an area which in fact we have no intention of going anywhere near. . . ."

One such area was, of course, the Pas de Calais, and within weeks Wulf Schmidt was reporting to Hamburg from Wye, a Kentish market town sixteen miles from Dover, on the steady build-up of an Army That Never Was. Activated as far back as October 18, 1943, at General Bradley's HQ in Bryanston Square, this was nominally the First United States Army Group (FUSAG), made up of the First Canadian Army, temporarily billeted in Kent and Sussex, and the Third US Army—supposedly headquartered at Chelmsford, Essex, but in fact 180 miles north-west in Cheshire. This was, in theory, an army eleven divisions strong, 150,000 men poised for the Pas de Calais, and its commander was a man known to every member of the *Abwehr*, Lieutenant General George S. Patton, Jr, a formidable opponent in Tunisia and Sicily, famous for his pearl-handled pistols, his lacquered helmet, his iron-fisted discipline, and his gruesome oratory—"We won't just shoot the sonsabitches—we're going to cut out their living guts and use them to grease the treads of our tanks."

His "Army" was a master-stroke worthy of Dr Josef Goebbels, Hitler's propaganda chief: 150,000 combatants did exist, but few of them were quartered in Kent and Sussex and few of

them would set foot in France before July. The trains that Schmidt reported on his journeys, supposedly helping out as an agricultural worker on a friend's farm, crammed with soldiers of the US 83rd Division, were figments of MI5's fertile imagination, and since "Big Week" had seen the slow erosion of the Luftwaffe, few reconnaissance flights were now flown over south-east England. To those few planes aloft, the fake landing craft moored in creeks and estuaries seemed real enough from 33,000 feet, down to the laundry drying on the halyards and smoke drifting lazily from the funnels.

"Something big is building in the Dover area," Schmidt, later to assume a new identity

Lieutenant General George S. Patton Jr: a front for the mythical First US Army. (US Army)

Dummy LCTs on the Medway River, designed to fool German photo-reconnaissance. (Imperial War Museum)

73

as Watford press photographer Harry Williamson, stressed in the four daily transmissions he averaged from Wye, and this was no exaggeration—a vast counterfeit oil dock covering three square miles of the foreshore, designed by Professor Basil Spence, RA, later the architect of the restored Coventry Cathedral. Aided by film set designers like Colonel Geoffrey Barkas (*King Solomon's Mines*) and illusionists such as Major Jasper Maskelyne, Spence had overseen a dock fully equipped with fake pipelines, storage tanks and jetties, all to be duly "inspected" over the weeks by King George VI, Eisenhower and Montgomery.

On April 24, when FUSAG's radio network took on a brisk life of its own—with all messages intercepted according to plan—only telegraphists who had served in North Africa and Sicily, their "fists" known to the Germans,

were on active duty, and this bustling activity was pointed up, all over the south-east, by ranks of plywood gliders and inflatable rubber tanks, their tracks created by a "simulator". West of Portsmouth, by contrast, encampment tents were darkened at night, cookhouses used only smokeless stoves, and khaki towels instead of white became standard issue.

Wulf Schmidt was only one link in this long chain of deception: at least three other "turned" agents reported themselves active in the Dover area. The Polish Wing-Commander Roman Garby-Czerniawski, now a West London printer, then MI5's "Brutus", had, he exulted, been posted as a liaison officer to FUSAG HQ. The 28-year-old Yugoslav playboy, Dusko Popov, whose love-life, he claims, inspired Ian Fleming to create James Bond, could keep track of troop movements as Assistant Military Attaché to the exiled Yugoslav Government. A 29-year-old journalist from Galicia, Juan Piyol Garcia, still active in Madrid until recently, used his job as an interpreter at the Ministry of Information to seek out other agents anxious to serve the Führer.

All three men, avowed anti-Nazis, had initially been approached by *Abwehr* agents in locations as far removed as Madrid and Belgrade. Prudently, each had agreed to play along—enlisting under the Allied banner as soon as contacts were feasible. Few among them proved as rewarding as Juan Garcia, known quaintly to his controllers as "Garbo". On his own initiative, the fantasy-loving Garcia had invented a network of almost thirty sub-agents throughout the United Kingdom: a waiter from Gibraltar, who worked in Services canteens, a

AWARD

FOR CARELESS TALK

DON'T DISCUSS TROOP MOVEMENTS · SHIP SAILINGS · WAR EQUIPMENT

Communist Greek sailor based on eastern Scotland, a Venezuelan businessman, living in Glasgow, even an Indian poet, with lodgings in Brighton, and a mistress well placed in the WRNS (Women's Royal Naval Service). By 1945, the *Abwehr* was to pay "Garbo" £20,000 for the 400 clandestine letters and 2000 wireless messages based on "secrets" that his "agents" had gleaned.

In reality, most of Robertson's agents lived lonely lives. Theirs was a shut-off world of "safe" houses such as Rugby Mansions facing Olympia, in West London, 39 Hill Street, Mayfair, or 64 Palace Gardens Terrace. Apart from Radio and Security (RSS) officers like Ronnie Reid or Russell Lee, who handled their transmissions, or "case officers' like Ian Wilson or Bill Luke, their contacts were few. Three times weekly they listened in for their call signs and coded instructions, rotating the tuner of a "Skyrider" radio through the 8650 metre waveband at midday or the 5000 band at midnight. Using orange sticks tipped with secret ink, they drafted in block letters the material that Robertson's aides provided: the hard core of messages routed to cover addresses in Stockholm, Madrid and Lisbon.

By contrast, their fantasy lives were lived to the full: a fictional montage of trains, clubs, messes and canteens, of conversations which reaped rich harvests of badges, vehicles, tanks and planes. Thus John Moe ("Mutt") and Tor Glad ("Jeff"), two Norwegians "turned" in April 1941, could give substance to the legend of a British Fourth Army based on Edinburgh Castle, since Moe was ostensibly a farm agent and Glad a Norwegian Army officer. This, they

could confirm, was no legend, but an army in its own right, 250,000 strong, destined to strike at Norway, with its own red, blue and gold insignia and its own tactical air command based on airfields near Glasgow. Its commander, Lieutenant-General Sir Andrew Thorne, was well known to the Führer; in 1934, the year that Hitler affirmed Germany's right to raise an army of 300,000 men, Thorne had served as Military Attaché in Berlin.

Few armies, it seemed, ever conducted a busier signals traffic—but whether in cypher, plain text or radiotelephony, all the messages struck a note of war in a cold climate: "Captain R. V. H. Smith, 10th Cameronians, will report to Aviemore for ski-training forthwith"—"80 Div. requests 800 pairs of crampons, 1800 pairs of Kandahar ski bindings". Reports of Fourth Army dances and football games featured almost weekly in the Perth and Dundee papers, and late in April came another tangible pointer: on the advice of the banker, Sir Charles Hambro, until recently head of Special Operations Europe (SOE), heavy purchases involving ten issues were made in London on the Stockholm Stock Exchange. Between May 9 and May 15, two of these stocks rose by just under 20 per cent: the Oslo City 1937 Loan and the 1935 loan of the Norwegian *Kommunalbank*.

Yet unlike FUSAG, Fourth Army, from first to last, had no basis in reality. As Colonel R. M. "Rory" MacLeod would later recall, the total staff at Edinburgh Castle consisted of twenty officers, "just a little beyond active service", under his command, other elderly officers holding a watching brief at Stirling and

Dundee, along with a handful of "madly indiscreet" wireless operators. But ultimately their presence tied down twelve German divisions in Norway: if the Pas de Calais seemed the real danger, a diversionary attack could never be discounted.

It was a ruse that had called for Russian complicity, but as Lieutenant-Colonel "Johnny" Bevan of the London Controlling Section discovered, the Russians, even as D-Day dawned, had a pace all their own. When Bevan and his American assistant, Lieutenant Colonel William H. Baumer, flew to Moscow on January 29, time was already running out; the whole success of the Fourth Army ploy, explained General John R. Deane, head of the US Military Mission, was dependent on two things. First, the Russians must launch a feint attack towards Petsamo, on the Arctic, in the late spring. A little earlier they must establish, briefly, a naval and military mission in Edinburgh. But almost a month had passed, while Stalin pondered the implications and Bevan and Baumer cooled their heels until finally, after a monumental feast of caviar and vodka, "which called to mind the banquet scene in Charles Laughton's movie *Henry VIII*," the Russians agreed to co-operate "lock, stock and barrel."

On March 6, dazed and weary, Bevan and Baumer flew back to London—the same day that Colonel MacLeod finally arrived in Edinburgh off the night train.

If this was, in the words of the historian, Sir Michael Howard, "perhaps the most complex and successful deception operation in the entire history of war," part of the success lay in the uncertainties created. If Wulf Schmidt and Juan Garcia pointed unwaveringly at the Pas de Calais, while John Moe and Tor Glad gave due warning on Norway, a 29-year-old Russian-born redhead named Lily Sergueiev was raising the spectre of Normandy.

Recruited in Lisbon by the *Abwehr's Major* Emil Kliemann, Lily Sergueiev was ostensibly another disaffected Ministry of Information worker with family friends at Wraxall, near Bristol, and thus, with legitimate reason to travel to the West Country. Any invasion pointed at Normandy, Kliemann knew, would call for troop movements to all the ports of Devon, Dorset and Cornwall. Thus Lily Sergueiev was to log all such movements in invisible ink, mailing them to her cover address.

By design, her reports were mainly contradictory, but soldiers wearing yellow, blue and red badges seen in the streets of Bristol suggested a Fourth Army presence here, too, and American soldiers wearing a large black "A" on their sleeves were another complication, so that even Normandy could not be ruled out.

On Friday May 26, the Allies compounded confusion: pedestrians crossing Harrow High Road, London, briefly glimpsed a well-loved figure in a black Tank Corps beret and a fleece-lined leather jacket, en route in a staff car to Northolt aerodrome. As his convoy of cars moved forward, a cheer burst out: "Good old Monty!"

The man who flashed the "Monty" smile and responded with the brisk "Monty" salute was just then as frightened as he had ever been. At this stage of the planning, General Sir Bernard Montgomery had already reached his advance Portsmouth headquarters, but his

What wonder . . . if the mind misses every impression except those to which it surrenders itself? The result is that we draw sweeping conclusions from trifling indications and lead ourselves into pitfalls of delusion.

(from *On The Nature of the Universe* Bk IV, by Lucretius)

. . . The great shadow-boxing match had to go on without a break. One bogus impression in the enemy's mind had to be succeeded by another equally bogus . . . there was always the necessity to do everything possible to induce him to make faulty dispositions of his dwindling reserves . . . Damned unsporting, of course, but that is the way it is in real war.

(from *Overture to Overlord* by Lieutenant-General Sir Frederick Morgan)

Our knowledge is a torch of smoky pine/That lights the pathway but one step ahead/Across a void of mystery and dread.

(from *Sonnets* III, by George Santayana)

Mystify, mislead—and surprise.

(—General Thomas J. 'Stonewall' Jackson)

"Monty's Double":
Lieutenant Meyrick
Clifton-James, Royal
Army Pay Corps.
(London *News Chronicle*)

"double," 41-year-old Lieutenant Meyrick Clifton-James, Royal Army Pay Corps, was embarking on the first stage of a 1000-mile journey to Gibraltar and Algiers. A Montgomery look-alike, who for years had toured the provinces as a small-part actor, Clifton-James was almost the last fling of the D-Day dice.

For plainly, if Montgomery was visiting Algiers, no assault across the English Channel could as yet be imminent.

Studying the general's mannerisms — the right hand weighing an invisible object when discussing a point, the slightly nasal high-pitched voice — Clifton-James had rehearsed the role for three weeks with ever-growing doubts. But as the roadside cheering redoubled, it was like a first night curtain rising: he was "on" and he was word perfect.

At intervals he would let drop khaki handkerchiefs initialled "BLM" like clues in a paperchase. He was to address Gibraltar's governor, Sir Ralph Eastwood, "Monty's" old Staff College crony, as "Rusty" and to talk openly of a mysterious "Plan 303." Despite the risk of snipers, he would travel always in an open car, so that German agents could train their telescopes on him. On Montgomery's insistence, he would even receive a general's pay — in the region of £8 a day — for every day on the job, but even this was scant compensation for the ordeal that would follow.

Only at the last moment had Clifton-James learned that "Monty" was both a teetotaller and a non-smoker, eschewing both meat and fish, and that ahead of him stretched a forty-eight hour tobacco-free nature cure, fortified by nothing stronger than ginger ale.

Reports like these — noted, if largely discounted — created an almost insuperable problem for *Oberst* von Roenne at Zossen. For months he had striven to create a *feindbild* — a picture of the enemy — yet by late May the messages pouring in were as shrill and confusing as static in the ether.

All told, some 250 largely conflicting messages had to be evaluated — pointing not only to the Pas de Calais and Normandy but to Norway, Denmark, Belgium, even the Balkans. And was an invasion even on the cards? Was the plan now to compel Germany to surrender by bombing alone — and to stage a series of mini-Dieppes as German resistance weakened?

Appropriately, the last word was with Juan "Garbo" Garcia. On the night of June 5, Eisenhower was to grant special dispensation for

Garcia to make one more contact with his control in Madrid—but not earlier than 3 a.m. on June 6, three-and-a-half hours before the first landings. With an RSS officer standing by, Garcia duly made this nick-of-time transmission: at Otterbourne, Hampshire, his waiter from Gibraltar had broken camp to report that Canadian troops had suddenly been roused and were on the move, armed with both rations and vomit bags.

It was an exclusive item to gladden any agent, but understandably, at 3 a.m., neither Wilhelm Leissner, the *Abwehr* chief in Iberia, nor Karl-Erich Kulenthal, based at Madrid's German Embassy, were tuned in. Not until 6.08 a.m. on June 6, did Garcia make contact, with a ringing rebuke: "This makes me question your seriousness and sense of responsibility. . . ."

From the British, his reward did not come for another eighteen months, when the Foreign Secretary, Ernest Bevin, decorated him with the King's Medal for Service in the Cause of Freedom. In this, at least, they lagged behind Hitler, who as early as July 29, had felt moved to make amends—"I am able to advise you today that the Führer has conceded the Iron Cross (Second Class) to you for your extraordinary merits."

Montgomery outside his trailer caravan with puppies "Rommel" and "Hitler." (Imperial War Museum)

"Freimut, mein liebe, ich schere mich den Teufel darum!"
(Frankly, my dear, I don't give a damn.)

THE PARTING WORDS of Rhett Butler to Scarlett O'Hara could rarely have been uttered in a stranger setting, a dining room where candle-light glowed on polished mahogany and faded Gobelin tapestries, the showpiece of the twelfth-century Château de la Roche-Guyon, fifty miles north-east of Paris and midway to the Normandy coast. The narrator, the jovial *Vizeadmiral* Friedrich Ruge, naval aide to *Feldmarschall* Erwin Rommel, was diverting his chief with their nightly entertainment: Ruge's blow-by-blow summary of Margaret Mitchell's *Gone With The Wind*.

Since November 1943, when Hitler had appointed him Inspector General of his much-vaunted Atlantic Wall, rare evenings like this had been Rommel's sole relaxation. At 53, "The Desert Fox" was, as so often in the past, facing a race against time: the fortification of almost 2500 miles of coastline, from the North Cape to the Bay of Biscay, above all the 800 miles from Holland to Brittany.

It was an assignment that Rommel had at first accepted with deep misgivings. "The war is as good as lost," he had told his interpreter, Dr Ernst Franz, on yielding up his temporary command in Italy, "and hard times lie ahead." Franz thought he knew why, for only recently Hitler's Chief of Army Personnel had noted for the war diary: "Unfortunately, *Feldmarschall* Rommel is still obsessed by the retreat from Africa"—recalling Rommel's crushing defeat at El Alamein one year earlier.

The attack will come; there's no doubt about that any more. . . . If they attack in the West, that attack will decide the War. If this attack is repulsed the whole business is over. Then we can withdraw troops right away.

(—Adolf Hitler, December 23, 1943)

Rommel's Wall: taking shape in April, 1944, as revealed by low-flying planes of 140 (Army Co-Operation) Squadron. (Author's Collection)

81

Feldmarschall Erwin
Rommel (L) with
Vizeadmiral Friedrich
Ruge, his naval adviser.
(Gen. Gunther
Blumentritt)

But Rommel had never yet resisted a challenge, and this was the challenge of a lifetime; appointed Commander-in-Chief of Army Group "B", which comprised the Fifteenth Army in the Pas de Calais and the Seventh Army in Normandy and Brittany, he had made his first whirlwind inspection of the Atlantic Wall in December—and what he saw staggered him. For all practical purposes, the Wall was not a wall at all. Only at a dozen points, like Cherbourg, had the Navy and the construction experts of the civilian Todt Organization come close to creating the impregnable fortress that Dr Josef Goebbels, as Minister of Propaganda, had celebrated so long and so loudly. Even those strongpoints under concrete had head cover only 60 cm thick, and while naval gun batteries were in steel cupolas, the army artillery, to ensure greater freedom of fire, had merely dug in. On this point, Rommel was in full agreement with his nominal superior, the ageing patrician Commander-in-Chief, West, *Feldmarschall* Gerd von Rundstedt.

For von Rundstedt, the blockhouses, casemates and gun emplacements of the Wall were a folly that had eaten up 3.7 billion Reichmarks, "an enormous bluff . . . more for the German people than the enemy". The Wall might "temporarily obstruct' an Allied attack; it would never stop it. "The Wall has no depth and little surface; it is sheer humbug."

This defeatist attitude shocked Rommel profoundly, but at 68, von Rundstedt was by now a commander steeped in cynicism. Confidants like *Generalmajor* Gunther Blumentritt, his Chief of Staff, knew that to von Rundstedt Hitler was always "that Bohemian corporal" (the Führer's rank in World War One), while Rommel was affably dismissed as the "Marschall Bubi" (the Boy Marshal). Rarely stirring from his headquarters at St Germain-en-Laye, outside Paris, von Rundstedt's pleasure was to dine early off his favourite *eintopf*, meat and vegetable stew, before an evening of browsing through piles of paperback whodunnits, with Agatha Christie for preference.

His thinking, though, had profoundly affected the entire concept of coastal defence: an invasion, if it came, could only be defeated *after* the Allies had landed, by a mass assault of troops, at first held back from the coast, then striking hard at the invaders' inadequate supply lines and disorganized bridgeheads.

Rommel would have none of this. The only way, as he saw it, was to smash the attack at the very outset—on the beaches. His aide, *Hauptmann* Hellmuth Lang, a former storekeeper from Gmund, near Stuttgart, always recalled how Rommel, stabbing at the sands with his black silver-topped marshal's baton, had summed up his entire credo: "We'll have only one chance to stop the enemy and that's while he's in the water . . . everything we have must be on the coast." Unwittingly, he coined a phrase that went down to history. "Believe me, Lang, the first twenty-four hours of the invasion will be decisive . . . for the Allies, as well as Germany, it will be the longest day."

Time and again, Rommel had exerted pressure—on von Rundstedt, on Hitler's Chief of Operations, *General der Artillerie* Alfred Jodl, on Hitler himself—to incorporate two hard-hitting mobile divisions into his coastal defence system: *Gruppenführer* Fritz Witt's 12th Panzer Division, based at Evreux, thirty miles south of Rouen, and *Generalleutnant* Fritz Bayerlein's Panzer *Lehr*, centred on Avranches. But Hitler, for one, was hostile to the concept of mobility. "Their part is to get killed behind the fortifications," he told Rommel coldly, on March 20. "So they've no need to be mobile."

Above all, there was the vexed question: where would the invaders strike? At Zossen,

Once a doctrine and its articles become a dogma, woe to the army which lies enthralled under its spell.

(—Major General J. F. C. Fuller)

They will be staking everything on one card . . . they will lose the war very quickly indeed if that card does not win.

(—Josef Goebbels, January 23, 1944)

83

opposite above
Rommel's Wall: one of
the so-called "Belgian
Gates." (Service
Historique de la Marine)

opposite below
Rommel's Wall: concrete
tetrahedra near Gold
Beach. (Service
Historique de la Marine)

Oberst Alexis von Roenne, who had so warmly welcomed Wulf Dietrich Schmidt's signal in mid-January, still favoured the Pas de Calais, and since Roenne was the man who had written off Allied intervention in Poland in 1939 and urged the great Sedan thrust of 1940, his stock was high. Von Rundstedt, too, saw this as logical: between Dover and Calais the Channel was at its narrowest, only twenty miles wide.

Since November 1943, the sites of Hitler's reprisal weapons, the V-1s and the V-2s, had sprung up all over the region: their capture must surely be an Allied priority. The Pas de Calais was equally the shortest route to the Ruhr, the industrial heart of Germany; given luck and daring, an invader might reach the Rhine in four days. This reasoning seemed foolproof: following Dieppe, four times as much concrete had been allotted to the Pas de Calais as to Normandy, and by June 1944, the Fifteenth Army, under *Generaloberst* Hans von Salmuth, was six weeks ahead of its Seventh Army neighbour in Normandy.

"The forefinger of High Command strategists moved . . . like an uncertain compass needle," noted the critic, Milton Shulman, then a Canadian Intelligence Officer, and Blumentritt, too, recalled Hitler's uncertainty. "His eyes were hopping all round the map."

Only as late as May 7 did Rommel achieve a compromise of sorts: three Panzer divisions, the 2nd, the 21st and 116th, were placed unreservedly at his disposal. But four remaining Panzer divisions were still held fifteen miles inland, as a High Command reserve, which meant, in effect, that only Hitler could ever authorize their dispatch.

Then, on March 4, Hitler, as was often the case, reverted to an earlier intuition, and the High Command's teleprinter wires hummed briskly once again: "The Führer . . . considers Normandy and Brittany to be particularly threatened by invasion because they are very suitable for the creation of beachheads." By March 9, Rommel had taken up permanent quarters at the Château de la Roche-Guyon, in a ground-floor office dominated by the portrait of the Duc de la Rochefoucauld, the seventeenth-century writer of maxims, whose castle this had been. "I'm raising plenty of dust," Rommel had written cheerfully to his son, 15-year-old Manfred, for now he had only one object in view: to refashion the Atlantic Wall after "The Devil's Gardens," which had come close to defeating the British at El Alamein.

"Let me see your hands," Rommel ordered *Leutnant* Arthur Jahnke, of the 919th Infantry Regiment, commanding Strongpoint No. 5, near St-Germain-de-Varreville on the Cotentin Peninsula, and only when Jahnke stripped off his gloves to reveal bloody calluses scored by barbed wire did he nod with satisfaction. "Well done. The blood on an officer's hands from fortification work is worth every bit as much as that shed in battle."

For what Rommel sought now was a hitherto-undreamt-of barrier of minefields, six miles wide, along the entire Atlantic Wall: 65,000 mines to a square kilometre, 200 million mines in France alone. It would be "a pre-coastal coral reef," he told Ruge confidently, where every beach, given precious time, would prove a graveyard. For Rommel, always single-minded, the Wall, in time, became an obsession. Pressed to visit the famous porcelain china works at Sèvres, he remained blind to the works of art. "Find out if they can make waterproof casings for my sea mines," was his only comment to his then Chief of Staff, *Generalmajor* Alfred Gause.

His ingenuity was boundless—"the greatest engineer of the Second World War," enthused his fortifications expert, *General* Wilhelm Meise—and the coastline of north-west Europe soon testified to that ingenuity. Among the deadliest obstacles were the Elements C, great iron gates, 15 ft long and 12 ft high, set 300 yards from high water mark, with powerful legs to brace them firmly against tidal pressure. There were "Czech hedgehogs,"

Modern observation platform for former US beaches at St Come-de-Fresne.

opposite above
Surviving German blockhouse with field gun on Juno Beach (St Aubin-sur-Mer).

opposite below
Surviving German blockhouse, Omaha Beach.

The fully developed man is, above all, provided with *weapons*: he is the man who *attacks*.

(—Friedrich Nietzsche)

The great distinction of this game is that it truly, when well played, determines who is the best man—who is the highest-bred, the most self-denying, the most fearless, the coolest of nerve, the swiftest of eye and hand. You cannot test these possibilities wholly, unless there is a clear possibility of the struggle ending in death.

(from *The Crown of Wild Olive* by John Ruskin)

wooden or steel triangles 4 ft high, with mines and a million obsolete French shells primed to explode on contact. There were curved rails, ramps fitted with blades and fat black Teller mines, and concrete pyramids called tetrahedra, all of them designed to wrench an Allied landing craft apart at the moment of impact.

And by degrees, it seemed, Rommel's enthusiasm was contagious. At Hardelot-Plage, as early as February, he rallied one detail to install stakes with fire-hoses instead of pile-drivers: it could be done in three minutes as opposed to forty-five, 100 stakes in a working day. When troops thus gave of their best, he was swift to reward: the third car in his convoy, where war correspondents like Lutz Koch and Baron Hans-Gertt von Esebeck rode in some discomfort, was always packed with harmonicas and accordions, prizes for the best divisions. The

reporters shrewdly noted the results: at Quinéville, on the Cotentin Peninsula, a double row of "hedgehogs" and tetrahedra, 2100 yards long, suddenly materialized within four April days.

"You'll find Rommel tiresome," *Feldmarschall* Wilhelm Keitel, the Chief of the Armed Forces, had warned von Rundstedt, but it was dilatory commanders in the field who most dreaded Rommel's headlong visits. All too often, the shortcomings were a legacy of von Rundstedt's initial strategy: at Fécamp, near Le Havre, the bunkers on the beach had been bricked in; at Dieppe, by ironic contrast, the bunkers remained but were now unoccupied. South of the mouth of the Somme, the barricades had been demolished and the main defence line moved inland, several miles from the beach. "There is still ignorance of a land front," was Rommel's acid rebuke to

Generalmajor Josef Reichert's 711th Infantry Division, sited east of the Orne River. "The foreshore has not yet been closed off with barriers."

The troops at his disposal lent urgency to Rommel's problems. "Many a man here has been living a soft life," he grumbled in one letter home, but many were all too frail to have lived otherwise. On a front normally boasting sixty divisions, only fifteen were divisions worthy of the name. While the average age was 36, many men were as old as 56, cast-offs from the Russian front, split, for administrative reasons, into units which bespoke their disabilities; "ear battalions" of deaf men, "white bread divisions" of men with stomach ulcers. Others

were ill-trained assortments of Russian prisoners-of-war—like Infantry Regiment 987 of the 276th Division, whose soldiers spoke thirty-four separate dialects from Armenian to Tartar.

"We are asking rather a lot," commented *Generalleutnant* Karl Wilhelm von Schlieben, of the 709th Division, "if we expect Russians to fight in France for Germany against the Americans," and there were covert hints of apathy in many coastal areas. Near Bayeux, Rommel had approved several cattle pastures duly signposted—"ACHTUNG MINEN. LEBENSGEFAHR"—unaware that once he had moved on, cattle would be grazing peacefully there until D-Day.

He was fully alive to the dangers of a parachute drop. On April 25, addressing the 346th Infantry Division at Bolbec, he told them with rare eloquence: "Like a cunning hunter we will have to lie in wait for the wild birds descending from the air. . . . Envision swarms of locusts falling from the moonlit sky." Already *Rommelspargel* (Rommel's Asparagus) were studding scores of inland fields, wooden poles 12 ft long, planted 2 ft deep and 30 yards apart, topped with a spider's web of mines to blow Horsa or Waco gliders to smithereens.

In all these weeks, Rommel, a devoted husband and father, never failed to write to his wife, Lucie-Maria, in Herrlingen, Germany, fifty letters in all, and it was as if, one biographer, David Irving, noted, a psychiatrist "had advised him to repeat two words over and over again to himself: think Victory!" "I think for certain that we'll win the defensive battle in the west," he had written as early as January 19, and on

March 31 the same aura of optimism prevailed: "I saw plenty to cheer me yesterday." On April 27: "We are now growing stronger every day": on May 15: "The enemy will have a rough time of it when he attacks and ultimately [he will] achieve no success."

Four days earlier, Army Group B's War Diary had recorded that 517,000 beach obstacles—30,000 of them fitted with Teller mines—had now been rammed and pile-driven into position. In Normandy, the work was still lagging behind, but Rommel did not worry unduly. He told himself there was still time.

"When they come it will be at high water," Rommel had told *Leutnant* Jahnke on one inspection trip and this mirrored the earlier thinking of *Admiral* Theodor Krancke, Naval Group West, who had predicted that the Allies would come by moonlight, at high tide, both to observe and float over the obstacles in the vicinity of a large port. They would need visibility of 5000 yards, winds of no more than 30 mph and wave heights no greater than seven feet.

On May 19, seated at his fine Renaissance desk, Rommel, for the first time in weeks, dared to think of a break from the front. "I'm waiting to see whether I shall be able to get away for a couple of days in June," he told Lucie-Maria.

And if possible one of those days would be Tuesday June 6, Lucie's fiftieth birthday; her present, a pair of hand-made grey suede shoes, size five-and-a-half, had already been ordered in Paris. This would mean leaving La Roche-Guyon for Herrlingen no later than the early morning of June 4, but the Weekly Report would stress that although the Allies had certainly reached "a high degree of readiness... according to past experience this does not indicate that an invasion is imminent...."

In their own good time, the Allies *were* coming—but Rommel, like a negligent host, would not be there to receive them.

9 EYES BEHIND THE WALL

View of the Channel
from the old German
batteries at Crisbecq,
Normandy.

André Dewavrin ("Colonel Passy"), chief of Free French Intelligence. (Author's collection)

EVEN AS WORK along the Atlantic Wall gathered impetus, *Vizeadmiral* Friedrich Ruge had the uneasy feeling that all was not well. The French civilians he encountered daily seemed *too* compliant, *too* docile. When Rommel's convoy of staff cars wound industriously along the Normandy coastline, from Honfleur to Ouistreham, through Port-en-Bessin to Crisbecq, Ruge had the sensation of eyes watching everywhere.

"It must have been fun for those on the other side of the Channel to carry on their intelligence activities," he would recall wryly. "The conditions which had developed during . . . four years of occupation . . . were a gift for every intelligence officer working in France. . . ."

Ruge was perceptive. Each day, for months on end, Mosquito and Spitfire reconnaissance aircraft hovered above the Wall, first at 40,000 feet, then, concentrating on verticals and obliques, more riskily: at wave-top height, three to four miles out, then, at zero feet, 1500 yards from the shelving coastline, finally 1500 yards inland, at a heart-stopping 2000 feet, rocketing along the Wall at 400 mph. Their prints, in due time, formed the basis of 170 million naval maps, but these were no more than double checks on what agents of the French resistance network, *Centurie*, the paragon of all the spy rings, had reported for nearly two years.

The concept of civilian agents, blending into the landscape because they were part of it, had been dreamed up as far back as July 1940—two weeks after the fall of France—in a dusty office in St Stephen's House, Westminster,

overlooking the Thames Embankment. It was then that a quiet, implacable young Assistant Professor of Fortifications from St Cyr, *Capitaine* André Dewavrin, one of 2000 Frenchmen who had rallied to General Charles de Gaulle, had sold the idea to his leader overnight. Nor was this surprising. As head of the newly created *Deuxième* (Second, or Intelligence) *Bureau*, the 28-year-old Dewavrin, code-name "Colonel Passy," was, at first, the Bureau's sole occupant—just as General Frederick Morgan, three years later, *was* "Operation Overlord."

Funds were never lacking. From the first, Sir Claude Dansey, Deputy Director of MI6, and

92

the chief of his French Section, Commander Wilfred Dunderdale, RNVR, were eager for short-spell agents to prospect the terrain for the new hit-and-run Commando raids—Winston Churchill's "steel hand from the sea." But in the long-term, Dewavrin's concept might have withered on the vine without Gilbert Renault, another Day One volunteer. A 36-year-old executive of the Eagle Star Insurance Company in Paris, Renault, "Colonel Rémy," to the underground, soon proved the agent-extra-ordinary. Smuggled back into France via Lisbon, he made the contacts which count-ed—port pilots, dockyard technicians—in the days when the Atlantic U-Boat war was the main threat to Britain's lifeline. By the autumn months of 1941—when the first Second Front demonstrations began—Renault's agents were dotted strategically through all the main U-Boat bases from Brest to Bordeaux, 100 men covering 500 miles of coastline. On that model he built up fourteen other networks.

But in April 1942, when Renault, through devious contacts, appointed a burly talkative cement salesman named Marcel Girard, to set up *Centurie*, a network based on the old Norman city of Caen, this was no more than prudent insurance. In the 200 miles between St Malo and Le Havre, no agents had existed until then, and Renault merely sought to plug the gap. And even after August 1943, when Normandy became the Allies' ultimate goal, neither Girard nor his agents were privy to that secret. Like the arc welders toiling on the pierheads of "Mulberry Harbour," they worked in the dark, sustained by faith, knowing nothing of the larger pattern.

The keynote, from the first, was normality. As the Government's Chief Engineer of Roads and Bridges, Eugène Meslin was the natural choice to head up *Centurie-Caen*; he had freedom to travel almost eighty miles of coastline, overseeing all non-military mainte-nance. In his quiet office by the Port de la Fonderie, spanning the Caen Canal, he and Girard at first envisaged a small-scale operation: no more than fifty men and women to cover 18,000 square miles, a territory roughly half the size of Ireland. This was a short-lived dream. Within weeks, travelling under his cover as a cement salesman, Girard was appointing agents in towns like Argentan and Le Mans, eighty miles inland; in time, *Centurie* would number 1500 agents.

It was Hitler who supplied the motivation. Pearl Harbor, coupled with setbacks on the Russian front, now made Allied invasion more than a possibility, and on March 23, 1942, the Führer issued his crucial Directive No. 40. To defend the French mainland to the death, from Nieuport to the Spanish frontier, was now priority, and a stocky eagle-nosed regular soldier, *Generalfeldmarschall* Erwin von Witz-leben, was dispatched on a tour with stark and simple terms of reference: the Fortification of the West.

At the same time, Meslin was appointing the kind of agents whom Dewavrin had seen as ideal—men with work-hardened hands, wearing labourers' denims, with valid reasons for travel. All of them blended imperceptibly into any provincial landscape. When Jean Chateau, the electricity board inspector, Léon Dumis, the garage proprietor, Roger Desch-

Yet, Freedom! yet thy banner, torn, but flying,/Streams like the thunder-storm *against* the wind.

(from *Childe Harold's Pilgrimage* Canto IV, by George Gordon, Lord Byron)

Ye are spies; to see the nakedness of the land ye are come.

(from *The Book of Genesis* xliii, 9)

. . . A spy has this strange and splendid characteristic: he never loses his temper. He has the Christian humility of a priest . . . he is brazen-faced against insults and goes straight for his goal like an animal whose strong carapace is proof against anything but a cannon-ball.

(from *A Murky Business* by Honoré de Balzac)

Three survivors of *Centurie* network: left to right, Léon Dumis, Léonard Gille and René Duchez, who stole the plan of the Atlantic Wall. (Léonard Gille)

A native of Lorraine, Duchez, at 40, still retained something of the language from the German occupation of his childhood, and this proved useful when carrying out minor decorations at the Todt Organization offices on the Avenue Bagatelle. One such occasion was on Friday May 8, 1942, when Duchez, submitting a lower estimate than any competitor, got the job of repapering two offices on the second floor—and established a good rapport with the Army liaison officer *Bauleiter* (Todt Major) Hugo Schnedderer.

It was in Schnedderer's office, while the Major was dictating an urgent letter to a clerk in the adjoining room, that Duchez spotted a pile of top-secret blueprints, labelled in red *Sonderzeichungen—Streng Geheim*—Special Blueprint—Top Secret—lying on the desk. At a glance he recognized the narrow bottleneck mouth of the Seine at Quillebeuf, and the cliffs north of Houlgate and Cabourg. The unbelievable had come his way: a Todt Organization map of the coastline of Normandy. As if by reflex, with the panicky bravado of a mischievous schoolboy, Duchez slid the topmost blueprint behind a heavy mirror 2 ft square that hung above the fireplace.

On Monday May 11, when he began work, there were complications. Schnedderer had been transferred to the main Todt HQ at St Malo, and his successor, *Bauleiter* Adalbert Keller, saw no reason to grant an audience to an importunate house-painter. Only when Duchez explained that as a gesture of goodwill he had offered to paint the commandant's office for free did Keller succumb to the bait. Thus far the map, one of a set of twelve duplicates, had not

ambres, the plumber, and Pierre Harivel, the insurance inspector, met for aperitifs and a game of dominoes in Caen's Café des Touristes, no Gestapo agent would spare them a glance. Even René Duchez, the house painter, with his twinkling blue eyes and non-stop banter, would pass off as an amiable buffoon, yet it was Duchez, entirely by chance, who achieved *Centurie's* most astonishing coup of the war.

been missed—and when Duchez finished work on the Wednesday, it was quietly spirited from the building in the cylinder holding his paint brushes.

Nobody—neither Girard nor any of his agents—knew enough German to assess the map's significance. In an ordinary week it would have reached Paris by the same routine means as all *Centurie*'s other information. From the broken-down boiler in the basement of the Café des Touristes, which was cleared weekly by the "duty postmen," Harivel or the advocate

Aboard the N51, June 20, 1942. The group includes Edith Renault; a sailor holding Michel, her baby; Gilbert Renault (wearing beret); Lieut. Daniel Lomenech, RNVR. (Daniel Lomenech)

Aboard the N51: Jean-Claude and Cécile Renault. Below the cardboard cartons holding Renault's despatches is the biscuit tin containing René Duchez's stolen plan of the Atlantic Wall. (Daniel Lomenech)

... The documents that we received from our agencies were read, classified, sorted, and then re-classified. ... The business was now taking on a regular commercial air ... every evening I received the messages that had come in. We were just like a large firm with many branches which kept in touch constantly by telegram. The head office, Free France, was in Carlton Gardens, London. Such an organization was entirely against all rules. But, such as it was, it delivered the goods. And I really believe that the fact it was organized contrary to the rules for intelligence networks, was a protection. ... This officelike operation ... helped us to lose that hole-and-corner mentality.

(from *The Silent Company* by Rémy (Gilbert Renault))

Léonard Gille, the dusty scraps of paper were taken, like the contents of some deadly suggestion box, to Meslin's office. These were classified under subject headings into a lengthy report, then passed to the courier Maurice Himbert, a motorcycle repair man, who had permission to buy spare parts in Paris. There Renault's agents took over. All told, it was a 600-mile journey before the information reached Dewavrin's London office, sometimes by maritime rendezvous with a fishing trawler, sometimes by Lysander pick-up from the landing-ground code-named "Guardian Angel," near Rouen. Two weeks later, a BBC "Personal Message" from the studios at Bush House, London, signalled safe arrival: "The three cabin boys lunched well in Dieppe."

Duchez's map entailed a more hazardous journey. By the time Girard himself took it to the capital, 32,000 Gestapo agents in Paris had Renault's description: one of his radio operators, caught in the act of transmission, had cracked under torture. Dewavrin's reaction was immediate—Renault must return to England without delay—not realizing that, as a family man, Renault would be travelling with his wife, Edith, his children, Jean-Claude, 13, Catherine, 12, Cécile, 10 and the baby, Michel, born eighteen months earlier. In the guise of a family picnic party, they had journeyed to Pont Aven, in Brittany, to board a leaky old lobster-boat, the *Deux Anges*, a 35-footer with a salt-crusted foredeck and only a 20 hp Beaudouin engine to reach a top speed of 13 knots. There followed a nightmare trip past German checkpoints, crammed in lockers six feet by three and a half by two like the living tenants of a coffin, before

they at last achieved a rendezvous off the Lorient fishing bank with the N51, a two-masted British trawler skippered by Lieutenant Daniel Lomenech, a Breton loaned by De Gaulle to the RNVR for special operations.

When the Renault family finally reached Tresco, in the Scilly Isles, at 10 a.m. on June 20, Duchez's plan had all along been secured inside a biscuit box of *Crêpes Dentelles*, a Breton delicacy, sealed with adhesive tape to keep out moisture.

Two months before the Dieppe raid, the code-name for all far-distant invasion plans was "Martian," and the "Martian Room," a bleak basement in Storey's Gate, St James's Park, otherwise Theatre Intelligence Section, GHQ Home Forces, was thus the plan's destination. "It scored a very great hit," the chief, Colonel John L. Austin, a peacetime don from Christ Church, Oxford, recalled later. "It turned attention sharply to this weakly defended sector ... showing that many earlier estimates of the strength had been alarmist ... and that a good deal of photographic interpretation had been in error." Another peacetime don, the historian M. R. D. Foot, then with Mountbatten's Combined Operations Staff, was to testify: "I used a well-thumbed copy, when helping ... to plan raids on the Channel coast."

Only by degrees did it dawn on the Allies that this plan, a gift from the gods, was an earnest of intention rather than an actuality: the Atlantic Wall had not yet been built.

In Caen, when the realization at last dawned that one blueprint had gone astray, reactions were understandably muted. The Todt HQ at St Malo was never informed, nor was the local Gestapo. A security detachment under *Sturmbannführer* (SS Major) Friedrich Riekert did stage a series of sporadic raids on the households of local draughtsmen but ultimately drew a blank. Neither von Rundtstedt—nor Rommel, when the time came—was ever aware that a plan had gone missing.

Since no one had alerted *Centurie* of their signal coup, they had decided to produce their own maps. The linchpin of this amateur service was 30-year-old Robert Thomas, then employed in the potato controller's office, yet still a frustrated cartographer, anxious to emulate his father, Louis, who worked under Meslin as an Inspector of Roads and Bridges. Papa Thomas had maps available only for eighty miles of coastline, but this was a start. The solution, as Thomas and Girard saw it, was simple: each agent living on the coast was given a square of mapping paper roughly eight inches by six. Based on the General Staff maps, serving the Government and the Army much like an English Ordnance Survey map, their scale was one-in-fifty-thousand, a little more than an inch to the mile. No man or woman would be asked to cover more than thirteen square miles of their own district. Details of a new blockhouse, an unfinished battery, could be noted on wafer-thin cigarette paper, then transferred to the map held at home. Normandy would become a living map.

All told, Thomas drew or supervised almost 4000 maps, but the watchword was always: Keep it normal. In the Prefecture at St Lô, twenty-five miles from the coast, Adolphe Franck, a Lorraine schoolmaster, who spoke German, used his interpreter's job to abstract a

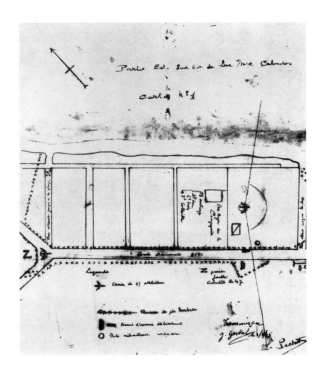

One of the 4000 maps prepared by *Centurie* network: a sketch plan of machine-gun and artillery posts plus the hidden petrol dump at Luc-sur-Mer, between Juno and Sword. (Robert Thomas)

plan of the locks at La Barquette, which controlled the tidal flow for twenty miles up the nearby Douve River. These became the D-Day target of the 501st Parachute Infantry Regiment, under Colonel Howard "Skeets" Johnson. Five hundred yards off the coastline, a one-time trawler skipper, Léon Cardron, now fishing from a battered 20-footer called *Le Maseu*, used a pre-war box camera tangled in his nets to register the now-desolate summer resort of Arromanches. This proved valuable, although in the autumn of 1942 nobody had conceived a harbour called "Mulberry."

In Port-en-Bessin, on the periphery of what became Utah Beach, Mme Olgvie Vauclin, a roof tiler's wife, was always knitting busily on her bus journeys, a pattern book spread on her knees; at intervals, she noted numbers in the

God send me to see such a company together agayne when need is.

(—Lord Howard of Effingham)

Fear has many eyes and can see things underground.

(from *Don Quixote* Pt I, Ch. 20, by Miguel Cervantes)

margin, 45-63-19. These were neither numbers of rows nor stitches but tactical items: the distance between the customs post and the path at the foot of the cliffs. In Bessin itself, François Guerin, a young student, had his music teacher, Arthur Poitevin, ostensibly riding pillion on his noisy velo-cycle, and Poitevin would memorize precise details of casemates and batteries from Guerin's murmured clues. The sentries paid no attention to the burly Poitevin with his white stick: the teacher had been blind for years.

When danger threatened, *Centurie* agents were there. Along with Duchez, Henri Marigny, a Caen bookseller, volunteered to serve as an air-raid warden in the bomb-battered port of Ouistreham, the ultimate objective for the

commandos of Lord Lovat's 1st Special Service Brigade. On their lonely night patrols, they spotted the 2-ft wide anti-tank ditch, the 300 yards of hotels and peacetime châlets demolished to make way for casemates, the flak batteries hugging the Casino. "We used a town plan that the tourist publicity office had issued before the war," Marigny recalled. "In that way we showed the pillboxes and barriers for every street."

No detail, Dewavrin's directives stressed, was ever too trivial. If barbed wire was involved, how high was the barrier? Was it triple dennert or otherwise? One of Meslin's staff, the engineer, Alex Jourdan, often took bread and sausage to the workmen's cafés in Ouistreham, to

Rommel's Wall: anti-tank ditches like this near Ouistreham were 15 feet deep, mined and flooded. (Service Historique de la Marine)

98

speculate on such technical matters as the thickness of a concrete blockhouse. "I'd guess 2 ft thick," Jourdan remembers, "and it never failed. 'Your eyes deceive you, monsieur. We've had instructions to build the wall 4 ft thick on all the blockhouses. . . .' "

Four miles south-east of Caen, at Ifs, Léon Dumis, the garage proprietor, was also busy — overtly on a temporary job checking the milk production of dairy cattle. As he tramped from farm to farm he chewed matches: a whole match equalled 100 yards, a half match 50 yards, a quarter match 25 yards, the distances between ack-ack batteries. Thus, the co-ordinates of almost forty batteries circling Caen passed to the Allies.

Fierce ingenuity went into plotting new hiding places for the control maps. Roger Deschambres, the plumber, packed his into a lead pipe, sealed it, then attached it to a windlass and let it down his well. Yves Gresselin, a Cherbourg wholesale grocer, buried his in flower pots. René Duchez and his wife Odette hid *their* maps beneath the reeking straw of the chicken run. Antonin Maury, an electrician in Ste Mère-Église, the D-Day focus of the drop by 13,000 US paratroopers, was among the most resourceful; scraping the cement bindings from the stones in his rockery, he lined it with control maps instead.

Jeanne Verinaud, then Meslin's trusted 17-year-old secretary, recalls the pressures vividly: "After May, 1943, London became insatiable. We'd send off reams of typed reports on an area, with maps and photographs, and suddenly, a few weeks later, they'd ask so many questions we might never have sent them a line."

The questions had an urgent hurry-up quality that brooked no delay, like these two from an inventory routed to Caen in August 1943:

What is the limit of the minefield on the beach west of Honfleur? Are they anti-tank or anti-personnel?

South of Morsalines you have signalled seven blockhouses. Are these not rather platforms for artillery? Give corrections and precise details.

By early 1944, it was plain that the Wall that Rommel was building apace was in essence the same Wall that had appeared on Duchez's

Hope is a tattered flag and a dream out of time . . . /The evening star inviolable over the coal mines . . . /The ten-cent crocus-bulb blooming in a used car sales-room./The horseshoe over the door, the luckpiece in the pocket,/The kiss and the comforting laugh, — / Hope is an echo, hope ties itself yonder, yonder.

(from an unpublished poem by Carl Sandburg, read over the CBS network on D-Day by Charles Laughton)

France, what of the night?/I watch and I do not sleep./I hear deep calling to deep,/I under the ocean drowned./ I hear the storm in the height:/My help will come from the sea,/ I working underground,/ I know I shall rise and be free.

(from *Song Before Sunrise* by 'Sagittarius' (Olga Katzin))

blueprint two years earlier. In a sense that was fortunate, for by November 1943, in Paris and all along the Wall, the Gestapo were swooping—"taken to hospital" was the underground code-name for an arrest. On November 16, 1943, Dewavrin signalled all his networks via the BBC the four-word alarm call to take cover: STORM IN THE WEST. Both Robert Thomas and Duchez escaped into hiding, until D-Day. Girard was lying low near Fontainebleu. Only Meslin, haggard with strain, still controlled a handful of agents along the Wall.

This was the ultimate irony. As D-Day approached, almost every battery, blockhouse or beach obstacle had been sedulously reported, but last-minute transfers of crack units presented more of a problem. At Grandcamp-les-Bains, midway between Omaha and Utah Beaches, the Mayor, Jean Marion, had crucial last-minute information for London: the sudden

Low-level panoramas showing strongpoints and batteries helped supplement reports by *Centurie* agents. (Air Historical Branch)

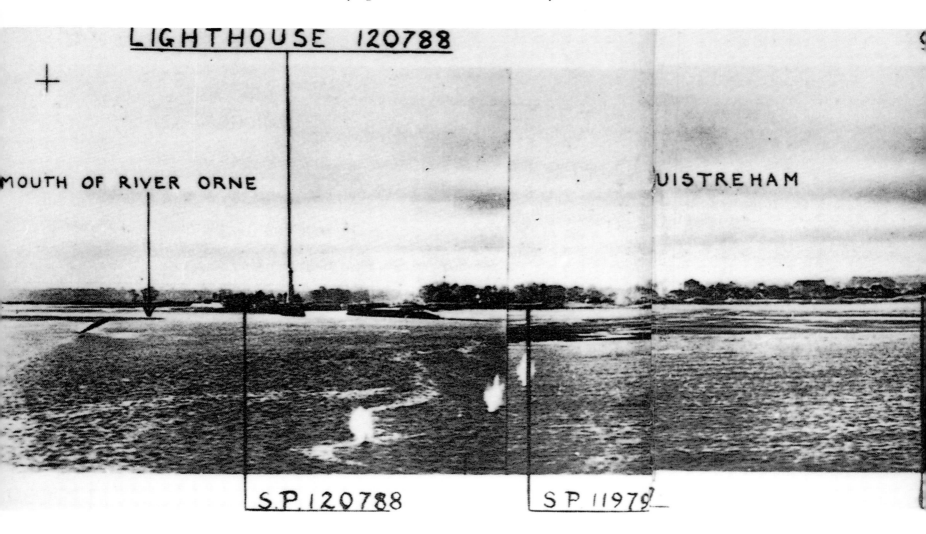

LIGHTHOUSE 120788

MOUTH OF RIVER ORNE

UISTREHAM

S.P. 120788

SP 11979

arrival of twenty-five ack-ack guns, five batteries, at the mouth of the Vire River, on which Grandcamp stood, and the puzzling absence of guns from the emplacements topping the 100-ft cliffs at Pointe du Hoc.

But one recent item that Marion had gleaned *had* reached the Allies. The tough battle-hardened 352nd Division, under *Generalleutnant* Dietrich Kraiss, who had survived the worst the Russian front could do to them, were no longer at St Lô. They were manning the defences above Omaha.

On June 3, Brigadier E. T. "Bill" Williams, Montgomery's senior intelligence officer, duly issued a warning of this in the *21 Army Group Weekly Neptune Intelligence Review*. But by then the troops were "sealed" into the forward areas called "sausages"; their dispositions could not be changed. Despite *Centurie*'s eleventh-hour warning, the Allies could do nothing at all.

Faith is the substance of things hoped for, the evidence of things not seen . . . these all died in faith, not having received the promises, but having seen them afar off, and were persuaded of them, and embraced them, and confessed that they were strangers and pilgrims on the earth.

(from *The Epistle of St Paul to the Hebrews* xi)

JRCH SPIRE 112784

GUN MED BTY 115799   113800   DEFEND

10 THE MEN AND THE BEACHES

Sword Beach, near Ouistreham, as it is today.

The Compleat Coppist: Lieutenant-Commander Nigel Clogstoun-Willmott models the wet suit, padded at elbows and knees, rubberized at wrists and face. (Author's collection)

FIVE HUNDRED YARDS off the Normandy coastline, a British LCN (Landing Craft Navigation) noiselessly weighed anchor—strategically short of the wheeling beam of the Pointe de Ver lighthouse. Beside the skipper, Lieutenant Commander Nigel Clogstoun-Willmott, two men clad like Martians in clumsy wet suits, padded at the knees and elbows, rubberized at the wrists and face, awaited his word of command.

As Willmott whispered, "Off you go," neither of the two—Major Logan Scott-Bowden and Sergeant Bruce Ogden Smith—saw themselves as pioneers. On this turbulent December night, cleaving through a Scale 5 sea in a sub-zero temperature, they were too dizzy and seasick, after a thirteen-hour journey from Portsmouth Harbour, to focus such a thought. They knew only that their mission on the beach at Ver-sur-Mer was crucial, for aerial reconnaissance had lately revealed broad dark stripes suggesting peat workings, fatal to the passage of tanks. The parting words of Brigadier E. T. Williams, Montgomery's intelligence chief, remained clearly in Willmott's mind: "If you only find out what those stripes mean—nothing else—it will be worth it."

Both swimmers were well equipped for the task. The pockets of their wet suits were crammed with paraphernalia specially designed for members of Willmott's COPP (Combined Operation Pilotage Parties), teams: waterproof torches, underwater writing tablets, meat skewers, augers for boring holes, sachets for storing samples, even cyanide capsules in event of capture. At each man's breast was a reel of fine sand-coloured fishing line, studded with a bead every ten yards—fashioned in the workshops of Ogden Smith's father, whose firm had supplied fishing tackle to the gentry of St James's since 1763.

Steadily, methodically, their senses attuned to the firefly flickers of sentries' torches farther inland, they began their survey. Working from the water's edge, they first skewered their fishing-lines, boring holes one foot deep, secured the cores in a waterproof bandolier, then moved on. Ten yards inland, a tell-tale bead signalled the time had come to extract a second sample. Thus they would proceed until the beach was charted, twelve samples in all—establishing that the alarming stripes were not peat bogs but firm hard rock.

It was Ogden Smith, glancing at the luminous dial of his wrist watch, who realized that it was one minute past midnight, and that this was not as other nights. Inching forward on his belly, he tapped the startled major on the shoulder. "What?" Scott-Bowden whispered, for torchlight was dancing very near and both men had frozen beneath the sea wall.

"Happy New Year, sir," Ogden Smith whispered back, for it was now January 1, 1944.

On this day, unknown to both men, the 24-year-old major and his irrepressible 22-year-old sergeant were putting the finishing touches to a survey that months earlier had set out to map the Bay of the Seine, yard by yard, for sixty-five miles from Barfleur to Cap d'Antifer. As early as 1940, following the disastrous Norwegian campaign, when officers had fallen back on 1912 Baedekers, Churchill had urged the creation of an Inter-Services Topographical Unit, to meet this crying demand. Headed by

Professor Freddie Wells, a retiring don, and Colonel Sam Bassett, of the Royal Marines, the Unit's first remit, in the quiet haven of the Ashmolean Museum, Oxford, was the topography of all coastal zones—but by 1943 the war had narrowed this down to just one stretch of coastline.

The British public, without knowing how or why, had played its part. Early in March 1942, a nationwide broadcast by Commander Rodney Slessor, RNVR, had told of a highly successful Commando raid on the German radar station at Bruneval, north of Le Havre—and of how thousands of photographs, including "holiday snaps," had made the raid possible. Would his listeners comb through their boxrooms and photo albums and write in describing what photographs they had? Within thirty-six hours, Colonel Bassett, at the Ashmolean, received "a frantic call" from the BBC: 30,000 letters had arrived by that morning's post. By 1944, the photos totalled ten million.

The beaches posed many moot questions, and both postcards and "holiday snaps" gave some of the answers. A woman's footwear, the height of her skirts when paddling, could sometimes indicate the gradient of a beach —usually a slope of one in eight to a height of six feet. Did parked cars feature in a picture? That, in itself, showed where the exits lay but would those exit roads carry tanks? Were matting roads laid alongside to carry wheeled vehicles feasible? Had old Roman peat workings become impassable mud-holes, as Willmott's COPPs had sought to discover? Were there hidden sand-bars close to the beach, for a man could drown in eight feet of water as easily as in eighty?

On March 3, a notable step was taken: the first invasion beaches received their mandatory code-names. Farthest to the east was Sword Beach, running roughly two-and-a-half miles from Riva-Bella to Luc-sur-Mer, the target of the British 3rd Division. Next came Juno Beach, where the Canadian 3rd Division would land on a four-mile stretch between the towns of Courseulles-sur-Mer and St Aubin-sur-Mer. Last in the British-Canadian sector came Gold Beach stretching from Le Hamel to La Rivière, where Scott-Bowden and Ogden Smith had taken soundings, for the 50th Northumbrian Division, on New Year's Eve.

In the American sector, the going promised to be tougher. Omaha Beach, stretching from Vierville to St Laurent, was almost four miles long. To the rear, four slightly wooded "draws," or exits, were flanked by slopes more than 100 ft high: behind the sands lay shale embankments up to fifteen yards wide. To the rear of Omaha, the 352nd Infantry Division, whose late arrival had been signalled by the *Centurie* agent, Jean Marion, were manning eight casemated batteries, thirty-five pillboxes, four field artillery positions, eighteen anti-tank gun positions, six mortar pits, thirty-eight rocket pits and eighty-five machine-gun posts. Here was a killing ground in the making. Even the most westerly American beach, Utah, a three-mile stretch behind the hamlet of La Madeleine, which Bradley and Montgomery had picked to speed up the capture of Cherbourg, was defended by twenty-eight batteries, with another eighteen batteries sited inland.

Look for me by moonlight;/Watch for me by moonlight;/I'll come to thee by moonlight, though hell should bar the way!

(from *The Highwayman* by Alfred Noyes)

. . . The three-o'-clock in the morning courage, which Bonaparte thought was the rarest.

(from *Walden, or Life in the Woods* by Henry David Thoreau)

Those who do not learn from history are condemned to repeat it.

(—George Santayana)

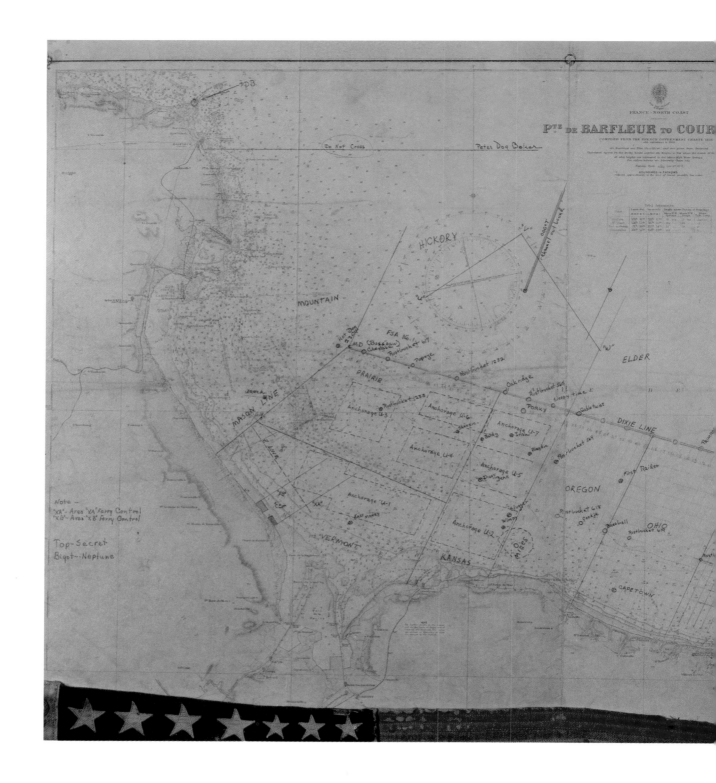

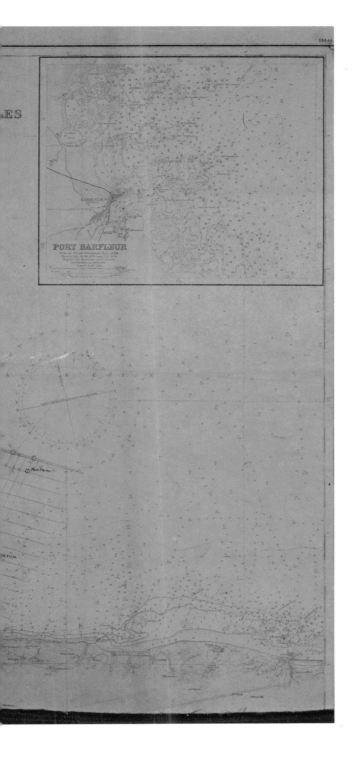

By now almost all these details were known to Eisenhower's planners. "They had been watching the coastal defences for more than three years," says Constance Babington-Smith, of the Central Interpretation Unit, "and constantly up-dating their records. They knew every gun emplacement, every pillbox, every wire entanglement and every trench system. . . ." This overall panorama, pieced together from aerial reconnaissance, from double-checks by *Centurie*'s agents, from pre-war geological surveys and old maps and guide-books, had now become the focus of tightly knit specialist teams like the COPPs, formed to wage the battle of the beaches.

At Dovercourt, on the Essex marshes, and on the Orford Peninsula in Suffolk, one such unit was in the final stages of its training: Major-General Sir Percy Hobart's 79th Armoured Division, the only armoured formation scheduled to take part in D-Day. The division had been formed as recently as March 1943, but Hobart, a difficult, dynamic exponent of the Armoured Idea, was already convinced that his "Funnies," as other units dubbed them, could provide the answer to most problems thrown up by Rommel's Atlantic Wall.

A "Hobo" unit like the 5th Assault Regiment, Royal Engineers, was typical; almost all its assault vehicles were the modern counterpart of a medieval siege-train. Thus, when the time came for the 79th to hit the British and Canadian beaches, minefields would hold few terrors for tank commanders like Donald Robertson and Bob Brotherton: the bows of their converted Churchill tanks, now known as "Crabs," were fitted with power-driven rollers

He was the mildest manner'd man/That ever scuttled ship or cut a throat,/With such true breeding of a gentleman,/You never could divine his real thought.

(from *Don Juan* Canto III, by George Gordon, Lord Byron)

Navigator's chart from a D-Day USN PT boat. By the time charts like this were issued, more than three years of pains-taking research and often dangerous recon-naissance had mapped every detail of the invasion beaches. (Hamilton Darby Perry)

107

. . . Leave off and list to me./That mean to teach you rudiments of war:/I'll have you learn to sleep upon the ground,/March in your armour thorough watery fens,/Sustain the scorching heat and freezing cold,/Hunger and thirst, right adjuncts of the war,/And after this to scale a castle wall,/Besiege a fort, to undermine a town,/And make whole cities caper in the air.

(from *Tamburlaine The Great* Pt II, III, ii, by Christopher Marlowe)

A green beret does not make you bullet-proof.

(—Major-General James L. Moulton, formerly OC No. 48 (Royal Marine) Commando)

Hobart's Funnies: the SBG (Small Box Girder) tank lowering a bridge over an anti-tank ditch. (Imperial War Museum)

inset
Hobart's Funnies: the Sherman DD (Duplex Drive) swimming tank, equipped with canvas skirts. (Imperial War Museum)

108

hung with chains like flails. Moving ahead of the main force, these whirling chains would scythe a path through the minefields.

Astern of them when the time came, aboard LCT 947, would be Jock Wingate's "Plough," a Churchill tank resembling an armoured lobster, its plough-like tines ready to churn the sand and hurl mines clear of advancing infantry. Close behind would follow Jock Charlton's SBG (Small Box Girder) tank, clamped with a device "reminiscent of the war towers of Cyrus the Persian": its heavy hornbeam-girdered ramp, detachable by explosive charges, would be thrown into position as a bridge across anti-tank traps 15 ft deep. The time was fast approaching when all these vehicles would be waterproofed with a tacky compound of grease, lime and asbestos fibres.

Major General Sir Percy Hobart, 79th Armoured Division, creator of "The Funnies." (Imperial War Museum)

Hobart's Funnies: Sherman "Crab" tank with chain flails churns through a minefield. (Imperial War Museum)

opposite
Hobart's Funnies: in action, the Crocodile flame-thrower could incinerate any obstacle within 360 feet. (Author's collection)

111

If a challenge arose at this late stage, it was Hobart's boast that he could meet it. As late as January 17, a three-day COPP sortie to the British beaches, working by night from the midget submarine X-20, revealed samples of soft blue clay—confirming geologists' predictions of the last traces of an ancient forest. When Hobart's men found identical clay on the beach at Brancaster, Norfolk, the problem was closer to solution. Before D-Day, REME (Royal Electrical and Mechanical Engineers) workshops had evolved the "Bobbin"—a Churchill fitted with an enormous spool of chestnut paling, coir matting and tubular scaffolding, a resilient carpet for any vehicles facing the hazards of blue clay.

Not all the "Funnies" were defensive. At Farnborough, Hampshire, Lieutenant Andrew Wilson, of The Buffs, was one of fifty tank commanders whose Churchill had overnight become a "Crocodile"—a slow infantry tank capable of only 15 mph but equipped with a towed trailer carrying 400 gallons of flame fuel. When the "Crocodile" went into action, as Wilson knew from trials just completed, a burning yellow rod shot from its nozzle "with a noise like the slapping of a thick leather strap." When it struck the concrete of a pillbox, "a dozen golden fingers leapt out from the point of impact, searching for cracks and apertures." It was claimed that a "Crocodile" could incinerate anything in its path up to a range of 360 ft—including German infantrymen. A stranger to battle until now, Wilson was wondering just how he would react to that.

Other teams were being assigned key roles. What Lord Lovat and Peter Young had achieved almost two years earlier against the Dieppe batteries of Varengeville and Berneval had earmarked the Commandos of the 1st Special Services Brigade for the hottest fire in the British sector. The sight of them scaling the 300-ft Brandy cliffs near St Ives, Cornwall, had convinced even Montgomery that they were "real proper chaps." Thus, on D-Day, the Commandos, singled out since 1943 by their distinctive green berets, would storm ashore on Sword Beach to "neutralize" the formidable Ouistreham Casino defences that René Duchez of *Centurie* had detailed so graphically. For this encounter they would be armed with Bren guns, 7-in Wilkinson fighting knives and in some instances 8-ft Bangalore torpedoes packed with 12 lbs of explosives. If all went well, they would then force-march four miles across hostile

Commandos display survival kit ranging from a folding bicycle to Craven A cigarettes.
(Imperial War Museum)

opposite
Commando training at Achnacarry: here, troops practise "unarmed" combat with 7-inch Wilkinson knives.
(Imperial War Museum)

Troops swarm ashore at the Commando Basic Training Centre, Achnacarry, Inverness-shire. (Commando Association)

Nothing is ever done in
this world until men are
prepared to kill one
another if it is not done.

(from *Major Barbara* Act
III, by George Bernard
Shaw)

country to relieve Major-General Richard Gale's
glider troops at the Orne and Caen Canal
bridges.

Forced marches had become a way of life
with the 1st Brigade. "[They bore] the same
relationship to the general army," thought their
historian, Hilary St George Saunders, "as a
monk or friar does to the ordinary Roman
Catholic," and on the Sussex coast at Bexhill, in
the spring of 1944, ten-mile daily speed marches
weighed down with 90-lb Bergen rucksacks
were routine. Even newcomers like the 171 Free
French commandos of *Commandant* Philippe
Kieffer accepted this stop-at-nothing philo-
sophy, typified by the slogan: "It's all in the
mind and the heart." In this spirit, one French
commando, Maurice Chauvet, completed a
speed march, his boot sodden with blood from a
burst carbuncle.

Many of the 600-strong brigade were
tough veterans of earlier, more elemental
struggles—Vaagso, Dieppe, Lofoten, St Naz-
aire—and this had annealed a rare bond
between officers and men. But by Lovat's
decree, no man who had slipped up on a raid
was ever given a second chance, and this
unforgiving mien made sense in terms of the
battle ahead. From October 18 1942, by
Hitler's decree, no soldier identified as a
commando any longer rated prisoner-of-war
status; he was to be shot out of hand. The
commandos' was a war of no quarter.

This *diktat* applied automatically to the
men of the 2nd Battalion, US Rangers, under
Lieutenant Colonel James Earl Rudder, a
33-year-old football coach from Brady, Texas.
First formed in 1942, as America's answer to the
Commandos, the Ranger Battalions had done
yeoman service in North Africa and Italy, and to
select 500 gung-ho fighting men from 2000
applicants Rudder had adopted the same un-
conventional yardsticks as Lovat and Young.
Volunteers like Private William "L-Rod" Petty,
rejected by the medics because of false teeth,
was at once signed on by Rudder; the private's
plea—"Hell, Sir! I don't want to bite 'em, I
want to fight 'em"—struck just the right
belligerent note that Rudder wanted.

But from the first Rudder tolerated nothing
less than perfection. His monthly "gripe
sessions," where every man could sound off on
injustices, won Rangers to his side—but
following one slovenly pass in review, the
outraged colonel threatened to fight every man
in the battalion. En route from Camp Forrest,
Tennessee, to Fort Dix, New Jersey, they initially

rode Pullman Class and used the First Class diner, until Rudder hauled them all off the train for a two-mile run: Rangers must be adaptable. At Fort Dix, wooden-walled tents and pot-bellied stoves were a touch of home—but one day Rudder banished them to the woods to subsist on squirrels and rabbits. Rangers must learn to live lean.

Only in January 1944, one month after settling to training sessions at Bude, Cornwall, did Rudder learn the Rangers' D-Day assignment. Behind drawn black-out curtains, in a second floor room at General Bradley's headquarters, 20 Bryanston Square, London, photos and maps were produced that for a moment left him dazed. Even his Executive Officer, Major Max F. Schneider—a veteran of

North Africa and promoted to command the 5th Rangers on D-Day — whistled through his teeth. A veteran of nothing but the football field and three years military training, Rudder thought that Bradley was playing an elaborate practical joke.

What Rudder was seeing for the first time were the casemates for six 155-mm guns above Pointe du Hoc. As yet, the guns were not *in situ*, but once they were their estimated range would be 25,000 yards, capable of devastating all landing areas along the coast from Port-en-Bessin, in the British zone, to Taret de Ravenoville, north of Utah. If bombers of the US Ninth Force plus heavy naval fire failed to destroy them, then the Rangers' mission, two hours before H-Hour, would be to finish the job — scaling the 100-ft-high cliffs on rope ladders and wiping out the German gunners.

It was potentially the most dangerous of all the D-Day missions — and it was to Rudder's credit that he soon afterwards sent two of his brightest men, Staff Sergeant Jack Kuhn and Pfc Peter Korpalo to liaise with the South London firm of Merryweather. As long-time suppliers of equipment to the London Fire Brigade, Merryweather had come up with a possible solution: a 100-ft fireman's extension ladder firmly mounted on the bed of a 2½-ton DUKW amphibious truck. If trials now under way at Swanage, Dorset, proved satisfactory, the 2nd Rangers would soar to the summit of Pointe du Hoc like firemen staging a rescue from a blazing tenement.

Another specialist team would work unenviably close to the target: the men of the Landing Craft Obstacle Clearance Units (LCOCUs), with their strange rubber diving suits and splayed web feet, known always to the Navy as "the frogmen." They, too, were a mystic elite, who had learned their craft at HMS *Appledore*, North Devon, close to the US Assault Training Centre. Almost all were "hostilities only" men, officers like Lieutenant Harry Hargreaves, a cotton salesman from Burnley, Lancashire, or non-coms like Sergeant Peter Jones, a Bournemouth carpenter, yet of the 100 volunteers who had gone through the earliest four-month course, only ten had lasted out. Every man, when the time came, would wear the newly devised "kapok jackets" beneath their frogmen's suits, protection against the fearsome explosions that would otherwise lift them bodily from the water: the frogmen's D-Day date was with Rommel's new-style "Devil's Gardens."

On that day, 120 volunteers such as Hargreaves and Jones, ten units of twelve men, between them cleared 2500 obstacles from Gold Beach alone, and in preparation for this all of them had done many hundred dives. Every obstacle — the Elements C, the "Czech Hedgehogs," the tetrahedra — must be systematically destroyed before the landing craft moved in; the most formidable of all, the Element C, weighing 2½ tons, needed thirty-six small charges, placed at vantage points, before it blasted apart. If the frogmen did their work as planned, no obstacle would protrude more than 18 in above the sea-bed at H-Hour.

But when *was* H-Hour — and when was D-Day? The key men were growing impatient for action. The initial target date — May 1, 1944 — had been projected as far back as May

1943, three months before the Quebec Conference. In January, Eisenhower had agreed to postpone until June 1, in the hope of a simultaneous drive on the Russian front. On May 8, this had been switched again, to June 5.

The date was of pressing concern to the crews of two midget submarines, X 23, under Lieutenant George Honour, RNVR, latterly a Schweppes area manager, and X 20, commanded by Lieutenant Ken Hudspeth, a quiet Australian. Their D-Day mission was to act as navigation markers off the coast at Ouistreham and Le Hamel, pinpointing the landing positions of Force S (for Sword) and Force J (for Juno) with automatic radio beacons and telescopic masts fitted with powerful lights.

But each midget, in one survivor's words, was "a tiny squalid steel chamber," with less than 5 ft of headroom, crammed with wires and pipes. Despite air purifiers, the foetid atmosphere could swiftly bring on dangerous hallucinations. It took two hours to struggle in and out of a rubber frogman's suit, and all the time the walls streamed with damp; blankets were moist and food grew soggy and unpalatable.

If D-Day was postponed yet again, Honour and Hudspeth and their three-men crews faced the most thankless vigil of all: thirty feet beneath the surface of the Channel for sixty-four hours, less than a mile away from Rommel's armies.

. . . this blow/Might be the be-all and the end-all here,/But here, upon this bank and shoal of time,/We'd jump the life to come.

(from *Macbeth* I, vii, by William Shakespeare)

Frogmen of the Landing Craft Obstacle Clearance Units (LCOCUs) in training at HMS *Appledore*, North Devon. (Author's collection)

IN A TIN-ROOFED brick-built office 20 ft square, lit by flickering fluorescent tubes, the man on whose decision the whole invasion hinged was working late. On the night of Friday April 28, at the new headquarters of the Allied Expeditionary Force, Bushy Park, near Kingston, Surrey, Eisenhower was a desperately worried man.

Ever since January, one problem had harassed him above all: security. In all the months of planning, several hundred personnel, code-named "Bigots," had of necessity known key facets of the assault—but how long could the presence of 250,000 fighting men and close to 7000 ships be concealed? Already, one American staff officer, Colonel Ralph Ingersoll, after viewing "the tiny harbours along the south coast and the big sprawling harbour of Southampton packed like miniature Pearl Harbors, with ships stacked gunwale to gunwale", had voiced what everyone felt: "No one . . . could believe that the invasion fleet would ever put to sea intact."

Ostensibly, security was now as tight as Allied Intelligence could make it. For ten miles inland, a 550-mile-long coastal strip was barred to all those without special identity cards. From April 17, to the fury of scores of foreign diplomats, the British authorities had summarily withdrawn the privilege of the diplomatic bag from all save Americans and Russians. Until the end of June, no coded messages could be sent and neither diplomats, their families nor even their servants could leave the British Isles. The clampdown was so tight that the Central Office of Merchant Navy Operations (COMNO) was even forbidden to tell shipowners the location of their vessels: LOOSE LIPS SINK SHIPS was the

. . . Golden care!/That keep'st the ports of slumber open wide/To many a watchful night!

(From *Henry IV* Pt 2, IV, v, by William Shakespeare)

Actors waiting in the wings of Europe/we already watch the lights on the stage/and listen to the colossal overture begin./For us entering at the height of the din/it will be hard to hear our thoughts, hard to gauge/how much our conduct owes to fear or fury.

Everyone, I suppose, will use those minutes/to look back, to hear music and recall/what we were doing and saying that year/during our last few months as people, near/the sucking mouth of the day that swallowed us all/into the stomach of a war . . .

(from *Actors Waiting in the Wings of Europe* by Keith Douglas)

Spring, 1944, and an invasion practice at Slapton Sands, Devon, is depicted by US Navy war artist Dwight Shepler. (US Navy Combat Art Collection)

Where are you going to, laughing men?/For a holiday on the sea?/Laughing, smiling, wonderful men,/Why won't you wait for me?

God, how I love you, men of my race,/As you smile on your way to a war./How can you do it, wonderful face,/Do you not know what's before?

(from *News Reeel of Embarkation* by Timothy Corsellis)

Put on the whole armour of God, that ye may be able to stand against the wiles of the devil. For we wrestle not against flesh and blood, but against principalities, against the rulers of the darkness of this world, against spiritual wickedness in high places. Wherefore take unto you the whole armour of God, that ye may be able to withstand in the evil day. . . .

(from the *Epistle of St Paul to the Ephesians* vi, featured in the pre-invasion prayers in US churches)

watchword of the time. As a result, COMNO's Leadenhall Street office was swamped with up to 13,000 anxious letters a day.

Yet there had been many grounds for long and wakeful nights. Early in March, a parcel of papers stamped "Bigot," bursting open in a Chicago mail office, had caused widespread panic until the mystery was solved. The hard-pressed chief clerk of the London Ordnance Supply Section, Sergeant Thomas P. Kane, had been worrying over his ailing sister's health: in a moment of aberration, he had mailed the package not to the appropriate US department but to her address in Chicago. Kane's security clearance was impeccable, yet he remained under routine surveillance — and his sister's house was watched by the FBI — for long after D-Day.

On April 18, in the dining-room of Claridge's Hotel, London, an old classmate of Eisenhower's, Major General Henry Miller, the Quartermaster of the US Ninth Air Force, was a guest at a dinner party given by Mrs Sloan Colt, of the American Red Cross. When his hostess apologized for the poor quality of the pastries, Miller was reassuring: at present cargo ships were limited to war supplies, but good pastries would be reaching Britain again soon after June 15. For this flagrant indiscretion, Eisenhower reduced Miller to his substantive rank of colonel and shipped him back to the States, but even while Miller was still in transit, a British "Bigot" had set the alarm bells ringing.

The culprit was a staff officer under Brigadier Lionel Harris, chief of "Overlord" telecommunications: somehow, he confessed, he had mislaid the entire communications plan

for "Operation Neptune" while on his way home. This was a weighty volume containing all the networks and naval ciphers for the assault, but before Harris could even alert Eisenhower, the Lost Property Office at Scotland Yard was on the line. A taxi-driver at Waterloo Station had just handed in a briefcase with papers stamped BIGOT — TOP SECRET left in his cab by a departing passenger. Had the driver examined them? Had a subordinate looked them over at the Yard? Neither Harris nor Eisenhower ever knew.

Predictably, worse was to come. No sooner had the final details of the airborne drop been clinched than a staff officer browsing through a London bookshop chanced on a manual entitled *Paratroops*, by Captain F. O. Miksche, a Czech serving with the Free French. Prominently featured was a map of the Cotentin Peninsula, showing drop and landing zones almost identical to those planned. Published in 1943, the book must long ago, through neutral sources, have reached Germany.

In fact *Generaloberst* Kurt Student, the founding father of Germany's airborne forces, had read the book, found it instructive and dismissed the Cotentin as an interesting sand-table exercise. But Eisenhower, not knowing this, was to anguish for many weeks ahead.

Only one day previously had come the biggest security scare of all: the tragic climax to an "invasion" exercise that had in itself gone disastrously wrong. South of Dartmouth, near the village of Slapton Sands, on the South Devon coast, one of ten simulated landings had taken place that Friday morning: the target, a coarse gravel beach stretching out towards a sheltered

PARATROOPS

*the history, organization,
and tactical use
of
airborne formations*

by

CAPTAIN F. O. MIKSCHE

with a preface by

CAPTAIN LIDDELL HART

FABER AND FABER LIMITED
24 Russell Square
London

THE TACTICAL EMPLOYMENT OF AIRBORNE TROOPS

capture such key-points ahead of the arrival of the retreating enemy, he can canalize the retreat along the course most favourable to himself; and perhaps force the enemy into a battle which will end in his annihilation. A perfect example of the way in which airborne troops should be used in the pursuit was given by the Germans at the Bridge of Corinth.

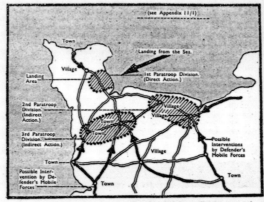

10. The Employment of Airborne Troops in Sea-Landing Operations

So much for the indirect action of airborne troops in the pursuit battle. But just as in the attack itself, so also in the pursuit airborne troops can be used to advantage within the tactical framework of the pursuing force. They land in small groups in the immediate rear of the retreating enemy and by sudden surprise attacks hasten the break-up of his formations. They interrupt any attempt he may make to reform his disorganized units or re-establish his position after his defeat.

Finally one can imagine cases in which airborne troops are used

64

An airborne landing scenario published by Captain F. O. Miksche in 1943 showed an unnamed but clearly identifiable Cotentin Peninsula. Fortunately, the German High Command dismissed it as a sand-table exercise. (British Library)

---

lagoon, was a credible substitute for Normandy. The landings—Operations Duck, Parrot, Beaver, Tiger, followed by the six-part Operation Fabius—were designed as a rehearsal in earnest for the beaches called Omaha and Utah.

But at 5 a.m. on April 28, along with Tedder, Montgomery, Bradley and Ramsay—each man aboard separate craft for reasons of security—Eisenhower on LCI (Landing Craft, Infantry) 495 had watched Operation Tiger fall ignominiously apart. For reasons unknown, the Hawker Typhoon fighters, due to swoop over the invaders at H-Hour, never arrived over the target. The skippers of many LCTs (Landing Craft, Tanks), ignoring all signals from the engineers already ashore, landed where they chose. From the start, naval fire support had been almost non-existent, since Admiral Don P. Moon, commanding Force U (for Utah) had postponed H-Hour for one hour, hoping the Typhoons would still arrive. The troops debarking from the LCIs ambled ashore, "almost like bathers," discarding their bedrolls at any convenient spot on the beach. Most had little idea of where to

121

inset
US Navy beach battalion "play dead" for Operation Tiger on Slapton Sands – foreshadowing 749 deaths that were soon reality. (U S National Archives)

Operation Tiger: US troops deploy across Dartmoor in simulated capture of "Cherbourg" (Okehampton). (Imperial War Museum)

123

obtain fresh ammunition, and few beach-masters were in evidence to guide them. Awareness of minefields seemed non-existent. "We are completely devoid of mine-consciousness," Major General Raymond O. Barton, commanding the US 4th Infantry Division, fumed to one umpire, "and a hell of a lot of us are going to get killed and you can put that in your book."

At Eisenhower's level, this concern was paramount. The "young American officers," the General's naval aide, Captain Harry C. Butcher, confided in his diary, "seem to regard the war as one grand manoeuvre in which they are having a happy time. Many seem as green as growing corn. How will they act in battle and how will they look in three months time?" But not until late on the night of April 28 did Butcher and his chief realize that 749 men would not react at all. They were already dead.

It had happened as early as 1.30 a.m., when convoy T-4, a straggling eight-strong assembly of LSTs spread out over three miles, was moving at a leisurely 6 knots through the darkness of Lyme Bay. Thirty-three miles ahead lay their destination, Slapton Sands. Survivors like Lieutenant David A. Roop, USNR, the chief engineer of LST 515, recall now that a pale moon had risen, and the ships' decks were opaque with fog. Due to structural damage, their main escort, the destroyer HMS *Scimitar*, was detained for repairs in Plymouth dockyard; the convoy's sole guardian was the corvette HMS *Azalea*. At this same hour, nine E-boats of *Kapitain zur Zee* Rudolf Peterson's Cherbourg-based 5th and 9th *Schnellboote* Flotillas, on a routine night patrol, sighted their quarry.

Closing in at 35 knots on powerful Daimler-Benz diesel engines, their torpedoes sought and found three of the slow-wallowing LSTs. Red and green tracer seared the night, and many young soldiers, hearing the order "Abandon Ship," jumped to their deaths, ignorant even of how to inflate their Mae West lifebelts.

Eisenhower was appalled by the news. Not only had 749 lives been lost, but among the missing men, ten officers of the 1st Engineer Special Brigade were classed as "Bigots." They knew the secrets of the DUKWs, the amphibious six-wheel-drive trucks, equipped with both rudder and propeller, that would carry the Rangers to below Pointe du Hoc. They knew the timing of the Utah and Omaha landings, and the exact lodgement of Major General J. Lawton Collins's VII Corps. If one of these officers fell alive into German hands and talked, the entire invasion plan was in jeopardy.

These thoughts, unspoken, were in every mind during the last full-dress "Overlord" conference, which was staged at 10 a.m. on Monday May 15, at Montgomery's old school, St Paul's, West Kensington. If the setting was prosaic—The Model Room, a circular class-room like a cockpit, panelled in pitch pine, with hard, narrow wooden benches rising in tiers—the company was illustrious. Only King George VI and Churchill aspired to armchairs; the remainder squatted on the hard benches, swathed in topcoats and blankets, for even in May the cold was bitter.

For every man taking part, this day would afterwards hold a special memory. For Rear-Admiral Morton L. Deyo, whose cruiser, USS *Tuscaloosa*, would lead the bombardment force off Utah Beach, it was the memory of Eisenhower's smile — "It had been said that (it) was worth twenty divisions. That day it was worth more." To General Sir Hastings Ismay, Assistant Secretary to the War Cabinet, it was the transformation of the Model Room's stage into a 30-ft scale model of the Normandy beaches, set on a slope, a Lilliputian landscape dwarfed by the giant figures of senior commanders such as Ramsay and Leigh-Mallory, as they swooped on key landmarks. Americans like Rear-Admiral Alan G. Kirk, of the Western Naval Task Force, and General Elwood P. Quesada, of the Ninth Army Air Force, long aware of Churchill's reservations, were moved by the conviction in the Premier's voice, as he told them: "Gentlemen, I am *hardening* towards this enterprise." On an impulse Churchill offered his services to Omar Bradley: he himself would ride with the Americans in the first wave.

Within two weeks, the bodies of the ten "Bigots" had been recovered, and they, along with 739 others, were buried in an unmarked mass grave inland from Slapton Sands, on what was later the sheep farm of Nolan Tope. ("They were laid out like rows of cordwood," says Dorothy Seekings, then a 23-year-old baker's daughter, who still had access to the area. "I was told never to mention what I'd seen.") Few fighting men knew this, then or even later; only the troops of Force U, confined for a month in a marshalling area ringed with barbed wire and guarded by 2000 Counter Intelligence Corps personnel, knew a mounting disquiet. But plainly this was the hour when the generals must take to the open road, like US politicians in the primaries, to reassure the troops on the task that lay ahead. Thus in time the men of Force U, as well as of Force O (for Omaha) took a long cool look at Omar Bradley, descending from his black Cadillac, and liked what they saw: a 6-ft-tall "doughboy's general," wearing a combat jacket under a stained trench coat, his GI trousers stuffed into his paratroop boots. At all times his optimism in off-the-record chats gave heart to his listeners: "This stuff about tremendous losses is tommyrot . . . some of you won't come back but it will be very few."

Soldiers surveying Montgomery took away a different picture. His set routine never varied: after talking to the officers, he walked up to half a mile between troops drawn up in hollow square, hands clasped behind him, piercing grey eyes in a lean, beaky face peering intently at each man. The inspection over, Montgomery, mounting a jeep with a loudspeaker, told the troops: "Break ranks and gather round me."

Then came an astonishing moment: 5000 men, in heavy boots, stampeded towards his jeep like charging buffaloes. Montgomery's address, delivered up to five times a day until a million men had heard it, never varied: "I have come out here today, so that I can get a look at you and you can get a look at me." A calculated pause — "Not that I'm much to look at" — followed by an easy ripple of laughter. "We have got to go off and do a job together very soon now, you and I . . . and now that I have seen you I have complete confidence . . . absolutely complete confidence . . . And you must have confidence in me."

And confidence they had in plenty. Politicians and even fellow generals never

Living on this little island just now uncomfortably resembles living on a vast combination of an aircraft carrier, a floating dock jammed with men, and a warehouse stacked to the ceiling with material labelled 'Europe'. It's not at all difficult for one to imagine that England's coastline can actually be seen bulging and trembling like the walls of a Silly Symphony house . . . the unspoken phrase 'second front permitting' is, more and more, tacked on to all minor plans for the future. . . .

(from *London War Notes* (May 21, 1944) by Mollie Panter-Downes)

Now all the youth of England are on fire,/And silken dalliance in the wardrobe lies;/Now thrive the armourers, and honour's thought/Reigns solely in the breast of every man. . . ./For now sits Expectation in the air/And hides a sword from hilts unto the point. . . .

(from *Henry V* II, Chorus by William Shakespeare)

The rainy summer of 1944 saw US artillery pieces waterproofed in Southern England gun parks. (Imperial War Museum)

wholly trusted Montgomery, but among Tommies and dogface GIs, he never lacked the common touch. "Seen the paper?" was one favourite gambit. "Here, take my copy," or, a true concession for a fanatic non-smoker, "Have some cigarettes? My lady friends send them to me." The 1st Welsh Guards never forgot the June day when "Monty", in the course of a 4 a.m. pep-talk, asked one man: "You. What's your most valuable possession?" "It's my rifle, sir." "No, it isn't, it's your life, and I'm going to save it for you. Now listen to me. . . ."

It was masterly psychology for men on the eve of an apocalypse. "Monty", like "Ike" and "Brad," was seen for what he was, a caring general.

By degrees, as D-Day approached, 250,000 men were shut off in private worlds of their own—"this great realm of Hush-Hush,"

Appledore Ebb by Dwight Shepler shows landing craft beached at low tide on the Devon coast where conditions resembled those on the Normandy target beaches sufficiently to make for effective dress-rehearsal. (US Navy Combat Art Collection)

At three o'clock in the afternoon the officers and ncos went for the briefing and came away looking secretive and important. At four o'clock the battalion filed past the pay table and were handed crisp, new, hundred-franc notes. At five o'clock they had tea — a huge festive meal was served to them to get rid of the battalion's spare rations. After tea . . . the Movement Order for the morning was read to them. Get to bed early tonight, lads, their officers told them, there's an early reveille in the morning. . . .

It was a strange, sad, beautiful feeling to know that this was your last evening in Blighty. It was like being very much in love, and very young, the evening before your wedding. . . . And it was such a lovely evening, clear and quiet and cool, with the tiny little ships moored in rows on the unruffled sea.

(from *From the City, From the Plough* by Alexander Baron)

as one regimental historian called it. For almost six weeks they remained isolated in wooded camps where the grass verges of the roadside had vanished, swallowed up beneath vast stands of ammunition. Wayside signs loomed large on aluminium tanks — "Do not drink this water without halogen tablets" — or cautioned truck drivers: "Know your distances. This is sixty yards from the last sign." Red crosses shimmered through woods misty with bluebells: hundreds of tents, hundreds of ambulances, waiting to bring the first wounded back.

In the last days of May, they would move to the forward assembly areas, called "sausages" from their shape on the map: from these sealed camps, where preliminary target details were revealed and "invasion francs" issued, they passed to the "hards," the sloping foreshore roadways where the landing craft were moored. Looking back over fifty years, most recall that their preoccupations then were with the minutiae of life. LAC Norman Phillips, an RAF technician in an advance party for Omaha Beach, was deeply suspicious of the sudden abundance of food — "as if we were being fattened like Christmas turkeys" — and this distrust was shared by Private John Schultz, a rifleman of the US Fourth Division. "Boy," he voiced his niggling doubts in an assembly area near Plymouth, "if they're starting to serve steak we're in trouble."

Private Lindley Higgins, of the same division, recently a shipping clerk in the Bronx, New York, admits now to being over-confident. As yet unblooded in battle, the sheer weight of US materiel deluded him. "We really thought we had only to step off the beach and all the

krauts would put up their hands." Others, who had known war for what it was, were less sanguine, but determined nevertheless. Major Harry Herman, of the US 9th Division Infantry, was thinking primarily of revenge. In January 1943, he had shared the humiliation of the US II Corps, when Rommel had won his last victory in Kasserine Pass, Tunisia, never believing until then that Americans, himself included, could throw away their arms and run for their lives. Now Herman was resolved that the time for running was past.

It was a gut-feeling he shared with Company Sergeant-Major Stan Hollis, of the Green Howards, a normally phlegmatic Yorkshire pub-keeper. In another disastrous retreat — Dunkirk — Hollis, then a dispatch rider, had chanced upon a cul-de-sac in Lille, choked with the dying bodies of a hundred French men, women and children caught in a machine-gun ambush. In the past four years, Hollis had avenged those deaths with the lives of ninety Germans. By D-Day's end, his Sten gun would account for twelve more.

None of these invaders were aware that successive security scares, even now, were imperilling the invasion.

On Thursday June 1, troops of the British 3rd Division, sealed up in the West Ham football stadium in London's East End, had already drawn their "invasion francs" and studied maps of the Ouistreham beaches, when the beer and cigarettes in the canteen abruptly ran out. Outraged at the prospect of a dry weekend, scores of men, armed with wire-cutters, snipped their way through the barbed wire and embarked on a memorable pub-crawl as far

128

June 3, 1944: GIs of Force U (for Utah) embark. (US Army)

Troops and vehicles board LCTs from concrete hards at Brixham, Devon. (US Army)

Slapton Sands, Devon, site of many invasion rehearsals, and of the disastrous loss of 749 men to a German E-Boat raid on April 28, 1944.

Slapton Sands:
US Army memorial to the civilian population of the area.

THIS MEMORIAL WAS·PRESENTED·BY·THE UNITED·STATES·ARMY AUTHORITIES· TO· THE PEOPLE· OF· THE· SOUTH HAMS·WHO·GENEROUSLY LEFT·THEIR·HOMES·AND THEIR·LANDS·TO·PROVIDE A·BATTLE·PRACTICE·AREA FOR· THE· SUCCESSFUL ASSAULT· IN· NORMANDY IN·JUNE·1944 THEIR·ACTION·RESULTED IN·THE·SAVING·OF·MANY HUNDREDS·OF·LIVES·AND CONTRIBUTED·IN·NO·SMALL MEASURE·TO·THE·SUCCESS OF· THE· OPERATION THE·AREA·INCLUDED·THE VILLAGES·OF·BLACKAWTON CHILLINGTON·EAST·ALLING TON·SLAPTON·STOKENHAM STRETE· AND· TORCROSS ·TOGETHER·WITH· MANY OUTLYING·FARMS ε·HOUSES

The five *Daily Telegraph* crossword puzzles from May 2 to June 2 that unwittingly spelt out the D-Day codes. (Ewan Macnaughton Associates)

PRIZE COMPETITION No. 5,797

Three prizes of books to a value of thirty shillings, to be selected by the winners from advertisements in THE DAILY TELEGRAPH on Fridays, will be awarded to the senders of the first three correct solutions opened. Solutions must reach THE DAILY TELEGRAPH, 135, Fleet Street, E.C.4, not later than first post on Thursday. Envelope must bear 2½d. stamp, and be marked Prize Competition in top left-hand corner. Winners' names appear on Friday.

NAME ....

ADDRESS ....

ACROSS

1 No half-baked praise (two words—4, 4)
5 The county of firm personnel (6)
9 Incog. (two words—3, 5)
10 Not apparently very high-class land (6)
11 —but some big wig like this has stolen some of it at times (8)
13 They may send one's temperature up, oddly enough (6)
14 It serves its turn in the opening episode (3)
16 Scattered inroad to order (6)
19 He has his duty to master (7)
20 "Die a V.C." (anag.) (improving words to a soldier?) (6)
21 It needs Erse to slander (3)
26 Need to come to signify (6)
27 When to change to the 31 across? (8)
28 To show grief about a lady is not fruitless (6)
29 What separates the novice from the adept (8)
30 No enemy allowed a bed (6)
31 Remote terminus don't mix around here (two words—5, 3)

DOWN

1 Cut out the chaff and do not delay victory (6)
2 The one that was left at the post? (6)
3 Hang up more than a corner (6)
4 They are probably prepared for floods in this English town (6)
6 Not prolonged enough to make the torso hot (two words—3, 3)
7 Not a strange spirit, apparently (8)
8 Entertainment that tells one what to do at it (8)
12 This Eastern is often in a whirl (7)
15 Is familiar with the cells from birth (3)
16 Reversed in 26 across (3)
17 Sounds a useful thing to wear, but no help (8)
18 There's no list for the ships on this (two words—4, 4)
19 Of secret composition and not taxed (two words—4, 4)
22 What a girl may expect if a sailor gives her the bird? (6)
23 Cool place to work in? (6)
24 Figure of speech is turned on quite a way (6)
25 Asked for convalescent patient's meal (6)

Y'DAY'S SOLUTION.—ACROSS: 1, Afterthought; 10, All ears; 11, Bladder; 12, Bucket; 15, Set off; 19, Decided; 17, Utah; 18, Feat; 19, Decorum; 20, Mace; 22, Amen; 24, Gainhad; 29, Sampan; 27, Ritual; 30, Equally; 31, Chablis; 32, Reinstatement. DOWN: 2, Feitura; 3, Elated; 4, Test; 5, Orby; 6, Graded; 7, Tadpole; 8, Harbour-master; 9, Front and loss; 13, Teheran; 14, Bivouac; 15, Secular; 21, Compute; 23, Maudlin; 24, Gallon; 25, Dasm; 26, Spit; 29, Scut.

Y'DAY'S SOLUTION.—ACROSS: 1, Long Island; 8, Idle; 10, Democratic; 11, Ruin; 12, Edge; 13, New York; 18, Alice; 19, Erect; 20, Breve; 21, Ingot; 22, Poser; 23, Union; 24, Green; 25, Usher; 26, Earnest; 30, Pelt; 32, Water-tight; 33, Kiwi; 34, Garden gate. DOWN: 2, Omen; 3, Grove; 4, Salt; 5, Actor; 6, Dose; 7, Flag; 9, Breaking up; 10, Diving-bell; 13, Dress-shirt; 14, Enterprise; 15, Neptune; 16, Ocean; 17, Keep out; 20, Brag; 27, Aster; 28, Nerve; 29, Sling; 33, Evil; 35, Twig; 35, Phut.

Y'DAY'S SOLUTION.—ACROSS: 1, Up to the mark; 9, Essen; 10, Melancholia; 11, Tesco; 12, Cedar; 15, Wells; 17, Air; 18, Muse; 19, Synod; 22, Pedal; 23, In use; 24, Tyros; 26, Sees; 27, The; 28, Navvy; 30, Style; 33, Tempo; 35, Thereabouts; 36, Ounce; 37, Done to a turn. DOWN: 2, Piece; 3, Omaha; 4, Hock; 5, Moose; 6, Keats; 7, Assiduously; 8, Incoherence; 12, Composition; 13, Daydreaming; 14, Rally; 15, Wear; 16, Leo; 20, Nasty; 21, Dives; 25, P.L.A.; 28, Noted; 29, Verge; 31, Trout; 32, Later; 34, Dago.

This was a localized matter, easily enough hushed-up in a wartime atmosphere of rumour and counter-rumour. But worse was to follow.

On Saturday June 3, in the Associated Press building off Fleet Street, Joan Ellis, a 23-year-old teletype operator, was carrying out a practice "dry run" of an invasion special on an unconnected teletype machine. At 10.38 p.m., a sub-editor threw her off balance with a hasty communiqué from the Russian front; forgetting her practice run, she fed the entire tape into a live transmitter. The desk men on five continents now read the electrifying news: URGENT PRESS ASSOCIATED NYK FLASH EISENHOWER'S HQ ANNOUNCES ALLIED LANDINGS IN FRANCE. Within seconds, Irene Henshall, a veteran teletypist, had spotted the error and broke into all circuits with the standard news agency panic-button transmission: BUST THAT FLASH . . . BUST THAT FLASH . . . BUST EISENHOWER.

The mistake was so swiftly rectified that no newspapers picked up the story, but the news had already reached both the Belmont Park racetrack in New York and the New York Polo Grounds, where the city's Giants were just then embroiled in a Saturday afternoon game with the Pittsburgh Pirates. Promptly, at the announcer's request, the crowds in both stadiums rose for a moment's silent prayer for the Allied success.

The chief of Eisenhower's Press Camp, Colonel Barney Oldfield, at once rang Captain Harry Butcher for clarification: had the Supreme Commander heard of the furore? "He sort of grunted," Butcher confirmed. "He has bigger worries."

afield as Limehouse and Canning Town—blithely offering invasion francs in payment. It took a posse of police under Chief Inspector Reginald Smith of Scotland Yard's "K" Division until 5 a.m. next day to coax them back into the stadium—along with two East End pub-keepers, who had accepted the francs.

It was true, and one of them, on Sunday June 4, was Leonard Sidney Dawe, a mild-mannered 54-year-old physics teacher from Leatherhead, Surrey. As compiler of *The Daily Telegraph* crossword puzzle for more than twenty years, along with his friend, Melville Jones, Dawe, in the past month, had somehow hit upon every key code-word for the forthcoming invasion. On May 2, the clue "One of the US" (17 across) had been, logically, "Utah." But on 23 May, the answer to 13 down, "Red Indian on the Missouri" had been, incredibly, "Omaha."

On May 27, Prize Competition Crossword No. 5797 had a truly arcane clue (11 across), "But some big-wig like this has stolen some of it at times." To those of like mind to Dawe, the answer to this could only be "Overlord"—a solution published on June 2 along with a new puzzle—15 down—"Britannia and he hold to the same thing." The seven-letter solution turned out to be "Neptune," and this was uncanny, for on May 30, the solution to 11 across—"This bush is a centre of nursery revolution"—was, disquietingly, "Mulberry."

The two MI5 agents who had questioned Dawe reported him as genuinely puzzled and distressed. He pointed out that some of the crosswords could have been completed many months before—when the code-words had not existed. Was it all, as Dawe himself suggested, a diabolical coincidence?

MI5 could form no judgement, any more than Eisenhower, but the tension stayed with him to the end. "This breach of security is so serious," he said, with palpable awe, "it practically gives me the shakes."

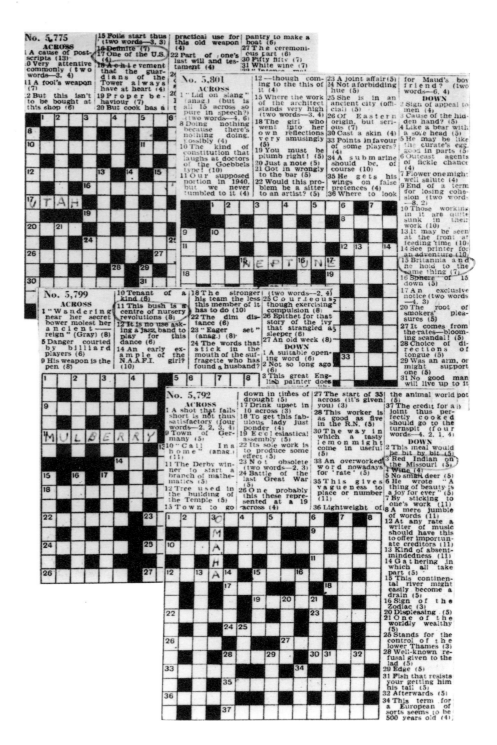

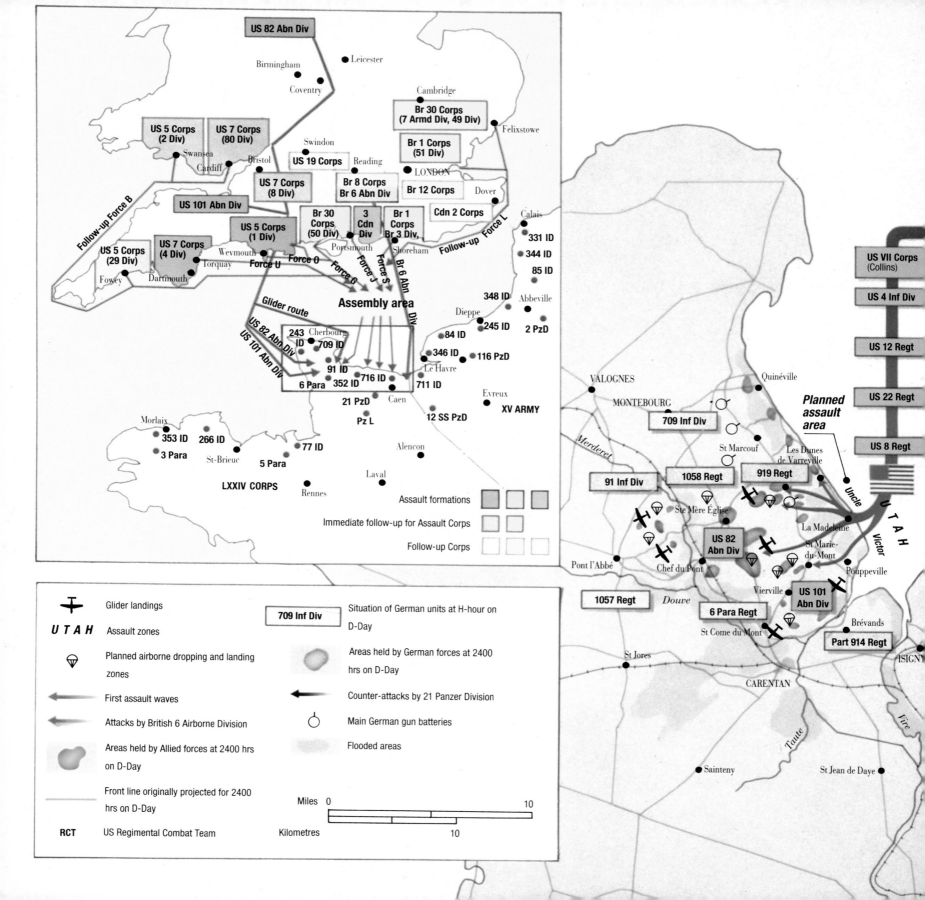

US 82 Abn Div

Birmingham
Leicester
Coventry

Cambridge
Br 30 Corps
(7 Armd Div, 49 Div)
Felixstowe

US 5 Corps
(2 Div)
US 7 Corps
(80 Div)
Swansea
Cardiff
Bristol
Swindon

Br 1 Corps
(51 Div)

Reading
US 19 Corps

LONDON
Dover

US 7 Corps
(8 Div)
Br 8 Corps
Br 6 Abn Div
Br 12 Corps

US 101 Abn Div

Cdn 2 Corps

Follow-up Force B
US 5 Corps
(1 Div)

Br 30
Corps
(50 Div)
3
Cdn
Div
Br 1
Corps
Br 3 Div,

Calais
331 ID
344 ID
85 ID

Force L
Follow-up

US 5 Corps
(29 Div)
US 7 Corps
(4 Div)
Weymouth
Torquay
Force U
Force O
Force G
Force J
Force S
Br 6 Abn Div
Portsmouth
Shoreham

348 ID
Abbeville
Dieppe
245 ID
2 PzD

Fowey
Dartmouth

Glider route
Assembly area

84 ID

US 82 Abn Div
243
ID
Cherbourg
709 ID
346 ID
116 PzD
Le Havre

US 101 Abn Div
91 ID
716 ID
711 ID

6 Para
352 ID
21 PzD
Caen
Evreux
XV ARMY

Morlaix
353 ID
266 ID
77 ID
Alençon
Pz L
12 SS PzD

3 Para
St-Brieuc
5 Para
Laval

Rennes

LXXIV CORPS

Assault formations

Immediate follow-up for Assault Corps

Follow-up Corps

Glider landings

UTAH Assault zones

Planned airborne dropping and landing
zones

First assault waves

Attacks by British 6 Airborne Division

Areas held by Allied forces at 2400 hrs
on D-Day

Front line originally projected for 2400
hrs on D-Day

RCT US Regimental Combat Team

709 Inf Div Situation of German units at H-hour on
D-Day

Areas held by German forces at 2400
hrs on D-Day

Counter-attacks by 21 Panzer Division

Main German gun batteries

Flooded areas

Miles 0 — 10

Kilometres 10

US VII Corps
(Collins)

US 4 Inf Div

US 12 Regt

VALOGNES
Quinéville

MONTEBOURG
709 Inf Div
St Marcouf

US 22 Regt

Planned
assault
area

91 Inf Div
1058 Regt
919 Regt
Les Dunes
de Varreville

US 8 Regt

Merderet

Uncle

U T A H

Ste Mère Église
La Madeleine

Pont l'Abbé
US 82
Abn Div
Chef du Pont
St Marie-
du-Mont
Victor

1057 Regt
Douve
Vierville
Pouppeville
US 101
Abn Div

6 Para Regt
Brévands

St Come du Mont
Part 914 Regt

St Jores
ISIGNY

CARENTAN

Sainteny
St Jean de Daye

Taute
Vire

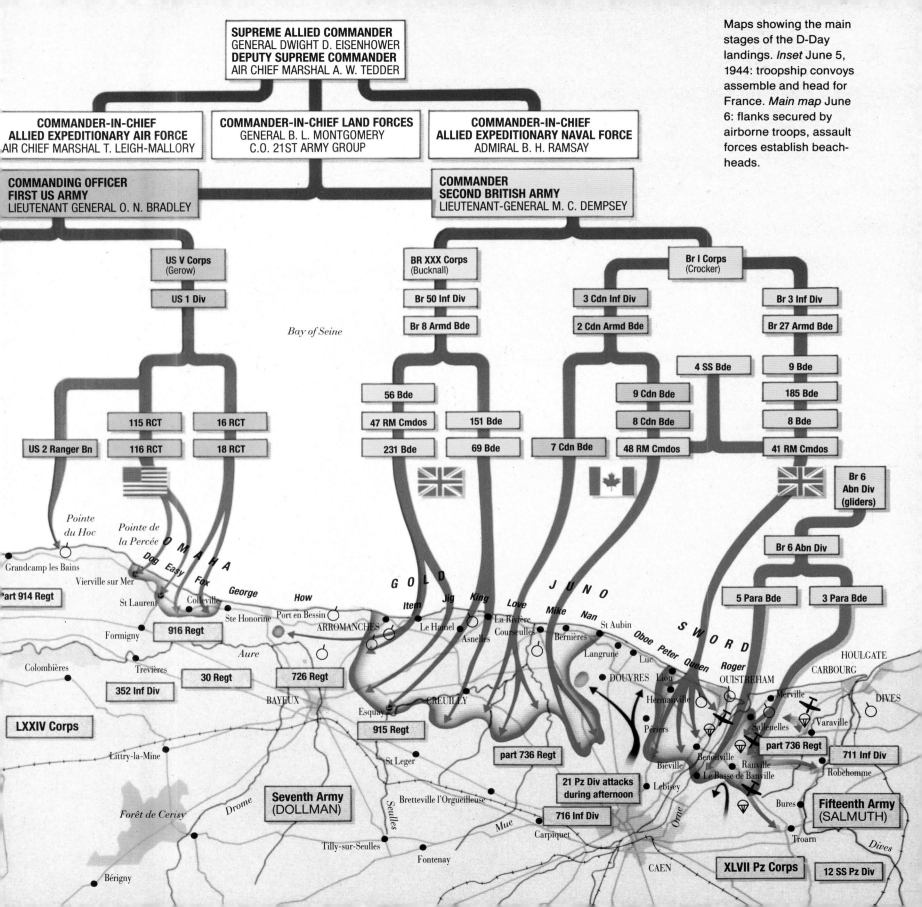

Maps showing the main stages of the D-Day landings. *Inset June 5, 1944:* troopship convoys assemble and head for France. *Main map June 6:* flanks secured by airborne troops, assault forces establish beach-heads.

Southern England, June 6: a last message from a forward assembly area. (Imperial War Museum)

ON SUNDAY JUNE 4, the strain increased perceptibly. As early as 5 a.m., in a darkened railway siding outside Southampton, General Sir Hastings Ismay, who had waited up all night on Churchill's private train, was listening intently to the metallic tones of Major-General Walter Bedell Smith, calling from Admiral Ramsay's headquarters, Southwick House, ten miles north-west of Portsmouth. There was news from the weathermen and all of it was bad: their forecast for D-Day, June 5, was uniformly pessimistic. A cloud base of 500 ft to zero and Force 5 winds would both rule out the use of aircraft and render naval gunfire ineffective.

Eisenhower and his commanders had been unanimous: without Allied air superiority, the landings posed too great a risk. A twenty-four-hour postponement had been agreed. For all naval units, the cryptic message, "BOWSPRIT" signalled this delay: for airborne divisions, "RIPCORD PLUS 24."

It was a move Ramsay fully endorsed. Since his move to Southwick House—"a stately home of many staircases and little plumbing," noted Mulberry's Captain Harold Hickling ruefully—the Admiral had left nothing to chance. His operational orders for "Neptune," issued on April 24, ran to 1000 pages, a volume 3 in. thick, the most detailed instructions ever issued by a naval Commander-in-Chief. While Rear-Admiral Alan G. Kirk's Western Task Force, Force O and Force U, stretched from Salcombe, Devon to Poole, Dorset, Rear-Admiral Sir Philip Vian's Eastern Force, Forces G, J and S, hugged the Solent and Southampton Water, with backup units as far east as Newhaven. That afternoon, all five forces had orders to rendezvous at

. . . The sun will not be seen to-day;/The sky doth frown and lower upon our army.

(from *Richard III* V, iii, by William Shakespeare)

Overleaf
The world-famous Overlord Embroidery, on permanent show at the D-Day Museum, Portsmouth, tells the story of the Allied invasion of Normandy in 34 panels. Here, the great invasion convoy, protected by 15 squadrons of fighters, sets course for France. (©Overlord Embroidery Trust)

137

Area Z, or "Piccadilly Circus," south-east of the Isle of Wight, where motor launches would shepherd them skilfully towards the ten mineswept channels called "the spout."

For all skippers, irrespective of age or rank, there were even "Mickey Mouse" diagrams, showing the position of each convoy at every hour of the passage, and it thus seemed likely that the boast of Rear-Admiral George Creasy, Ramsay's Chief-of-Staff, at his final press conference, would be made good: "Gentlemen, what Philip of Spain failed to do, what Napoleon tried and failed to do and what Hitler never had the courage to try, we are about to do, and with God's grace we shall."

Yet the whole vast enterprise must wait upon the weather.

It had been a fraught decision, for every hour was crucial: how long could the gigantic secret be kept? Already huddles of loaded transports and supply ships were collecting at the Nore, Milford Haven, Plymouth and South-ampton. Hundreds of LCTs, moving south from the Combined Operations Training Base at Inveraray, and the Clyde base of Troon, were assembled, camouflaged with netting, off the mud-flats of Portsmouth, in secluded coves at Shoreham, Lymington and Weymouth. On these craft the men already embarked fought a miserable retching battle against nausea and seasickness.

There were other all-too-obvious signs that invasion was imminent. On airfields from Debden in Essex to Honiton in Devon, the warning red cross of St Andrew loomed on the signals area outside every Watch Office: airfield unserviceable, landing forbidden. Scores of

trains had been cancelled without notice; London's main termini now resembled huge frowsy dormitories as stranded passengers caught a few hours sleep.

All that Sunday afternoon the preparations continued—hoping against hope. Since before dawn, ground crews of the Eighth Air Force on the east coast had been busy breaking open a paint consignment labelled "For the cake walk," daubing black and white stripes 2 ft wide on the wings and tail booms of Lightnings, Mustangs and Thunderbolts. Late that afternoon, the same instructions reached Joe Hann and other glider mechanics of the Ninth Troop Carrier Command, based at Exeter: identical stripes were to be painted on the wings and fuselage of every Waco and Horsa glider. All told, 10,000 aircraft would use up 100,000 gallons of paint, singling them out from Luftwaffe planes.

As the day wore on, the weather worsened perceptibly.

At 9.15 p.m., rain lashed the pine trees outside Southwick House; behind the heavy blackout curtains of the library, flurries of rain rattled like buckshot against the window panes. It was a large comfortable blue-carpeted room, dominated by a table with a green baize cloth, set about with easy chairs and sofas; dark oak bookshelves lined the walls. Tonight, every man present had been a participant in that momentous St Paul's School conference of May 15, when the biggest problem had been security: Bedell Smith chatting with the pipe-puffing Tedder, Montgomery in corduroy slacks and a roll-topped sweater, Ramsay and Leigh-Mallory, formally clad as always.

All of them awaited Eisenhower—and, above all, Group Captain James Stagg, the tall, serious RAF meteorologist.

Promptly at 9.30 p.m., trim in a dark-green battledress, Eisenhower entered. There was the faintest hint of a rueful grin—"When I die they ought to bury me on a rainy day in a ceremonial coffin shaped like a landing craft," he had joked earlier—but his face was set and worried. Shortly the three senior meteorologists, led by Stagg, reported with their briefing.

As Stagg later recalled it: "No one could have imagined weather charts less propitious." Two depressions over the North Atlantic were in themselves mid-winter phenomena, and while all three forecasters were confident that the stormy cold front would traverse the Channel overnight, none of them could predict the sequel.

"There have been some rapid and unexpected developments in the situation," Stagg told the hushed assembly. In two to three hours, the rain would cease, followed by thirty-six hours of less clear weather with moderate winds. Bombers and fighters should be able to operate on Monday night, June 5, though hampered by cloud.

At its simplest, it boiled down to one unenviable option: tolerable weather, far below minimal requirements, would pertain for little more than twenty-four hours.

No sooner had Stagg finished than the questions erupted. Could the forecasts be wrong? Had reports been checked with all available sources? Still Eisenhower hesitated, as someone asked Stagg, "What will the weather be on D-Day in the Channel and over the French coast?" It was fully two minutes before Stagg replied, "To answer that question would make me a guesser, not a meteorologist."

It was an awesome decision for any man to take. Eisenhower looked questioningly at Bedell Smith. "It's a helluva gamble but it's the best possible gamble," Smith replied. Next it was Montgomery's turn. "I would say—Go!" was his incisive verdict.

The minutes ticked by, while Eisenhower wrestled with it. Another postponement would mean two weeks delay, with less favourable moon conditions, and thousands of troops had already embarked and been briefed. Watching his chief, Bedell Smith felt pity for his "loneliness and isolation," sitting with his hands clasped before him, staring at the green baize cloth.

"The question is," Eisenhower mused, as if to himself, "just how long can you hang this operation on the end of a limb and let it hang there?"

At length he looked up. The decision was taken: "I am quite positive we must give the order. I don't like it, but there it is."

But at 4.15 a.m., on June 5, when the weathermen once again faced the commanders, the tired face of Group Captain Stagg bore the ghost of a smile. "I think we have a gleam of hope for you, sir," he could now tell Eisenhower.

Stagg confirmed that the mass of weather fronts coming in from the Atlantic was moving faster than anticipated. Everything suggested fair conditions beginning late on 5 June and lasting until the morning of June 6, with a drop in wind velocity, some break in the clouds, and a ceiling of 3000 feet.

The dummy parachutist at the church at Ste Mère-Eglise, Normandy, symbolizes, to this day, the moment of liberation and salutes those who died.

Paratrooper Channel ferry: a C-47 transport preserved in the museum at Ste Mère-Eglise.

143

Utah, 5.50 am: US troops on the final run-in aboard an LCA. (US Army)

... And ships, by thousands, lay below,/And men in nations;—all were his!/He counted them at break of day—/And when the sun set where were they?

(from *Don Juan* Canto I, by George Gordon, Lord Byron)

Eisenhower sat lost in thought. The minutes ticked by—so remorselessly that Air Vice-Marshal James M. Robb of Leigh-Mallory's staff, took note of their passage. Eight minutes had elapsed before Eisenhower very quietly but quite audibly, said, "OK, let's go."

★   ★   ★

The word was passing. All over southern England, men, hearing the news, came to terms with what they had to do.

Aboard the LSI (Landing Ship Infantry) *Empire Lance* in Southampton Harbour, the men of the 6th Battalion, The Green Howards, heard the Senior Naval Transport Officer's measured tones over the loudspeaker: "At 17.45 hours, this ship will weigh anchor, and, in passage with the remainder of the armada, sail for the coast of France." As this news was broken, an eerie hush fell upon the ship. On other ships, a few men, understandably, had reservations. "We felt that we'd done our war, we should go home," remembers Major Frank Colaccio, of the US 1st Division, which had fought all through Tunisia and Sicily. "We kept reading in the papers about the huge increase in US strength." A chosen few felt a rare elation. As Lord Lovat's Commandos, whistling *Lilliburlero*, embarked at Southampton, it seemed to their Adjutant, Captain Tony Smith,

144

"more like a regatta than a page of history," hearing that an Admiral had thrown his hat in the air, Smith confessed, "I never loved England so truly as at that moment." Aboard the USS *Augusta*, the flagship of Rear-Admiral Kirk, in Plymouth Harbour, Lieutenant John Mason Brown, USNR, noted, by contrast, a reflective mood. "D-Day is a more potent revivalist than Moody, Billy Sunday, or the McPherson who was Aimee Semple," he reflected, "Men begin going to church in droves."

For many, their first sight of the ships pointed up the immensity of the whole enterprise. "Big ships, small ships, odd ships, plain ships, freak ships and graceful ships," marvelled Captain Hugh Gunning, an observer with the British 3rd Division, for the whole channel of the Solent seemed choked with "the far-stretching grey Armada of Operation 'Overlord'." Aboard HMS *Goathland*, in Portsmouth Harbour, Captain Eric Bush, RN, felt the same; a 45-year-old veteran of Gallipoli, commanding the Naval Assault Group for Force S, even Bush had "never . . . seen so many ships together at one time . . . thousands and thousands of ships of all classes stretched from horizon to horizon."

Some commanders, in these last hours, sought to play down the hazards that lay ahead — "just the spring housecleaning that we used to do under Mother's direction when I was a little boy at home," wrote Colonel Paddy Flint of the US 9th Division soothingly to all the wives and mothers of his officers. Others were more forthright. In the aft wardroom of the USS *Carroll*, Brigadier General Norman Cota warned his 29th Division, bound for Omaha: "You're going to find confusion. The landing

SUPREME HEADQUARTERS
ALLIED EXPEDITIONARY FORCE

Soldiers, Sailors and Airmen of the Allied Expeditionary Force!

You are about to embark upon the Great Crusade, toward which we have striven these many months. The eyes of the world are upon you. The hopes and prayers of liberty-loving people everywhere march with you. In company with our brave Allies and brothers-in-arms on other Fronts, you will bring about the destruction of the German war machine, the elimination of Nazi tyranny over the oppressed peoples of Europe, and security for ourselves in a free world.

Your task will not be an easy one. Your enemy is well trained, well equipped and battle-hardened. He will fight savagely.

But this is the year 1944! Much has happened since the Nazi triumphs of 1940-41. The United Nations have inflicted upon the Germans great defeats, in open battle, man-to-man. Our air offensive has seriously reduced their strength in the air and their capacity to wage war on the ground. Our Home Fronts have given us an overwhelming superiority in weapons and munitions of war, and placed at our disposal great reserves of trained fighting men. The tide has turned! The free men of the world are marching together to Victory!

I have full confidence in your courage, devotion to duty and skill in battle. We will accept nothing less than full Victory!

Good Luck! And let us all beseech the blessing of Almighty God upon this great and noble undertaking.

Dwight Eisenhower

craft aren't going in on schedule, and people are going to be landed in the wrong place. Some won't be landed at all. . . ."

For the men who would form the invasion spearhead — more than 1000 glider pilots, 13,000 American paratroopers and 4255 British — this last day was the longest they had ever known. If the British 6th Airborne Division's role was as onerous as any — the destruction of the four-gun Merville battery, the seizure of the bridges across the Orne River and the Caen Canal — at least they knew the odds. Only three days earlier, Major-General Richard Gale, the divisional commander, revealing final details of their destination, had told them: "The

Hun thinks only a bloody fool will go there—that's why I am going!" To Gale's briefing, Brigadier James Hill, of the 5th Parachute Brigade, added a caution to rival Brigadier General Cota's: "Gentlemen, in spite of your excellent training and orders, do not be daunted if chaos reigns. It undoubtedly will!"

The American airborne troops were ready too. On a score of airfields pivoting on Newbury, Berkshire, paratroopers smeared their faces with cocoa and linseed oil or with the ashes from spent fires; others carefully shaved their heads, leaving only a Mohawk scalp look. At Honiton, in Devon, Private Donald Burgett, the young paratrooper who knew death as an old familiar, smiled wryly at one group of buddies "doing the Jolson bit, singing 'Mammy', waving their hands and blinking white-looking eyes in blackened faces." But Burgett's real concern was with his equipment. By take-off time—towards 11 p.m.—he and all the others were weighed down with packages like walking Christmas trees.

Aside from his suit of olive drab, worn under his jump suit, Burgett was wearing helmet, boots, gloves, a main parachute, a reserve parachute, and a Mae West. He was armed not only with a rifle, a .45 automatic, three knives and a machete; he was further burdened with a cartridge belt, two bandoliers, almost 750 rounds of ammo, both .30 and .45, a Hawkins mine to blow the tracks off a tank, four blocks of TNT, an entrenching tool, three first aid kits, two morphine needles and a gas mask. He had nine separate grenades, five days' rations, a canteen of water, a change of socks and underwear and 200 cigarettes.

It was small wonder that when the order came, "Emplane," two Air Corps men lifted Burgett and the rest of his "stick"—eighteen men—bodily into the C-47. Once there, many knelt as if in prayer; it was the easiest way to ride.

Though Burgett only glimpsed him, Eisenhower was briefly at Honiton—and at Welford, Tarrant Rushton, and all the airfields ringing Newbury. "If it goes all right," his driver, WAC Lieutenant Kay Summersby, had told him, "dozens of people will claim the credit. But if it goes wrong, you'll be the only one to blame." Yet nothing of this showed in the Supreme Commander's face as he moved through the twilight among the black-faced troops, like an echo of Shakespeare's Henry V on the eve of Agincourt: a little touch of Eisenhower in the night.

"What is your job, soldier?"
"Ammunition bearer, sir."
"Where is your home?"
"Pennsylvania, sir."
"Did you get those shoulders working in a coal mine?"
"Yes, sir."
"Good luck to you tonight, soldier."

No man who saw him could have guessed that earlier this day, anticipating the possibility of failure, as all commanders must, Eisenhower had drafted a message of defeat. In part it read, "Our landings in the Cherbourg-Havre area have failed to gain a satisfactory foothold and I have withdrawn the troops . . . If any blame or fault attaches to the attempt it is mine alone."

Eisenhower's June 5 draft of an order to withdraw the troops, preserved by his naval aide, Capt. Harry C. Butcher. (US Signal Corps)

At dawn of D-Day, the US Army's Pocket Guide spelt out the aims of Eisenhower's great crusade. (US Army Military History Institute)

Our landings in the Cherbourg — Havre area have failed to gain a satisfactory foothold and I have withdrawn the troops. (This particular operation) My decision to attack at this time and place was based upon the best information available. The troops, the air and the Navy did all that Bravery and devotion to duty could do. If any blame or fault attaches to the attempt it is mine alone.

For some paratroop commanders, it was a time for fervent exhortation. In the 101st Airborne Division Area, Colonel Howard "Skeets" Johnson, commanding the 501st Parachute Infantry Regiment, brandished his jump knife like a beserk cheer-leader, rallying his troops in a frenzied chant of "We're the best! We're the best!" In the 82nd Airborne Area, Lieutenant Colonel Edward Krause, of the 3rd Battalion, 505th Parachute Infantry, held aloft a folded Old Glory and solemnly vowed: "Tonight . . . we're going to liberate the people [of Ste Mère-Église] and fly this flag from the tallest building." By dawn on June 6, they would have done just that.

At Broadwell, Gloucestershire, Captain John Gwinnett, a chaplain of the 6th Airborne,

"You will probably get a rousing welcome from the French."

2

A POCKET GUIDE TO

France

WAR AND NAVY DEPARTMENTS, WASHINGTON, D. C.

PROPERTY OF US ARMY

I

WHY YOU'RE GOING TO FRANCE

YOU are about to play a personal part in pushing the Germans out of France. Whatever part you take— rifleman, hospital orderly, mechanic, pilot, clerk, gunner, truck driver—you will be an essential factor in a great effort which will have two results: first, France will be liberated from the Nazi mob and the Allied armies will be that much nearer Victory, and second, the enemy will be deprived of coal, steel, manpower, machinery, food, bases, seacoast and a long list of other essentials which have enabled him to carry on the war at the expense of the French.

The Allied offensive you are taking part in is based upon a hard-boiled fact. It's this. We democracies aren't just doing favors in fighting for each other when history gets tough. We're all in the same boat. Take a look around you as you move into France and you'll see what the Nazis do to a democracy when they can get it down by itself.

5

☆ U. S. GOVERNMENT PRINTING OFFICE: 1944   —O— 567341

dedicated the divisional flag of Bellerophon mounted on the winged horse Pegasus, using as text: "Fear knocked at the door. Faith opened, and there was nothing there." At Honiton, Second Lieutenant Joshua Logan, later a noted Broadway producer, having briefed the paratroopers on escape and evasion techniques, handed over to the group chaplain. Suddenly the padre's prayer tailed off in a high-pitched scream: "Get in there and kill them! Kill them! Go over there and kill 'em!"

"Scared the hell out of everybody," Logan was to recall.

The secret could no longer be kept from the world at large. At Littlehampton, on the Sussex coast, Sister Brenda McBryde, of No. 75 British General Hospital, who two weeks later would herself embark for France, was one of a group who left a crowded dance floor to cool off on the flat roof; the muffled beat of the Palais Glide came faintly on the evening air. Suddenly they were conscious of a new vibration growing louder by the minute.

As Sister McBryde watched, a cloud of tiny specks in the sky inland fanned out and multiplied; formation after formation of planes was throbbing overhead. The noise grew deafening; dancers were flocking up from the ballroom floor, "moon faces turned up to the sky." Wave after wave of Lancasters, Blenheims and Halifaxes thundered above them, all of them towing Horsa or Hamilear gliders, moving purposefully across the sky, heading for France: a great V-shaped arrowhead, made up of many smaller arrowheads, only the tiny purple lights on the wing-tips keeping the planes apart.

A great drawn-out sigh went up from all the watchers; it was, Sister McBryde recalled, "like the Ah-ah-h-h that follows a firework display."

Unknown to the airborne troops—and initially to the Germans—D-Day had already dawned on French soil.

For all the citizens of Caen, Bayeux, St Lô and other coastal towns, the night of June 5, endured behind tight-closed shutters, was airless and oppressive. But for the men and women of the Resistance network *Centurie*, it was equally a testing time. In the 9000 square miles between Cherbourg and Le Havre and forty miles inland, as far as Argentan, they sensed their hour had come.

Crewmen of the USS *Augusta* hear their destination over the ship's PA system. (US Navy)

On the night of Thursday June 1, the BBC had broadcast certain personal messages. The first held an ominous note: "The hour of combat is at hand." Others were more in keeping with spring and a young man's fancy: "The flowers are very red," "Eileen is married to Joe." Then three days had passed, and still they waited for messages with meaning for Normandy.

Now, at 10.15 p.m., German Central Time on June 5 — one hour earlier than British Double Summer Time — came a string of personal messages that had a ring of *Alice in Wonderland*, two of them at least with significance for every Norman resistant. In the kitchen of his house on Route Nationale 13, the Paris-Cherbourg highway, Jean Chateau, a burly electricity board inspector, was eating an omelette with his wife, Albertine. Tense with emotion, Chateau said, "Why — I think this is it."

In the wine cellar of his bicycle shop in Bayeux, Georges Mercader, intelligence chief for the coastal sector between Vierville and Port-en-Bessin — the region of Omaha Beach — had

carefully removed his secret radio set from behind two convincingly dusty bottles of claret. "It is hot in Suez," Mercader heard then, "It is hot in Suez." To the bicycle merchant, it was heart-stopping news: the long awaited signal for "The Violet Plan," or sabotage of underground Post Office cables.

"The dice are on the table," said the voice, "The dice are on the table." For Mercader this was enough, and he snapped off the tuner; the second message denoted "The Green Plan," mass railway sabotage. "I have to go out," he told his wife, Madeleine, "I'll be late tonight." Then, wheeling out a low-slung racing bicycle, he pedalled off to alert his sector leaders. A former Normandy cycling champion, who had represented the province in the Tour de France, Mercader knew that no German curfew applied to him; impressed by his prowess, the local commandant had given him *carte-blanche* to practise day or night. It was, after all, in keeping with the maxim which had enabled *Centurie* to somehow survive until now: Keep it normal.

Now the days of subtle stratagems were past. It was time for action. In the darkness along the coast, teams of five men armed with charges and detonators went quietly from their houses to carry out the first instalment of "The Green Plan." (Within three weeks, 3000 rail cuts had been accomplished.) At Caen's *Gare Centrale*, the stationmaster, Albert Augé, and his team, first destroyed all the yard's water pumps, then pulverized the steam injectors on every locomotive. Explosions erupted along Rommel's Wall as teams led by the Cherbourg grocer, Yves Gresselin, dynamited the Paris-Cherbourg line above Carentan and the line

between St Lô and Coutances. Other teams moved in, blowing the lines between Caen and Bayeux, between Caen and Vire, forty miles south.

Nor was "The Violet Plan" neglected. In the heathland above Omaha Beach, André Farine, the proprietor of the Café de l'Étanville, near Grandcamp-les-Bains, split forty men into eight teams of five before they melted discreetly into the darkness. Armed with shears and other tools, they cut the mighty telephone cable that ran from Cherbourg to Smolensk in eight 2-in. sections. At St Lô, another team made ready to sever the vital military telephone between German 84th Corps and the 91st Divisional HQ near Valognes. Gresselin's men demolished the St Lô—Jersey cable and the long distance line from Cherbourg to Brest. The initial sluggishness of German reaction in the Cotentin Peninsula would owe much to these men.

Five miles north-east of Caen, strange things were also afoot. In the village of Ranville, 11-year-old Alain Doix sat up in bed transfixed; the big brass knobs of the bedpost seemed to have come alive, quivering with the brilliant light of chandelier flares. Towards the Channel, flak flickered and danced in the sky like summer lightning.

Six thousand feet overhead, a lively chorus of "Abie, My Boy" came to an abrupt halt; unseen by the Doix household, six Halifax aircraft from Tarrant Rushton, Dorset, were releasing the tow ropes of six Horsa gliders. Swooping eerily towards the earth like kestrels over a farmyard, plainly visible to Alain and his father René, the gliders were heading as if magnetized, towards the bridges spanning two parallel waterways, the Orne River and the Caen Canal, still and refulgent in the moonlight.

The 6th Air Landing Brigade, 150 men under Major John Howard of the Oxford and Buckinghamshire Light Infantry, were on time for their D-Day rendezvous.

As Howard's lead glider neared the canal bridge, the night was strangely silent. No firing from the ground rose up to greet them. Next instant, in a grinding, rending landfall for which no one was quite ready, more than 6000 lbs of men and glider struck the bridge head-on, swaying and shuddering, splintering like matchwood, the barbed wire that guarded the approaches snapping like twine under the impact of the 88-ft wingspan. As the perspex cockpit canopy sprayed into glittering shards, both pilots were hurled clear of the wreckage into the wire. Behind them a muffled thudding signalled the landfall of the gliders in their wake.

"Come on, lads," Howard yelled, and now men were tumbling out, some through the door, some through the buckled cockpit, pouring across the bridge. In this carefully contrived chaos, surprise was total; some Germans, asleep in their gunpits, knew nothing until hurtling grenades blasted them awake, others came to, only groggily, staring down the glinting barrels of Sten guns. Now forty men under Lieutenant Danny Brotheridge pelted like furies for the vital far bank. As they ran, a German sentry was clearly visible, Very pistol held high. Forty Bren guns, fired from the hip, opened up simultaneously; even as the flare burst into the night sky the man fell dead. Seconds later, Brotheridge, too, fell, mortally wounded in the throat.

As a warning to the Orne Bridge garrison, 500 yards away, the flare was fired too late. In what Leigh-Mallory later acclaimed as "the finest piece of airmanship thus far," the pilots had crash-landed on a sloping landing zone just 300 yards long. Both bridges had fallen as one.

Ironically, neither could have been blown, even had the Germans been alerted. Sappers surveying the scene found that though demolition preparations were completed, no explosive charges had yet been placed. They were stored in a cottage near by.

Now there was nothing left to do but hold the bridges and wait—for the small-hours arrival of a seventy-two-strong glider supply train led by Major-General Richard Gale, who to ensure good luck was bringing along amulets as various as a four-leafed clover and a miniature crusader's sword plus a tin of treacle for sustenance. By 1 p.m. Lord Lovat's commandos would provide further reinforcements. In a captured pillbox, Corporal Edward Tappenden was calling into his walkie-talkie radio D-Day's first success signal: "Ham and jam . . . ham and jam." A few enterprising souls knocked at the door of Georges Gondrée's tiny *estaminet*, nestling beside the bridge. When Gondrée, reluctantly opening up, heard the reassuring words, "It's all right, chum," he burst into tears of relief, then busied himself uncorking ninety-seven bottles of champagne hoarded against just such a moment.

It was 12.35 a.m., and D-Day's first battle had ended. It had lasted scarcely fifteen minutes.

★   ★   ★

They must not go alone/into that burning building!—which today/is all of Europe!

Say/that you go with them, spirit and heart and mind!/Although the body, grown/too old to fight a young man's war; or wounded/too deeply under the healed and whitened scars/of earlier battles, must remain behind. . . .

(from *Poem and Prayer for an Invading Army* by Edna St Vincent Millay, read over the NBC network on D-Day by Ronald Colman)

They never go to battle, but other in defence of their own country, or to drive out of their friends' land the enemies that be comen in, or by their power to deliver from the yoke and bondage of tyranny some people that be oppressed with tyranny.

(from *Utopia* Bk II, by Sir Thomas More)

153

German beach defences: these Teller mines – each capable of destroying a tank – symbolized the High Command's conviction that Allied landings in Normandy would swiftly be repulsed. (Service Historique de la Marine)

On the German side of the hill, there had been no premonitions. From Paris to Brest, no man from senior commanders to soldiers in their concrete dug-outs expected anything but the quietest of nights.

There was heavy cloud; in some coastal sectors it was drizzling. A wind of Force 5–6 was churning the sea to a turbulent Scale 4–5. In his office overlooking the fine cathedral of St Lô, *Major* Friedrich Hayn, intelligence officer at HQ 84th Corps, knew for certain that the weather ruled out all chances of a landing. In Strongpoint No. 5, on the east coast of the Cotentin Peninsula, *Leutnant* Arthur Jahnke was equally sanguine. The Allies would come at high water and at any moment now the tide would turn.

The lower echelons of Army Group B were equally unconcerned. Many men, like *Gemeiner*

Soldat Heinz Walz, a 266th Artillery private in the eastern Cotentin, were more fearful of a comb-out; as a veteran of the Russian front, Walz dreaded a transfer back more than any onslaught by the Allies. Another east front survivor, *Leutnant* Rudolf Schaaf, now limped so painfully he knew he could never return; he recalls relishing Normandy above all for the abundance of farm food. Although Rommel had told his regiment, the 1716th at Ouistreham, "If they come, they'll come here." Schaaf found this too vague to credit. *Feldwebel* Helmut Gunther, of the 17th SS Panzergrenadiers, was wary of a different kind of war — "In Russia, we had fought men against men . . . in Normandy it would be men against machines." On this score, *Hauptmann* Eberhard Wagemann, of the 21st Panzer Division, was fatalistic. "It wasn't in our interest to think too much about our feelings. We were conscious that neither our men nor our tanks were good enough."

At the Luftwaffe's Paris headquarters, the Palais Luxembourg, the chief meteorologist, *Oberst Professor* Walter Stöbe, even doubted that Allied planes would be airborne on June 5. On the strength of this, many anti-aircraft crews were stood down. At Cap de la Hague, Cherbourg, weathermen assured *Konteradmiral* Walter Hennecke, Naval Commander, Normandy, that invasion conditions could not prevail again until the second half of June.

Oddly, Hennecke was one of the few senior commanders on the spot to hear such intelligence. Rommel, later intending to confer with Hitler, had already left for Germany, to join his wife, Lucie — as had his operations officer, *Oberst* Hans Georg von Tempelhof. Von Rundstedt's intelligence chief, *Oberst* Wilhelm Meyer-Detring, was on leave; *Admiral* Theodor Krancke, commanding Naval Group West, had left for Bordeaux.

And still more men were preparing to depart. At 10 a.m. on June 6, a *Kriegsspiel* (map exercise) was scheduled to take place in Rennes, Brittany, almost 100 miles away, chaired by the paratroop general, Eugen Meindl; virtually every divisional commander was expected to attend, along with two regimental commanders. *Generalleutnant* Carl von Schlieben, in command of the 709th Division, near Valognes, had left that afternoon; *Generalmajor* Wilhelm Falley, of the 91st Air Landing Division, near Château Haut, had moved off at nightfall.

Incredibly, the message that spelt out the Allies' precise intentions had been intercepted, and decoded by 11.37 p.m. on June 4, then filed in twenty-three separate pigeonholes — a masterpiece of bumbled bureaucracy.

As far back as October 14, 1943, *Oberstleutnant* Oscar Reile, of the *Abwehr*'s Paris-based Section IIIF, the bane of the French underground, had filed a report based on interrogations of two captured resistants. The password for the Anglo-American invasion of France would be six lines taken from Paul Verlaine's sonnet, *Chanson d'Automne*:

> *Les sanglots longs*
> *Des violons*
> *De l'automne*
> *Blessent mon coeur*
> *D'une langueur*
> *Monotone.*

(The long sobbing of the autumn violins,
Wounds my heart with a monotonous languor.)

The first part of the signal, Reile reported, up to and including the word "l'automne," would be broadcast by the BBC on the first and fifteenth days of given months. The second would be broadcast when the landings were scheduled for the next forty-eight hours — the time to be counted from midnight of the day of the initial transmission.

Thus on June 2 Reile had alerted his chiefs that on the day preceding, the BBC's Bush House, via radio station Daventry, had repeated the first segment several times between 1.20 and 2.30 p.m.

On June 4, Reile informed twenty-three addressees that the second part of the alert had been broadcast no less than fifteen times between noon and 2.30 p.m. and June 3. Among the recipients were *General der Artillerie* Jodl at Hitler's headquarters, von Rundstedt, Rommel's Army Group B, *Oberst* Meyer-Detring, and *Oberstleutnant* Hellmuth Meyer, intelligence chief of Fifteenth Army.

In some instances — as in *Oberst* Alexis von Roenne's office at Zossen — the messages were filed and forgotten. In others they were disclaimed: "the immediate 'invasion' is not yet apparent," Meyer-Detring noted as his leave began. In one instance, there was plain disbelief. *Generaloberst* Hans von Salmuth, Fifteenth Army's commander, disturbed at a bridge party, commented disdainfully, "I'm too old a bunny to get too excited about this." But as a precaution he did place Fifteenth Army — well outside the invasion area — on full alert.

Almost every other move seemed destined to abet the Allies. Of the 160 serviceable fighters left in France, three squadrons of *Jagdges-chwader* 26 had now been ordered away from the coast — to Metz, Rheims and Marseilles. The wing commander, *Oberstleutnant* Josef "Pips" Priller, had been left with just two planes at Lille to stave off an invasion. In the Omaha Beach region, half the ammunition supplies of the 352nd Artillery Regiment had been moved several miles inland — to safe ammunition dumps. To the chagrin of the 709th Division they were still patrolling, as they had always done, with blanks in their rifles; their live ammo, for conservation reasons, was stowed in their haversacks.

At St Lô, the imminent target for 13,000 US paratroopers, the commander of 84th Corps, *General der Artillerie* Erich Marcks, had other things on his mind. At dawn he, too, was departing for Rennes to take a leading role in the *Kriegsspiel*, a role which intrigued him. Marcks was to represent the Allies in the forthcoming war-game, staging an invasion in which a paratroop assault would be followed by a landing from the sea. There was no doubt that *General* Meindl had set him a thorny problem: the hypothetical invasion area was Normandy.

Unknown to Marcks, a surprise party was in the offing for his fifty-third birthday, June 6. *Major* Hayn had secured several bottles of well-chilled Chablis, to celebrate that moment: precisely at midnight, before the corps commander left for Rennes. A shade uneasily, Hayn and the chief of staff, *Oberstleutnant* Friedrich von Criegern, were wondering how Marcks would react. An austere, stern-faced man, who restricted all meals to official rations, Marcks, who had lost a leg in Russia, was in no sense demonstrative.

But as the solemn knell of the cathedral bells tolled midnight, the little group decided to go ahead. With Hayn in the lead, bearing the Chablis and a tray of glasses, they marched into their chief's room. His artificial leg creaking as he rose to greet them, Marcks peered through his spectacles, then gestured them to be at ease. All of them stood, raising their glasses solemnly, toasting his health.

It was 12.02 a.m.—the moment that Major Howard's raiding party, forty miles to the east, were readying for that long last glide towards the bridges.

By any criteria, Howard's men were lucky. They had gained their objectives. Due to many factors, thousands more airborne men would always recall D-Day as a night of wild terror and confusion, of muddle and fouled-up planning. All Eisenhower's reservations on the wisdom of a paradrop seemed amply justified.

Scores of transport aircraft, chary of an assignment which pinned them to a height of 600 ft and a speed of 120 mph—sitting ducks for fighters and ack-ack—dropped their paratroopers miles wide of their targets. More than one plane load of troopers was dropped in the English Channel, never to be seen again. A fate as gruesome awaited Colonel Robert Sink's 3rd Battalion, 506th Parachute Infantry; dropping into a field ringed by burning oil-soaked barns, more than twenty of them were wiped out. If Colonel Howard "Skeets" Johnson's men did land in the right zone, this was purely by accident; a bundle of K-rations, blocking the doorway for thirty crucial seconds, prevented everyone from jumping. When Johnson and his troops followed it into space, they were over the field assigned to them.

The Pathfinder system on which Bradley had pinned his hopes went sadly awry. Of 120 hand-picked American pathfinders, only 38 landed squarely on their targets. Others tumbled on to rooftops, or fought their way loose from the branches of tall trees; the first American to land in Normandy, Captain Frank Lillyman, of the 101st, was one of the few to set up a lighted "T" on Drop Zone A. Others, like Private Fayette Richardson, of the 82nd, did set up a DZ as instructed—but found only one plane load of troopers descending that whole night.

Some thirty men of the 82nd Airborne landed not in one of the six drop zones ringing Ste Mère-Église but squarely in the town itself, where a hailstorm of German fire met them. One man, Private John Steele, of the 505th Regiment, hung for two hours suspended from the church steeple, so benumbed he never remarked the monstrous tolling of the bell. Pfc Ernest Blanchard, tangled in a tree, sawed so desperately at his harness that he sliced off the top of his thumb. He, too, was so deep in shock it was hours before he realized it.

Many men were swept by high winds into the flooded valley of the Merderet River—"ground here probably soft," the 660th US Engineers had noted—to drown in slimy ditches 7 ft deep by 4 ft wide. Among the survivors was Brigadier General James M. "Jumpin' Jim" Gavin, of the 82nd, who recalled with bitter exasperation how one man in his group, Lieutenant James H. Devine, had to strip naked, then dive repeatedly into "the vast expanse of water" to retrieve bundles of bazookas, radios and mines—bundles essential to the capture of Ste Mère-Église. Five miles east, Father Francis Sampson, the 101st chaplain, dived more than five times into the waters of the Douve to retrieve his Mass kit—reflecting on those confident youngsters who had wisecracked as they emplaned, "No Heinie bullet has my name on it, Father." That was true, Father Sampson thought; instead the waters of the Douve had claimed them.

Thus most Americans were hitting the dirt to fight battles which the planners had never envisaged—with commanding generals conspicuous among them. Major-General Maxwell D. Taylor, of the 101st, stumbling through a darkened field, at first met up with no one but a lone private; overjoyed to find a kindred spirit, the two men hugged one another like bar-room buddies. An hour of tramping revealed most of Taylor's key staff officers but few paratroopers; with only 2500 located by D-Day's end, Taylor was moved to comment, "Never in the history of military operations have so few been commanded by so many." Matthew B. Ridgway, of the 82nd, shared that feeling; the only shape he encountered, groping through darkness, was a lone cow. The general barely refrained from embracing it—a cow, above all, meant an absence of mines—but after that he was virtually in the dark for thirty-six hours. With his radio lost, he could only estimate that 4000 of his men had gone missing.

It was only logical that the glider trains, in turn, ran into trouble. Of 102 gliders that made up the first 4 a.m. train, only six landed in their allotted fields; with the Pathfinders dropped

At the end of Pegasus Bridge stands the Cafe Gondrée, first French household to be liberated by Allied forces. A part of the interior has been preserved much as it was on June 6, 1944.

twenty miles off course, few Landing Zones had been marked to guide them in. "I probably could have cracked walnuts with my fanny," recalls Flight Officer George Buckley, after running the terrifying gauntlet of German flak for the first time, and others in the train knew that fear. Major Mike Murphy's Waco slid 800 ft over dew-soaked grass before smashing into trees at 50 mph; as Murphy toppled from the cockpit with both legs broken, he was too dazed to realize that one passenger, Brigadier General Donald F. Pratt, of the 101st, was dead in the seat behind him. Flight Officers Oliver Farris and John Jackson, piloting a Horsa, cut their landing so fine that a poplar tree, shattering their perspex canopy, literally passed between pilot and co-pilot.

It was a noncom arriving to survey the wreckage of a Horsa piloted by Lieutenant Hayden G. Haynes who struck the right note of outraged disbelief: "Man, you guys gotta be crazy to fly these damn things."

Most of the missing troopers, like Private Donald Burgett, were by now engaged in a gigantic lethal game of hide-and-seek over a chequerboard of fields and marshes ten miles square, identifying friend from foe only by the snapping of a toy "cricket": one snap to be answered by a double snap, then a password, "Flash," followed by "Thunder." Burgett knew accurately enough the task facing the two divisions: somehow in the five hours scheduled by the planners they must carve out an "airhead" roughly twelve miles long by seven miles wide, securing the five narrow causeways dominating Utah Beach.

The problem was: How?

From the moment the green light flashed on in his C-47, and Lieutenant Muir, the platoon leader, yelled, "Let's go," it had been like every Fort Benning practice drop Burgett could recall: air, solid and rushing, wrenching the parachute from the bag, battering the lungs to emptiness, the crackling of the 28-ft canopy as it unfurled, the sizzling sound of twenty-eight separate suspension lines, taut silk supporting his swaying descent, the connector links whistling past the back of his helmet. Cursing, he hit the pastureland too hard, with a force that almost stunned him. Briefed to drop them at 700 ft, the pilot had come as low as 300 ft, more intent on evading the flak.

It was a bad beginning. As Burgett struggled free of his harness, watching a sky "lit up like the Fourth of July", he sensed the vague shadowy figures of other troopers plunging downwards, men who had been dropped so low their chutes had no time to open. Almost simultaneously, seventeen men hit the soft pasture. In the mild June night they made a sound "like large ripe pumpkins being thrown down to burst."

"Dirty son of a bitch pilot," Burgett swore, close to tears.

Now he knew he was quite alone. This one he would have to play by instinct all the way.

Hours of cautious inching forward seemed to follow: through hedgerows, across the short grass of grazed-over pasture, wet with dew that soaked his knees and elbows. A long way off, ack-ack rolled like kettledrums, and machine-gun fire stitched the darkness. By degrees, the cautious snapping of Burgett's "cricket" brought welcome reinforcements from "A"

Company: "Slick" Hoenscheidt, "Red" Knight and Private Hundley. Crawling forward, the four of them prepared to lie low. Huddled against a hedgerow, soaked by a light rain, they waited patiently for the grey light of the false dawn.

Instinct proved them right. Breasting through hedgerows, they struck a dirt road, where a group of troopers, blackened faces streaked with sweat, had assembled. Some were men from the 82nd, some from the 101st, but most reassuring of all, they were reunited with Lieutenant Muir.

"Just the four of us," Burgett answered his officer's query.

"Swell," Muir enthused, "there's seven of us here; we're going to attack that town; you can come along if you want."

All the time the road curved gradually right, until suddenly they had reached the outskirts of a medieval town: grey stone houses, barns, sheds, interlocked by narrow streets. A natural fortress, Burgett thought, his stomach tense for snipers.

But what materialized instead was three teen-age girls, armed with a jug of wine, crying *"Vive les Américains,"* smothering him with hugs and kisses. Where were they? Lieutenant Muir wanted to know, and to help them get their bearings, the girls brought an old woman who had taught English in school. Even then the name meant nothing, until the teacher located it on Muir's map: Ravenoville, north-west of Ste Mère-Église, towards the coast.

Muir let loose a string of oaths, all of them directed at the US Air Corps. "They dropped us all over the whole damned Cherbourg Peninsula," he raged. "Who the hell's side are they on anyway?"

Plainly, whoever was to secure those causeways, it would not be Lieutenant Muir's little band. "Now we've got to fight through nine towns and twelve miles of enemy country just to get to where we were supposed to land and start fighting in the first place."

Scores of Allied paratroopers, like this soldier of the 82nd Airborne, dropped in flooded ground, to drown in less than 5 feet of water. (US Army)

ABOARD THE SHIPS, there was no way of knowing that D-Day was verging on catastrophe.

At midnight on June 5, it was more than six hours since the first convoys had headed for the five buoy-marked lanes south-east of the Isle of Wight, there to split into ten channels—two for each beach—that led to Normandy. As Beachy Head came in sight, the order "Darken ship" echoed over every megaphone; soon only tiny blue lights low down aft, markers for the next vessel astern, were visible. On Hartland Point, South Devon, Eric Crofts, an RAF technician, was conscious that for the first time in weeks his radar screen was suddenly mysteriously blank—"sobering to know that so many men . . . were heading for a hell ahead . . . ."

To all who glimpsed them they were an unforgettable spectacle. All told, the armada was spread out across thirty miles of Channel water—the mighty command ships, bristling with antennae, bone-white hospital ships with scalloped green lines and stacked cans marked "Whole Blood," shallow-draught landing ships, 350 ft long, rusty decrepit little minesweepers, destroyers, heavy cruisers, Channel steamers and coasters, self-important little tugs fussing like ducklings on a pond. "We must have seemed to ooze, the thousands of us, like a stream of dark oil," remembered William Golding—not then Sir William, Nobel Prize winner, author of *Lord of the Flies*, but a 33-year-old rocket ship lieutenant, frightened not of the mines of the shore batteries ahead "but of being late and jeered at."

Many ships, after four years of war, were already a part of history: in 1941, the USS *Augusta* had carried Roosevelt to Placentia Bay,

Western wind, when wilt thou blow,/The small rain down can rain?/Christ, if my love were in my arms/And I in my bed again!

(—Anon, from The Oxford Book of 16th Century Verse)

In this painting by Canadian war artist Tom Wood, Royal Navy LCIs carrying Canadian troops sweep in to the Normandy beaches. (Canadian War Museum)

163

Landing craft churn past the cruiser USS *Augusta*. (US Navy)

Newfoundland, for his first "Atlantic Charter" meeting with Churchill. The USS *Nevada*, sunk at Pearl Harbor in that same year, was now raised to fight again; the light cruiser, HMS *Ajax*, had hunted down the pocket battleship *Graf Spee* in Montevideo Harbour, following the Battle of the River Plate, as far back as December 1939. Heading for the British beaches in his flagship, the cruiser HMS *Scylla*, was another figure from history, Rear-Admiral Sir Philip Vian; after ending the "phoney war" in February 1940 by boarding the German prison-ship *Altmark* in neutral Norwegian waters, Vian, in 1941, had led his 4th Destroyer Flotilla to victory over the battleship *Bismarck*.

And history was playing its part in the skies above the Channel; the air superiority on which the planners had pinned their hopes was about to pay off. Ahead of the real airborne drops, four

squadrons of RAF Bomber Command, unimpeded by the Luftwaffe, were dropping scores of dummy paratroopers fitted up with firecrackers—as far north as Yvetot, inland from Dieppe, as far south as Marigny, west of St Lô. Moving at an equivalent steady 7–8 knots, other bombers of No. 617 Squadron, under Group Captain Leonard Cheshire, VC, dropped streams of "Window" (thin lengths of wire) to simulate to enemy radar a seaborne convoy heading for Fécamp. At daybreak, 3000 British and American fighters and fighter bombers, patrolling in nine squadron strength, would be manoeuvred from a Combined Control Centre, 50 ft below ground, at 11 Group, Uxbridge, where Winston Churchill had witnessed the Luftwaffe's last sortie on Battle of Britain Sunday. After four long years, history had come full circle.

Impressions of that night would remain inescapably vivid. Aboard USS *Augusta*, Lieutenant John Mason Brown, USNR, remembered the low murmur when Brown, as Admiral Kirk's Executive Officer, announced, over the PA system, "We are bound for the beaches in the Bay of the Seine," and the silence as men digested this news, in the red oases cast by battle lamps burning below decks. Aboard the 3rd (Canadian) Division ship, HMS *Hilary*, heading for Juno Beach, the war correspondent Ross Munro, a veteran of Dieppe, recalled how "the wind howled through the wireless masts . . . the sky . . . black as the inside of a gun barrel, and spray and rain lashed the deck." Colonel Ralph Ingersoll, too, recalled the noise of the wind: "There was no room left in the air for any other noise; the noise of the wind and the water—and the low throbbing from the Diesels. . . ." Aboard LCT 947, a British naval lieutenant, Lambton Burn, listened with fascination as Lieutenant-Colonel A. D. Cocks briefed his 5th Assault Regiment, Royal Engineers, under the single light of an electric lamp: "Look at your maps. Caen is Poland, Hermanville is Mexico . . . All bogus names to be destroyed tonight . . . 0430 all troops to be issued tea or hot soup."

Conditions varied markedly from ship to ship. Aboard the USS *Chase*, a solidly built mother-ship ferrying many assault barges, *Life* photographer Robert Capa marvelled at the nonchalant way the mess boys at 3 a.m. served hot cakes, sausages, eggs and coffee, wearing neat white jackets and white gloves. Aboard HMS *Ben Machree*, though, Lieutenant-Colonel James Rudder's men breakfasted more meagrely. By order of Captain Walter E. Block, the battalion physician, the Rangers were restricted to a 2 a.m. snack of flapjacks and coffee.

On the American bridges, look-outs gazed in wonder at the lighthouse of Cap Barfleur, east of Cherbourg, still burning brightly in the night as if to guide them in. Below decks, a few men settled to urgent last-minute tasks: Major C. K. "Banger" King, of the 2nd East Yorks, was memorizing Henry V's speech to his troops on Saint Crispin's Day: "He that outlives this day, and comes safe home/Will stand a tip-toe when this day is named . . . ." If all went well, he planned to recite it over the loud-hailer as the ship neared Sword Beach. Aboard LST 302, like others with time on their hands, Flight-Lieutenant Alan Caverhill, RAF, browsed idly through his official D-Day phrase book—everything from "*Encore une verre du vin rouge, s'il vous plaît, Mademoiselle*" to "*Hande hoch.*" On other transports, men chatted aimlessly, played cards or wrote eleventh-hour letters—though few were as optimistic as Staff Sergeant Larry Johnson, of the Rangers. Dropping a line to a former girl-friend in Paris, Johnson was seeking a date—early in June.

For those in the flimsier craft, it was a never-ending nightmare. In LCT 777, Signalman Third Class George Hackett, Jr, remembered waves so high they smashed from one end of the heaving craft and rolled out the other. Sergeant Morris Magee of the Canadian 3rd Division found the wallowing of his landing craft "worse than being in a rowboat in the centre of Lake Champlain." He was so far gone he could no longer vomit. One man, Second Lieutenant

The big guns of the *Texas* and *Arkansas* that sounded as though they were throwing whole railway trains across the sky were far away as we moved on in. They were no part of our world as we moved steadily over the gray, white-capped sea toward where, ahead of us, death was being issued in small, intimate, accurately administered packages. They were like the thunder of a storm that is passing in another county whose rain will never reach you.

(from *Voyage To Victory* by Ernest Hemingway, *Collier's* magazine, July 22, 1944)

It was no good looking in any direction, watching for any sign, speculating upon the nearness of the moment. When the time came the blackness would overwhelm silently the bit of starlight falling upon the ship, and the end of all things would come without a sigh, stir, or murmur of any kind, and all our hearts would cease to beat, like run-down clocks.

(from *The Shadow-Line* by Joseph Conrad)

A battle exists on many different levels. There is the purely moral level, at the Supreme Headquarters perhaps eighty miles away from the sound of the guns, where the filing cabinets have been dusted in the morning, where there is a sense of quiet efficiency, where soldiers who never fire a gun and never have a shot fired at them, the high Generals, sit in their pressed uniforms and prepare statements to the effect that all has been done that is humanly possible. . . .

The Generals have all studied from the same books at West Point and Spandau and Sandhurst, and many of them have written books themselves . . . and they all know what Caesar did in a somewhat similar situation and the mistake that Napoleon made in Italy. . . . So they sit back in their offices, which are like the offices of General Motors or the offices of I. G. Farben in Frankfurt . . . and look at the maps and read the reports and pray that Plans I, II and III will operate as everyone has said they

Headed for France, June 6, 1944. A sombre dawn breaks ahead of an American LST, depicted by US Navy war artist Alexander Russo. (US Navy Combat Art Collection)

Joseph Rosenblatt, Jr, remembers polishing off seven helpings of chicken à la king and never feeling better, and Lord Lovat, aboard HMS *Astrid*, kept down hot ship's cocoa and oily tinned sardines. But they were the notable exceptions. Most men were so racked with nausea they now longed to reach the beaches they had dreaded—"bacon and eggs, pork chops and plum pudding, they all went the same way," one survivor recalled with misery.

Only the captains of the pitching craft, who had sweated it out on their bridges for fifty-six hours now, could have put their minds at rest; they had known the timing ever since breaking the seals of the bulky "Package A," nearing Land's End. "Serial One in force," ran the cryptic message. At 3 a.m. on June 6, this meant D-Day for the American beaches was still three-and-a-half hours distant; for the hapless British another four-and-a-half hours of suffering.

By 1.11 a.m. the Germans were coming alive to the danger. In St Lô, *General der Artillerie* Erich Marcks, still concentrating ferociously on the forthcoming *Kriegsspiel*, took a phone call from *Generalmajor* Wilhelm Richter, whose ill-trained 716th Division were massed on the coast above Caen. The news suggested a war game transmuted into grim reality. "Parachutists have landed east of the Orne," Richter reported. "The area seems to be around Bréville and Ranville. . . ."

Marcks and his staff were galvanized. The corps commander at once called *Generalmajor* Max Pemsel, chief of staff of Seventh Army. On Marcks's orders, Pemsel signalled *Alarmstruffe*

II, Coastal Alarm—the code-word for invasion—to all Seventh Army units.

Pemsel was one man who never doubted that the invasion's main thrust was here and now. First he called his own C-in-C, *Generaloberst* Friedrich Dollmann: "General, I believe this is the invasion. Will you please come over immediately?" Next 84th Corps was again on the line: "Parachute drops near Montebourg and St Marcouf". Both were locations on the Cherbourg Peninsula. At 1.35 a.m., Pemsel alerted *Generalmajor* Hans Speidel, Rommel's newly appointed chief of staff at Army Group B.

Others were less certain. From Fifteenth Army headquarters on the Belgian border, *Generaloberst* Hans von Salmuth called *Generalmajor* Josef Reichert, whose 711th Division were stationed east of the Orne. Earlier Reichert had reported British paratroopers landing with apologetic aplomb on his front lawn — "Awfully sorry, old man, but we simply landed here by accident." Egocentrically, Reichert believed his own headquarters had been singled out for airborne attack.

"What the devil is going on down there?" von Salmuth wanted to know.

"If you'll permit me," Reichert answered, "I'll let you hear for yourself." To von Salmuth, the distant hammering of machine-gun fire came clearly up the wire. He, too, lost no time in calling Army Group B.

But Speidel was a hard man to convince. At 2 a.m. Pemsel had called him again: naval radar at Cherbourg was picking up ships near the Bay of the Seine. "The air landings," he insisted, "constitute the first phase of a larger enemy action." Speidel thought otherwise: the

will operate back on Grosvenor Square and the Wilhelmstrasse. . . .

The men on the scene see the affair on a different level. . . . They have not been at the conferences in which was discussed the number of divisions it would be profitable to lose to reach a phase line one mile inland by 1600 hours. There are no filing cabinets on board the landing barges, no stenographers with whom to flirt, no maps in which their actions multiplied by two million, become clear, organized, intelligent symbols, suitable for publicity releases and the tables of historians.

They see helmets, vomit, green water, shell geysers, smoke, crashing planes, blood plasma, submerged obstacles, guns, pale senseless faces, a confused drowning mob of men running and falling. . . . To a General sitting before the maps eighty miles away, with echoes of Caesar and Clausewitz and Napoleon . . . matters are proceeding as planned, or almost as planned, but to the man on the scene everything is going wrong. . . .

When he is hit or when the man next to him is hit, when the ship fifty feet away explodes, when the Naval Ensign on the bridge is screaming in a high, girlish voice for his mother because he has nothing left below his belt, it can only appear to him that he has been involved

action was still "locally confined." "For the time being," the War Diary noted, "this is not to be considered as a large operation."

At 3 a.m. there was still dire if understandable confusion. Among the senior officers only Pemsel was convinced that the Allied *Schwerpunkt*—the main thrust—was indeed to be Normandy. The myth of the Pas de Calais, so sedulously nourished by Wulf Dietrich Schmidt and others, died hard: supposing the paratroops were only a diversion to mask a massive thrust against Fifteenth Army?

At von Salmuth's HQ his Chief of Staff, *Generalmajor* Rudolf Hoffmann, was so sure of it he called up Pemsel solely to place a bet that he was right. He proposed a really first-class dinner as a stake. But Pemsel knew it in his bones: this was the real thing.

Before disconnecting, he told Hoffmann: "This is one bet you're going to lose."

Behind Sword Beach, the assault's easternmost flank, the British side of the invasion was in jeopardy six hours before the British had come ashore.

At 1 a.m. on June 6, Lieutenant-Colonel Terence Otway, whose 9th Parachute Battalion was charged to destroy the guns of Merville, had bitter cause to recall the parting words of Brigadier James Hill, CO of the 5th Brigade: "Do not be daunted if chaos reigns. It undoubtedly will!"

And undoubtedly it had. Though Otway and his batman, Corporal Joe Wilson, had baled out near the drop zone—Wilson emerging unscathed after plunging into a green-

house—raw RAF crews had contrived to scatter the bulk of his men over fifty square miles. Thus, at 2.35 a.m., one-and-a-half hours after the drop, only 150 out of 750 men had reached the rendezvous. Worse, an eleven-strong glider supply train, bringing such vital paraphernalia as anti-tank guns, scaling ladders, flame throwers and Bangalore torpedoes, had failed to arrive.

At first Otway saw nothing for it but to do the best he could with the men available—men armed only with rifles, Sten guns, grenades, twenty Bangalore torpedoes and one heavy machine-gun against the deadly obstacles and a garrison 200 strong.

Crouched at the edge of the battery's barbed wire, Otway saw the carefully wrought plan, rehearsed on the Berkshire downs time and again since April, falling apart by the minute. The bombing raid ordered by General Gale had failed abysmally; not one bomb had hit the battery. The glider train was still missing. Of the three gliders scheduled for the crash landing on the guns, only two had arrived—and Otway was powerless to signal them. The crash dive was to be triggered by a star shell fired from a mortar—and Otway had neither star shell nor mortar.

Already his men had done much to redeem the disasters. With wire cutters they had sliced through the outer barricade and placed their Bangalore torpedoes in readiness. Lacking both mine detectors and tape, a group under Captain Paul Greenway had done it the hard way: prodding for trip-wires with bayonets, denoting the cleared passage with heel-marks in the mud.

Towards 4.30 a.m. Otway saw his last

hopes vanish. As the gliders circled, vainly seeking a signal, German machine-guns opened up on them with 20-mm tracer. Promptly, one took evasive action, landing unscathed four miles away; the second, shearing into an orchard, caught fire within seconds of the crew jumping clear.

In the silence that followed, Otway's second in command, Major Allen Parry, whispered, "Have you decided what to do, sir?"

"Do?" said Otway sharply. "Attack in three minutes, of course. Pass it on."

Now, above the crackle of small-arms fire, the coughing rasp of mortars, one sound stood out above all the rest: the shrill, long drawn-out cry of a hunting horn, blown by Lieutenant Alan Jefferson. Seconds later came Otway's stentorian summons to battle: "Everybody in! We're going to take this bloody battery!"

Pandemonium reigned. With a searing whoosh, the Bangalore torpedoes blasted the wire. Through wreathing smoke, whooping and yelling, Otway's paratroopers hacked their way forward, firing as they went, splitting into four assault parties, headed for the guns. Piling into the anti-tank ditches, other paratroopers fought hand to hand with the Germans, kicking, gouging, lunging. Cries of *"Paratruppen, paratruppen"* grew in volume, and Private Sid Capon, surprising two men in a trench, could see why. One, raising a Red Cross box above his head in a gesture of surrender, was crying, *"Russki, Russki"*; not every man in this garrison had stomach for defending Rommel's Wall.

Inside the battery defences, bomb craters, loose wires and mines contrived to hamper the assailants. Lieutenant Alan Jefferson fell wounded, but still the hunting horn remained at his lips, the weird, haunting notes resounding amid the screams of dying men, the crump and flash of grenades. Machine-gun fire glittered in a bright stream, and Major Allen Parry felt as if "someone had kicked me hard in the leg"; collapsing momentarily into a bomb crater, he resourcefully used his whistle lanyard as a tourniquet. Painfully hobbling towards No. 1 Casemate, he beheld a scene of ultimate slaughter: the dying and the wounded, among them eighty-five of Otway's men, lay everywhere.

But for the most part the battle was petering out. The guns—not, ironically, German 150-mm but ancient French 75-mm—had been destroyed by Gammon grenades, lumps of plastic explosive encased in a stockinette bag. With almost classic British *sang-froid*, Lieutenant Mike Dowling, his right hand clasped to his left breast, reported to Otway: "Battery taken as ordered, sir. Guns destroyed." Promptly, Otway fired a yellow flare—a signal of success—from his Very pistol. Noted by an RAF spotter plane, it was radioed just in time to HMS *Arethusa* offshore. In little more than half an hour, *Arethusa*'s guns were slated to open up on Merville, in the hope of accomplishing what Otway's party had now achieved. Turning, Otway realized that Dowling was lying dead at his feet.

For many who came ashore on Sword, expecting a holocaust, the final landing, thanks to Otway's men, was almost an anti-climax. But on Bloody Omaha it was to be a different story.

★　　★　　★

in a terrible accident. . . . it is inconceivable . . . to believe that there is a man eighty miles away who has foreseen that accident . . . and who can report, after it has happened . . . that everything is going according to plan.

(from *The Young Lions* by Irwin Shaw)

far left top: The fearsome
Pointe du Hoc.

far left below: Omaha –
shell-pitted ground left
as it was at the end of
D-Day.

left: Omaha – view from
a German lookout
position as it appears
today, complete with
preserved barbed-wire
defences.

171

It was 5.45 a.m. Off the American beaches the naval bombardment would soon begin. For the 3000 men of the first assault wave, H-Hour was only forty-five minutes distant. Aboard the flagship *Augusta*, Lieutenant-General Omar Bradley methodically plugged his ears with cotton wool, blotting out the last-minute pep-talks which every unit commander had somehow felt impelled to deliver: "Keep in line! Keep in line!" . . . "Rangers, man your craft!" . . . "This is it, men, pick it up and put it on, you've only got a one-way ticket and this is the end of the line" . . . "I'll do your praying for you from here on in. What you're going to do today will be a prayer in itself" . . . "Now hear this! This is probably going to be the biggest party you boys will ever go to—so let's all get out on the floor and dance!"

Now the invasion barges, swinging on their cranes, were descending like slow-moving elevators. Painfully, as the light broke in the east, troops laden down with up to 300 lbs of equipment each inched their way down cargo nets, into the heaving craft. The most final of messages passed from ship to ship: "Away all boats!"

All this time, Bradley was nourishing the hope that the naval assault, combined with massive air cover, would neutralize the tough opposition of the recently reported 352nd Division. Abruptly, at 5.50 a.m., the terrible storm of the first bombardment began, drowning the rattle of chains, the squeal of winches. Six miles offshore, the battleships *Texas*, *Arkansas* and *Nevada*, the cruisers *Tuscaloosa*, *Quincy* and *Black Prince*, pounded the shore batteries and the coastal battery on Pointe du Hoc with "the streaking arcs of hundreds of rockets," blinding, breathtaking waves of fire—"enough fire to avenge the Alamo," thought John Mason Brown. Then tragedy struck. The air cover on which Bradley had pinned so much hope—a force of 329 Lancasters, Fortresses and Liberators—lost its

Omaha, 6.30 am: H-Hour as seen from the bows of an LCT. (US Army)

174

opposite above
Marble and enamel
campaign map in the D-
Day memorial at St
Laurent-sur-Mer.

Opposite below
Omaha Beach today.

The Allied war cemetery
at St Laurent-sur-Mer,
with 9386 graves of
servicemen who
perished during the
Omaha landings and
their aftermath.

inset
Omaha, H-Hour +15.
Troops seek cover
behind obstacles of
Rommel's Wall. (US
Engineers)

D-Day, 5.50 a.m.: the
battleship *Nevada*, Pearl
Harbor veteran, opens
fire on the American
beaches. (US Navy)

way in low cloud. Hopelessly overshooting their target, the bombers ended by dropping 13,000 bombs up to three miles inland.

Ahead of the plunging ranks of the first assault craft, dominating the 7000 yards of beach, Rommel's finest fortress loomed still intact, with eighty-five machine-gun posts, thirty-eight rocket pits, and four field artillery positions, poised to fire.

Behind Omaha, in Strongpoint 62, *Leutnant* Friedrich Frerking lifted his field telephone: "Target Dora, all guns, range four-eight-five-zero, basic direction twenty plus, impact fuse." Then "Wait for the order to fire." Behind his MG-42, *Gefreiter* Hein Severloh waited nervously; the moment must be coming; already the Americans of the first wave, tiny ant-figures, were knee-deep in water. "Target Dora—fire!" Frerking shouted, and Severloh curled his forefinger round the trigger. By noon, Severloh was only one of many to have pumped 12,000 rounds into the American ranks.

All through the shallows men fell dying, and as the tide swept them inshore they nudged with ghastly importunacy against the living, as if still seeking human kinship. Everywhere off the American beaches landing craft were foundering and capsizing—ten off Omaha alone. For the US Navy's Lieutenant Dean L. Rockwell, this was an appalling dilemma; he alone had overall charge of the sixteen landing craft from which thirty-two Duplex Drive amphibious tanks were to be launched—but in the pounding surf, twenty-seven had foundered before the first troops had landed.

It was a reverse that Admiral Ramsay had long predicted—yet his cautions had always fallen on deaf ears. Curiously, of all Major-General Hobart's "Funnies," the DD "swimming" tanks, with their ungainly canvas skirts, were the only ones that had caught the Americans' fancy; at Eisenhower's insistence, 300 had been ordered. But while the DDs performed sturdily in calm waters, they were at all times vulnerable in rough seas—yet the Americans, intent on evading the shore batteries, had launched them three miles out.

From the mayhem ensuing, men retained brief and awful vignettes: a man shot through the head, "spinning round like a chicken," a captain, both cheeks pierced by shrapnel, blood spouting as he rallied his troops to charge, an operator, tugged under by his heavy radio, screaming, "For God's sake, I'm drowning!" Weird irrelevant fancies assailed the mind: Captain Carroll Smith saw his friend Captain Sherman Burroughs of the 29th Division lolling inertly in the surf and thought that never again would Burroughs be doubled up by one of his migraine headaches. He had been shot through the head.

From the USS *Chase*, *Life*'s Robert Capa, boarding an invasion barge as it descended from its crane, had the uneasy feeling "this would develop into the father and mother of all D-Days." Nor did Capa's instincts play him false. As they lay pinned down by withering fire, an Army lieutenant whispered to him: "Do you know what I see? I see my ma on the front porch, waving my insurance policy."

What Capa saw through the viewfinder of his Contax camera over the next six hours was a "foreground . . . filled with wet boots and green faces": above those boots and faces "the picture

176

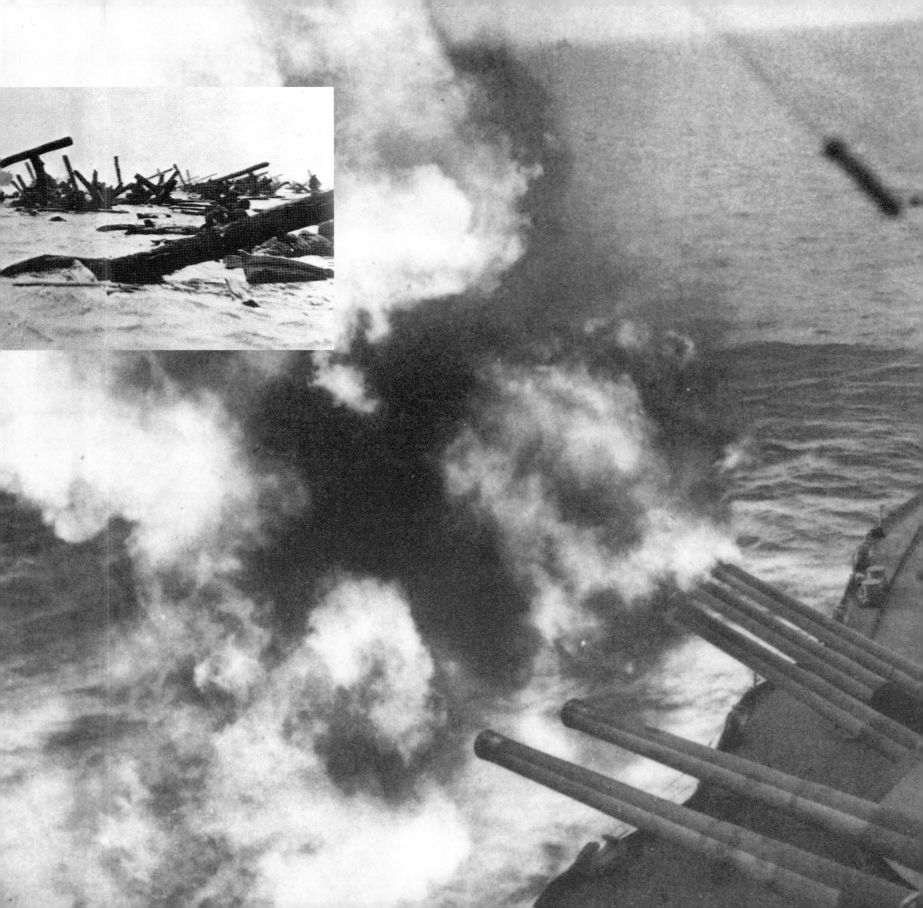

frame was filled with shrapnel smoke; great tanks and sinking barges formed my background." Then the camera jammed, the roll was finished, but as Capa reached in his musette bag for a new roll, his "wet shaking hands" ruined the roll before he could insert it. Then, as he later admitted, his nerve broke. A Red Cross LCI was rolling with the waves, and he ran for it. By sheer chance it delivered him, along with many wounded men, back to the USS *Chase*. The white jackets of the mess boys who had served coffee at 3 a.m. were now smeared with blood, and they were busy sewing the dead into white sacks.

Aboard *Augusta*, confusion was almost total; such messages as came from the shore were notably laconic: "Obstacles mined, progress slow. . . ." Reinforcing troops, reported one staff colonel from an amphibious DUKW, were held up in LCTS, milling offshore "like a stampeding herd of cattle." Another war correspondent, Don Whitehead, of the Associated Press, who had gone ashore with Brigadier General Willard G. Wyman, of the 1st Division, saw the situation clearly: "Men dug in on that narrow strip of beach by the thousands, shoulder to shoulder. But nothing was moving off the beach. The battle was being fought at the water's edge."

Omaha had become a battle stalled in the shallows, a battle where attackers had given way to survivors.

Hundreds never achieved the initial slog over 300 yards of wet sand to shelter beneath the cobblestoned sea wall. Pfc Henry Meyers, a signaller, came ashore struggling with half a mile of telephone wire; his orders were to set up a

France was a land, England was a people, but America, having about it still the quality of the idea, was harder to utter — it was the graves at Shiloh, and the tired, drawn, nervous faces of its great men, and the country boys dying in the Argonne for a phrase that was empty before their bodies withered. It was a willingness of the heart. . . .

(from *The Crackup* by F. Scott Fitzgerald)

Utah Beach today: unlike at Omaha, landings were swift, with comparatively light losses.

179

telephone link somewhere inland, but so far as Meyers could see, no one had even crossed the first belt of shingle.

The combined force of Army-Navy demolition engineers—272 men under Commander Joseph H. Gibbons—whose task was to blow a path through the beach obstacles fought a losing battle from the first. Brought in minutes behind schedule, they had to battle more than Teller mines and Elements C: struggling infantrymen blocked their progress and soldiers cowered behind obstacles they were due to blow. Out of sixteen gaps allotted to Gibbons's sixteen teams, only five were ever wholly cleared and two partially; thirty minutes after they set to work, 111 of Gibbons's men were dead. Enemy fire took toll of their equipment, too. Of sixteen bulldozers earmarked for Omaha, only three ever went into operation.

For Rudder's Rangers, it was equally a near-run thing. Although nine LCAs made it to the shingled shelf below Pointe du Hoc, two had shipped water and capsized with all hands before the remaining 225 Rangers piled ashore. Lieutenant George Kerchner remembers thinking even then: "This whole thing is just one great big mistake . . . we'll never make it." But somehow, dodging from cover to cover as the cliff-top Germans lobbed "potato masher" hand grenades or fired Schmeissers, they did. Although slippery clay made free-climbing impossible, an unexpected landfall of grey wet clay helped Corporal George Putzek, in the lead, to support a 16-ft extension ladder. Then some grapnels finally caught, and men began swarming, among them Pfc Harry Roberts; twice the Germans cut his ropes, as Rangers in

their death throes were hurtling past him, but after three tries Roberts made it to a cratered niche below the edge of the cliff, the first man to do so. For one Ranger at least, Lieutenant Jacob Hill, the transition from manoeuvres at Swanage to the real thing proved almost too abrupt. He grumbled disbelievingly, "Those crazy sonsabitches are using live ammunition."

The Germans were fighting back desperately now, but yard by yard the Rangers were gaining ground. Again and again their rockets soared, hurtling ropes and rope ladders with grapnels attached up the nine-storey-high cliff. All were determined to make it to the summit, spurred on by the reported gibe of one naval lieutenant: "Three old women with brooms could keep the Rangers from climbing that cliff." The shore itself, cratered like a moonscape with shellholes, blocked the access of the 2½-ton DUKW amphibious trucks with the London Fire Brigade ladders, but one Ranger, Staff Sergeant William J. Stivison, refused to give ground. Scaling a ladder to a height of 80 ft, while the DUKW bobbed frantically in the waves, he raked Pointe du Hoc with the steady fire of two Lewis guns, oblivious to an answering chain of glittering tracer. To Pfc John J. Gilhooly, scrabbling to keep a toehold on the same craft, Stivison looked like nothing so much as "a circus performer."

Everywhere Rangers were gaining the heights and seeking urgent cover in shell holes. Pfc Carl Weast, for one, thought the Germans were giving up the unequal struggle; as he and his company commander, Captain George Whittington, circled a machine-gun nest, manned by three Germans, one of them, seeing the

Americans, screamed, *"Bitte! Bitte! Bitte!"* Whittington's Tommy gun had killed all three before he asked Weast, "I wonder what *bitte* means?"

At last, Colonel Rudder had established his first command post, another niche at the cliff's edge; from there a hasty signal was flashed to the battleship *Texas,* "Praise the Lord." Although this was the code for "All men up the cliff," Rudder was stretching the truth. At the cliff's edge, Captain Walter E. Block would minister throughout the day to 130 men who were dying or already dead—in a valiant if useless cause. The guns which *Centurie* sector chief Jean Marion had reported missing from the emplacements were found more than a mile inland—too late to defend the heights of Pointe du Hoc.

Rudder's Rangers scaling the 100ft-high Pointe du Hoc. (US Army)

Omaha H-Hour + 25. First Army-Navy demolition teams move in. (US Engineers)

Omaha, late a.m.: Medics administer blood transfusions. (US Army)

In a situation like this, rank no longer counted. One of the first to move—and inspire others to follow suit—was Private Vincent Dove, who had steered a bulldozer across building sites in Washington, DC, for fifteen years before joining the Army. Climbing into the seat of an abandoned 'dozer, Dove now began to grind out a lone roadway off Omaha—the first road on which trucks and tanks and guns could move inland.

Once the realization of stalemate sank in, the Navy was swift to react. At 10.30 a.m., two young skippers, Lieutenant Sidney Brinker, commanding LCT 30, and Lieutenant E. B. Koehler, of LCI 554, came ashore with all guns blazing at German strongpoints, ramming their 400-ton craft through beach obstacles that the demolition engineers had yet to reach. Simultaneously, Rear-Admiral Carleton F. Bryant, aboard USS *Texas*, hailed his destroyers: "Get on them, men! Get on them! They are raising hell with the men on the beach, and we can't have any more of that!" With this, at least eight destroyers—*McCook* and *Carmick*, *Frankford* and *Emmons*, *Doyle*, *Harding*, *Thompson* and *Baldwin*—steered within 900 yards of the shore, close to running aground, to pump thousands of rounds of 5-in. shells at the shore batteries, filling the breach left by the capsized DUKWs and DDs.

Despite the havoc of the night, the same spirit prevailed inland. Cut off from their leaders, let down, as they saw it, by their own Air Corps, the airborne troope were finding their own solutions. A score of paratroopers, dropped all too close to the target, lay dead in the main square of Ste Mère-Église, but Lieutenant

On the beaches below, the issue was still in doubt.

"The battle belonged that morning," Bradley wrote later, "to the thin, wet line of khaki that dragged itself ashore on the Channel coast of France." More accurately, it now belonged to the movers and shakers among the American ranks: men like Willard G. Wyman and Colonel George A. Taylor of the 16th Regimental Combat Team, who realized that there was no place to go but forward. "Two kinds of people are staying on this beach," Taylor was rallying all those who could still listen, "the dead and those who are going to die. Now let's get the hell out of here!"

Colonel Edward Krause of the 505th did make good his vow; at 5 a.m. on D-Day the Stars and Stripes was flying from the flagpole of the town hall, the first in France to be liberated by the Allies. The way was clear for General J. Lawton Collins's VII Corps to advance from Utah Beach. The Merderet causeway was taken by the enterprise of a lone rifleman, Private James L. Mattingly, a lead scout, who had killed one German and wounded two before five others surrendered without a fight. Many men, anxious for leadership, tagged on to any scratch formation they could find, though still soaking wet and blue with cold from the waters of the Merderet or the Douve. Some were as matter-of-fact as Lieutenant John H. Dolan, of the 505th, holding the bridgehead at La Fière, though down to 81 men from 147: "I don't know a better spot than this to die."

The flamboyant Colonel Howard "Skeets" Johnson, and his 501st Parachute Infantry, had also achieved their goal, the locks at La Barquette, the key to the flooding across the neck of the Cotentin. Despite the darkness and the roar of water from the weirs, Johnson felt a speech was called for. "Hereafter this is known as Hell's Corners," he told his men, "We dig in and we hold on," and history has recorded that they did.

With some units securing their targets, while others overshot them, it was hard for any airborne man to know how the battle was going. (General Ridgway of the 82nd thought the invasion had failed and the fleet withdrawn.) Yet by dusk on D-Day, a captain in Colonel Robert Sink's 3rd Battalion, 506th Parachute Infantry, was convinced it had succeeded. At a crossroads

north of St Côme-du-Mont, in German hands until June 8, Captain Joe MacMillan spotted a parked convoy of eight trucks that had obviously bowled through the town unscathed, trucks packed with such vital supplies as razor blades, shaving cream and candy.

"Don't you know," MacMillan asked the lead driver rhetorically, "you're the spearpoint of the American advance, out in front of the whole army?" "Captain," the GI begged him, "don't kid me."

But it was true.

Off Utah Beach, one man's unwitting error had, in fact, saved thousands of lives. Blinded by the smoke from the naval bombardment, tugged by a strong current, an anonymous control boat officer had brought the first assault wave on to a beachhead almost 2000 yards south of the original Utah—away from the firepower of twenty-eight heavy batteries but away, also, from two of the crucial five causeways that the US Airborne were struggling to secure.

From the first, the men of Force U, unlike their brothers on Omaha, seemed to bear a charmed life. General J. Lawton "Lightning Joe" Collins, after watching the DD tanks perform at a Slapton Sands exercise, had urged the Navy to bring them within fifty yards of the shore—saving lives and DDs. Unlike Omaha, the naval firepower on Utah had been devastating, as *Leutnant* Arthur Jahnke, in Strongpoint No. 5, could testify. With all his 50-mm guns wrecked by shells and bombing, Jahnke saw resistance was hopeless. The man whose calloused hands had won a spontaneous tribute from Rommel found himself one of a long straggling line of American prisoners of war.

Brigadier General Theodore Roosevelt, Jr, of the 4th Division, a distant cousin of the President's, a man so homely one GI mistook him for "a frazzle-arsed old sergeant," thus faced a snap decision. Any moment now, wave after wave would be landing — 30,000 men, 3500 vehicles. Should they pile into this relatively peaceful area, with its one causeway — or switch back to the causeways of the original Utah? The question was no sooner posed than answered: "We're going to start the war from here."

Soon, on the one open causeway that the beach afforded, two generals — Roosevelt and his CO, Major General Raymond O. Barton, commanding the 4th — were standing side by side engaged in traffic cop duty, speeding long steady lines of men, and trucks christened "Filthy Flora" and "Ten Shilling Annie," inland to victory. The casualties on Utah had been less than 200 men.

Two German commanders remained completely in the dark. Sometime after 1 a.m., *Generalleutnant* Edgar Feuchtinger, whose 21st Panzer Division, once an element of Rommel's tough *Afrika Korps*, was scattered through all the villages twenty-five miles south-east of Caen, had received word of the British paratroop drop. At once Feuchtinger awoke the division's Panzer Regiment commander, *Oberst* Hermann von Oppeln-Bronikowski, an Olympic Gold

Medal equestrian. "Imagine," he said, "*they* have landed." In a strikingly short time, officers and men had mustered, alert beside their tanks, engines revving, waiting to move out. Soon orders *must* come — to close in and drive the Allies back towards the coast. But the night ticked away, and no word came.

Precious time had thus been lost before Feuchtinger, at 6.30 a.m., acted on his own initiative; Bronikowski was at liberty to set his Mark IVs rolling. But from that moment on, Feuchtinger imposed radio silence; all further orders were passed by dispatch riders. There was thus no way for Bronikowski to know that he was moving against the wrong enemy. Oblivious to the fact that Gold, Juno and Sword Beaches would soon come alive with men, Bronikowski's 120 Panzers were moving northeast — to challenge Major Howard's hold on the Orne and canal bridges.

At 5 a.m., in his blockhouse headquarters sited beneath a girl's school in St Germain-en-Laye, twelve miles from Paris, *Feldmarschall* von Rundstedt had also decided to act. Still convinced that Normandy was a diversion, he was even so taking prudent precautions. The 12th SS and the Panzer *Lehr* — the two divisions Rommel had for three months sought to integrate into his coastal defence system — were both ordered to rush to the coast. Technically, both, as reserve divisions, were under Hitler's command, but von Rundstedt thought it unlikely the Führer would impede their dispatch. His teletype message requesting their release was strictly for the record.

Von Rundstedt had discounted one factor; at Hitler's Berchtesgaden headquarters, the

Omaha, late p.m.: Evacuating the wounded by LST. (US Navy)

atmosphere was what the Field Marshal liked to call *Wolkenkuckkucksheim* (cloud cuckoo-land). Staff who received the message in the office of *General der Artillerie* Alfred Jodl decided that it was still too early to wake the Führer. Only Jodl could clear it with his master, and the insomniac Hitler, asleep with his mistress Eva Braun, three miles away in his mountain retreat, the Obersalzberg, had not retired until 4 a.m. Nobody would disturb him for another five hours.

Nor was von Rundstedt aware that Army Group B had not yet alerted the man most intimately concerned—*Feldmarschall* Erwin Rommel—and from the German standpoint this was an oversight. Rommel was a master of "the spoiling attack," and the American plight on Omaha that morning cried out for exploitation.

By noon, as Bradley later recorded, the men of Force O had gained just ten yards of beach in six hours. For the first time, Bradley was forced to contemplate the hitherto unthinkable: the total evacuation of Omaha, the diversion of those Americans still clinging to life to Utah and the British beaches.

AT 4.45 A.M., one mile off the coast, two midget submarines surfaced through chilly darkness on to a heaving sea. Astride the casing of X 23, Lieutenant George Honour and his four-man crew, in their tight-fitting rubber frogmen's suits, were adjusting their five-foot telescopic mast to throw a powerful beam of green light five miles to seaward off the port of Ouistreham. Twenty miles west, off Le Hamel, the crew of X 20, under Lieutenant Ken Hudspeth, were going through the same motions. Now the British-Canadian assault zones were clearly marked. All they could do was cling to the guide rails and wait.

They saw the boats long before they heard them. When the sighing of the great shells from the Naval Assault Groups began, passing far overhead, all sound was blotted out by the thunder inland. Then, almost before they realized it, the assault craft were in focus, long serried lines of them arising from the mists of the morning, streaking in from the bobbing hulls of the mother ships. Off Le Hamel, Hudspeth's No. 2, Robin Harbud, after sixty-four hours beneath the Channel, found his emotion too great to contain. "You beauties," he screamed at them, naval decorum cast to the winds. "You bloody little beauties!"

On most mother ships, until now, the mood was one of total absorption. The last-minute checks that save lives were evident on ship after ship: testing the tips of bayonets, sealing weapon muzzles with adhesive tape, to ward off salt or sand, checking automatic springs. By degrees, subliminal sounds became apparent: the muffled buzz of the ship's telegraph, the shrill of the bos'n's pipe, the

These D-Day veterans form part of a memorial at Utah Beach – where the first Allied transport and armour rolled ashore and on to inland objectives.

187

On the bright and awful morning of D-Day, *Saltash* found herself, for the first time in many months, in unfamiliar waters. She was one of a number of support groups, patrolling in a wide ring across the mouth of the English Channel: they were there to intercept any U-boats that might be tempted to leave the dubious shelter of the Atlantic and make for the invasion beaches. They were, in fact, on guard at the back door. . . . It was the first time any one of them had felt involved in any theatre of war except their own. But on this day the great Atlantic was nothing: all the sea war and all the land had shrunk down to a few miles of beach, a few yards of shallow water, and nothing else counted at all.

(from *The Cruel Sea* by Nicholas Monsarrat)

vibration of steel plates lessening. The transfer to the LCAs was imminent: thirty-five men packed on hard bench seats, one row to port, one to starboard, one along the centre, loaded down with rucksacks, Bren guns, rifles, Tommy guns. It was now that the banter began:

"Will I need my water-wings, Sergeant?"
"Tell the driver to wait, my good man, I won't be a minute."
"Wait for you? How can you ask such a thing? . . . If there's any chance of our *Astrid* being raped, we'll be off."

It was almost compulsive, thought Lieutenant Denis Glover, a New Zealander commanding one LCA, this need to be facetious — "Why," he asked himself, "must I give way to this affectation of flippancy?" Then he came to terms with it; it was the one way he and all the others could forget they were "running on a timetable towards terror," forget "those bristling stakes . . . the mines on them look as big as planets." So Glover joked relentlessly all the way in: "How do you feel, Middy? Myself, I wouldn't be elsewhere for a thousand quid. Well, not for a hundred anyway" . . . "Cox'n, you're a lucky man. Not everyone gets paid for taking a trip to the Continent." But in his mind, another train of thought was moving altogether as swiftly as an unravelling spool of film: Speed, more speed . . . weave in and out of these bloody spikes, avoid the mines, avoid the wrecked craft and vehicles . . . GET THESE TROOPS ASHORE.

Now, all along the British and Canadian beaches, other sounds were discernible: "all the mad dogs of hell, barking over a bone on the invisible beach," the searing sound of sand, scraping against ships' bottoms, cog teeth chattering on oiled chains, ramps yawning open. Then they were out, and bounding towards the beaches and barbed wire 100 yards away, "bent like half-shut knives."

It was H-Hour.

And now the mood was veering subtly from beach to beach, from sector to sector. On all the beaches, "Hobart's Funnies" were more than proving their worth: Churchill tanks carrying "Petards," short-barrelled mortars that lobbed "flying dustbins," heavy high-explosive charges, against concrete bunkers and casemates, other vehicles laying bundles of wood, called "fascines," in the path of any tank likely to bog down. On one half of Juno, Canadians of the 3rd Division, their path thus smoothed for them, mopped up all resistance in the town of Courseulles in two hours. On Gold, at Ver-sur-Mer — site of the first Scott-Bowden-Ogden Smith survey — the going was tougher; on the western half of the beach, stalled by hedgehogs and tetrahedra, the men of the 1st Battalion, The Hampshire Regiment, took almost eight hours to knock out the defences of Le Hamel, suffering 200 casualties as they fought.

On Sword, from the first, a strange élan prevailed — as if to vindicate the heroism of Otway's men at Merville. For some survivors music was the keynote of that morning: a wheezy record of *La Marseillaise*, played over and over on an old horn gramophone from the village of St Aubin, Captain Hutchinson Burt's men singing *Jerusalem* as they piled in "like the fierce Covenanters of old." On another LCA,

Major C. K. "Banger" King was rallying the men of the 2nd East Yorks: "We would not die in that man's company/That fears his fellowship to die with us." And aboard LCT 947, Lieutenant Lambton Burn watched the Commandos of Lovat's Brigade disdaining steel helmets, in their trim green berets, striding through the surf "with shoulders hunched like boxers ready for in-fighting"; as they waded, Piper William Millin, waist-deep in water, oblivious to the scream and splash of shells, paraded up and down the shoreline, keening *The Road to the Isles*.

As relaxed as a man on a holiday beach, Colonel Derek Mills-Roberts, another veteran of Dieppe, remarked conversationally to a corporal, "Seems ages since we had a dry landing. D'you find the sea cold?" Another Lovat contingent, the 171 French Commandos under *Commandant* Philippe Kieffer, were equally in good heart. Told that he would lead the attack on the gambling casino at Ouistreham, one sergeant, *Comte* Guy de Montlaur, was overjoyed. "It will be a pleasure," he told Kieffer, "I have lost several fortunes in that place."

Through mud and blood to the green fields beyond.

(Motto of the Royal Tank Regiment)

Juno Beach, 7.30 a.m.: troops disembark from the HQ ship HMS *Hilary*. (Royal Canadian Navy)

There was cause for jubilation. On Sword, in contrast to Omaha, the timing was exactly right; at first, the senior sector engineer, Colonel R. W. Urquhart, spotting stakes and ramps topped with mines and shells just visible above the wavetops, dived overboard with his men and swam from stake to stake, cutting the mines away. But soon the arrival of an armoured breaching team, with sixteen flail tanks and eight armoured bulldozers, saw five exits clear—at a cost of machinery, not lives. Inland, the same success story was by degrees visible: signs reading "*Achtung Minen*" gave place to "Verges Clear To Twenty Feet."

From every beach men bore away a patchwork of impressions. In the Ouistreham half of Sword, soldiers of the East Yorkshire Regiment remembered scything waves of machine-gun fire which within minutes cost them 200 dead at the waterline. To Captain Henry Ryan Price, a pre-war racehorse trainer, whose supply ship had been sunk at sea, the East Yorks' tragedy was his opportunity; doubling among their ranks, he re-equipped his commando troop with the small arms of the dead. Others recall an almost unnatural courtesy even under fire. Aboard a sinking LCI off Juno, Lieutenant Michael Aldworth held back his men from disembarking prematurely with a gentle, "Wait a minute, chaps. It's not our turn." From the bowels of the craft, a voice queried, "Well, just how long do you think it will be, old man? The ruddy hold is filling up with water."

Some men were single-minded from the first. Captain Hutchinson Burt, too impatient to

190

await the arrival of the "Funnies," led his Commandos through the dunes fronting Ouistreham by perilously hugging the barbed wire fence separating one minefield from the next. Others followed suit, before the bloody battle of Ouistreham was fought from pillbox to pillbox, from house to house. Then the speed march to the Orne bridges was on, four miles across rugged country to reinforce Major Howard's men. "We were only two-and-a-half minutes behind schedule," Derek Mills-Roberts recalls, but this did not spare them from ribald cries of "What kept you?"

Older British campaigners gave priority to creature comforts. Sergeant Henry Morris, of the 13th/18th Hussars, whose Duplex Drive tank had been launched 4000 yards off Sword, was quite determined to make it to the beach

Troops of the German 711th Infantry Division counter-attacking near Sword Beach. (Bundesarchiv-Koblenz)

because he wanted a proper breakfast; the tinned steak-and-kidney pudding in his ration pack had been no fare to tempt a seasick man. Company Sergeant Major Harry Bowers, of the Hampshires, fought his way forward on Gold with one object in mind; his feet were killing him and he wanted a nice soft pair of German boots. Scaling a pillbox and dropping a grenade through the firing slit, he stripped them from the first Russian prisoner to emerge.

On Gold, despite the deaths, there was an acute sense of anti-climax. Captain Roger Bell, of the Westminster Dragoons, commanding a flail tank, always remembered the eastern flank of Gold because a green smoke canister, used to signal an advance to the infantry, burst open on the floor of his turret; thereafter, for Bell, Gold Beach was the battle he fought with an emerald green face, hair and moustache. To Trooper

Norman Smith, of the 5th Royal Tank Regiment, Gold was the beach where his Cromwell tank, buffeted by 5-ft waves, foundered even as it left its LCT. Settling for the night into an abandoned German slit trench, with his tank commander, CSM "Knocker" Knight, Smith thought glumly, "*This* is hardly the way we planned to come ashore."

On Sword, as the day wore on, a heady air of carnival prevailed. Heedless of the danger from mines, groups of Frenchmen crying "*Vive les Anglais*" swarmed on to the beach, ready to hug and kiss any unwary Englishman they met. From Colleville-sur-Orne, a mile inland, the Mayor himself, sporting the big brass helmet of a fire chief, turned up to welcome the invaders. One artilleryman, Captain Gerald Norton, was even accosted by four Germans, suitcases already packed, waiting to board the first British boat available. Already, scenting victory, the long khaki-clad files were moving inland, towards Caen, Bayeux and Périers.

Devotion to duty was so commonplace that morning it was often unrecorded until later. When a heavy sea wrenched away the steering wheel of LCA 786, the coxswain, George Tandy, a 19-year-old Royal Marine Corporal, acted for four-and-a-half hours as a human rudder—slipping over the stern to stand with one foot on the rudder guard, guiding the rudder with the other. On the seven-mile run-in from the mother ship, the surging waves first lifted him high in the air, then plunged him breast-deep in water, but Tandy hung on until thirty-five men were delivered off Sword, then fought the LCA back to the mother ship—this time with the wind and the sea against him.

At 4 p.m. that day, *General der Artillerie* Erich Marcks halted the bulk of the 21st Panzer Division in their drive towards the Orne bridges. The bulk of their armour, he thought, was needed at the coast, and he told *Oberst* Oppeln-Bronikowski flatly, "If you don't succeed in throwing the British into the sea, we shall have lost the war." Yet many on both sides now concede wryly that in those first hours of crisis they thought and acted like civilians. For the Allies, there had been the long months of training, for the Germans, the stagnation on a quiet front—and both had combined to stifle the killer instinct.

Gefreiter Werner Kortenhaus was one of the 21st Panzer troops still moving towards the Orne when he and his men spotted two lone Britons standing by the roadside, hands raised in surrender—two more 6th Airborne men who had been dropped wide. With no inclination either to kill or take prisoners, the Germans studiously ignored them, hastening on. Medical orderly Fritz Müller, finding an unconscious American paratrooper in the woods near Ste Mère-Église, was giving first aid when cigarettes suddenly showered on him from the branches; fellow Americans, trapped in the trees above, were showing their gratitude. *Gefreiter* Anton Wuensch, of the 6th *Fallschirmjäger* Regiment, was combing the woods for Americans north of Carentan, along with six others, when they chanced on a parachute container. Faced with

Utah, 8.30 a.m.: troops of the 8th US Infantry Division move inland. (US Navy)

opposite above
German forward observation and gun bunker ahead of the main batteries commanding Gold beach.

opposite below
Remains of German battery at Le Chaos (Gold beach).

Remains of German bunker at Graye-sur-mer (Juno beach).

195

canned pineapple, orange juice, chocolates and cigarettes, they put the war aside for an orgy of gluttony. Washing powdered Nescafé down their throats with condensed milk, they felt that life could offer no greater bliss.

With Allies, too, civilian habits died hard. At dawn on June 6, snipers in the church tower at Le Port were harassing the men at the Orne bridges so severely that Corporal Jim Killeen, of Howard's party, blew the tower to smithereens with a bomb from a Piat mortar, killing twelve snipers. But later, entering the church to assess the damage, he did reverently remove his steel helmet. It was the same with Private James R. Blue, of the 101st Airborne, adrift, like most of his fellows, in the countryside near La Fière. When a bazooka shell from his company set a French farmhouse on fire, and a German officer and fifteen men surrendered, Blue's first instinct, as a North Carolina farm boy, was to beg forgiveness of the old French couple whose home had been destroyed.

But at 9 a.m.—8 a.m. German Central Time—one German at least was not thinking like a civilian. At Lille, *Oberstleutnant* Josef "Pips" Priller, commander of *Jagdgeschwader* 26, and his sole pilot, *Feldwebel* Heinz Wodarezyk, were making ready to strafe the invaders with just two Focke-Wulf 190 fighters. It would be a last symbolic sortie for the once-mighty Luftwaffe, a two-man gesture of defiance against General Carl Spaatz.

Thirty minutes after heading west, the invasion was spread before them like a diorama—ships by the hundred, stretching out of sight beyond the horizon, landing craft chugging for the shore as sedately as ferries, mile upon mile of sand black with men. "We're going in!" Priller hailed his sergeant, "Good luck!", and at 400 mph in they went, streaking over the British beaches, lower than 150 ft, guns hammering. As the fleet recovered from the shock, every ack-ack gun opened up as one, but at the end of their run the two fighters soared for the clouds, unharmed.

But again the reaction was totally civilian: one sportsman acknowledging the prowess of another. "Jerry or not," said Leading Stoker Robert Dowie, aboard HMS *Dunbar*, "the best of luck to you. You've got guts."

On Bloody Omaha, men were awakening slowly, as if from an anaesthetic. Rallying by degrees, more and more were coming to realize they must fight their way inland or perish. Earlier the commander of the 16th Infantry Regiment, Colonel George A. Taylor, had made that plain; now two other commanders, Colonel Charles Canham, of the 116th, and Brigadier General Norman Cota, of the 29th Division, roaming the beach, oblivious to the deadly fire, added their voices to Taylor's. "They're murdering us here!" Canham raged repeatedly. "Let's move inland and get murdered!"

All along the beach, officers and non-coms took their cue from the three—storming, swearing, urging shell-stunned men to struggle to their feet: "Get your arse on up there!" . . . "This is what separates the men from the boys" . . . "Let's see what you're made of." And gradually, as morning gave way to afternoon, barbed wire was cut, beach exits opened up—often so narrow, Lieutenant

Franklyn A. Johnson, of 1st Division, saw, that engineers were delicately draping unexploded mines with handkerchiefs and toilet tissue. "Flames everywhere," Major Stanley Bach, the 1st's liaison officer, had noted at 1.20 p.m. "Men burning alive..." But by 3.40p.m.: "Infantry moving by us on path over crest ... We get to open field—follow path— see one man that had stepped on mine; no body from waist down.

Yet by 4.50 p.m. Bach himself had reached St-Laurent, three-quarters of a mile inland; Colleville had fallen and so had Vierville-sur-Mer. Even on Omaha, at a cost of 2500 dead, wounded and missing, the Atlantic Wall was irreparably breached.

Again and again, Rommel's driver, *Gefreiter* Daniel, sounded the horn. Beside him in the

Landing craft form queue off Juno Beach, late June 6. (Royal Canadian Navy)

speeding Horch, the Field-Marshal was urging repeatedly, "*Tempo! Tempo! Tempo!*" Driving his gloved right fist into the palm of his left hand, he muttered bitterly, "My friendly enemy, Montgomery."

It was all too late, as Rommel had guessed it would be. Not until 10.15 a.m., still in his red-striped dressing gown at the family home in Herrlingen, had Rommel heard from *General-major* Speidel that the invasion had been launched. "How stupid of me," was almost his only comment. Now he was racing back to resume command, but the delays would be fatal. Hitler—whose only reaction had been, "Well, is it or isn't it the invasion?"—had waited until 3.40 p.m. before releasing the vital Panzer divisions, the 12th SS and Panzer *Lehr*. Now the 12th SS could not hope to reach the coast before June 7. The Panzer *Lehr*, strafed repeatedly from the air, would not make it until June 9.

The one unit that might have exploited an eight-mile gap which British Commandos had not closed between Juno and Gold, the 21st Panzer, had been diverted to the coast too late—fated to lose sixteen tanks in as many minutes to the British guns.

Twisting round in the Horch's front seat, Rommel spoke feelingly to his aide, *Hauptmann* Hellmuth Lang. "Do you know, Lang," he said, "if I was commander of the Allied forces right now, I could finish off the war in fourteen days."

The world at large was slow to react. In Moscow, Josef Stalin was sitting up late in the Kremlin and

Old men forget: yet all shall be forgot,/But he'll remember with advantages/What feats he did that day.

(from *Henry V* IV, iii, by William Shakespeare)

opposite
Invasion pattern – Normandy by Eric Aldwinkle. A Hawker Typhoon flies in over the Normandy beaches. (Canadian War Museum)

P-51Bs of the 359th Fighter Group, under 1st Lt John H. Oliphint, blast an ammo train near Le Mans on D-Day. (USAF)

We who are left, how shall we look again/Happily on the sun or feel the rain,/Without remembering how they who went/Ungrudgingly, and spent/Their all for us, loved too the sun and rain?

. . . How shall we turn to little things,/And listen to the birds and winds and streams/Made holy by their dreams,/Nor feel the heart-break in the heart of things?

(from *Lament* by Wilfrid Gibson)

drinking deep with his Foreign Minister, Vyacheslav Molotov and Milovan Djilas, Marshal Tito's Yugoslav emissary to Russia. A dispatch had arrived from Churchill announcing the landings, and at once Stalin began to scoff: "Yes, there'll be a landing, if there is no fog . . . Maybe they'll meet with some Germans! What if they meet with some Germans! Maybe there won't be a landing then, but just promises as usual." Only when D-Day was an accomplished fact, did he consent to release a suitably fulsome tribute.

Meanwhile, Churchill had returned from Southampton to London, to pace the Map Room of "The Hole," the six-acre honeycomb of offices below Whitehall, where one in ten of War Cabinet meetings were held. He had "hardened to this enterprise," but in the small hours doubts once more assailed him. In his mind echoed the tramp of ghostly legions from A. E. Housman's *A Shropshire Lad*:

> *Far and near and low and louder*
> *On the roads of earth go by,*
> *Dear to friends and food for*
> *   powder,*
> *Soldiers marching, all to die.*

It was late, and Clementine Churchill had joined him. "Do you realize," her husband asked, "that by the time you wake up in the morning, twenty thousand men may have been killed?"

But later that morning, facing the House of Commons, his old aplomb was once more apparent, though tradition decreed that Prime Minister's Question Time must first run its course: one paramount demand was that charwomen and charladies should henceforth

be known as Office Cleaners. Only then could Churchill make D-Day official: "The commanders who are engaged report that everything is proceeding according to plan. And what a plan!"

In the United States, the truth dawned more slowly. At 12.37 a.m. East Coast time the German Transocean News Agency put out an urgent flash from Berlin: American landings had begun on the shores of north-western France. But the Columbia Broadcasting System, for one, mindful of the Joan Ellis scare, reacted with wary scepticism—"there is as yet no reason to believe that this . . . is anything more than a German propaganda move." Night birds among their listeners relaxed once more as the Lennie Conn orchestra swung into (*I'll Always Remember*) *The Forget-Me-Nots in Your Eyes*. Not until 10 p.m. did Franklin Roosevelt lead the nation in a cautionary prayer from the Oval Office of the White House: "Their road will be long and hard. For the enemy is strong. He may hurl back our forces. Success may not come with rushing speed, but we shall return again and again. . . . "

In Berlin, although the news came later, the implications registered more swiftly—most especially with all those in the German underground who had plotted Adolf Hitler's downfall. One of them, Ruth Andreas-Friedrich, an editor with the Ullstein publishing house, awoke in her apartment as early as 6.30 a.m. on June 7 to a call from a fellow conspirator, *Major* Hinrichs, of the Luftwaffe: "Oh, by the way . . . the shipment got in . . . by the early morning train." But in the suburb of Steglitz, *Frau* Andreas-Friedrich noted, it was 11 a.m.

200

before the first editions hit the news-stands—to be confiscated by fast-moving police before the bundles were even untied. It as noon before the first newspaper headlines appeared on the streets of the German capital—"Invasion by order of Moscow!"—but as the day wore on, no further bulletins followed. The time-limit once forecast by Hitler—"within nine hours we will throw them back into the sea"—had long passed, Ruth Andreas-Friedrich noted in her diary. "The people with swastikas in their buttonholes look uneasy . . . still there is no sign that the enemy is drowning in the Channel."

For the men who had made part of this "great crusade" it was still too early to assess the magnitude of what they had done. Since reaching Ravenoville, Private Donald Burgett had been as confused as any man. At the end of the day, Burgett had to grope back to think just what his outfit had achieved.

It had not taken long for the company to swell to three officers and seventeen men—nor to discover that all Ravenoville from this point on was a German fortress. But as Lieutenant Muir argued, "That's what we came here for, to kill Krauts, and from the looks of it, there are plenty to go around."

As Muir led them all in a head-on attack against a group of houses across an apple orchard, it seemed as simple as that. Yelling and screaming at the pitch of his lungs as he ran, Burgett saw his first German victim running through trees; stopping short, he "took a good sight on him and squeezed the trigger." Afterwards he never recalled feeling the recoil or even hearing the shot: just the man spinning sideways and falling face down out of sight.

Another German rounded the building, then stood stock-still, staring dazedly at his dead comrade. Carefully sighting on his chest, Burgett squeezed the trigger again and this man, too, fell forward.

Then the fighting grew so feverish that Burgett lost all count of his personal toll of dead; darting from house to house with a captured haul of German "potato masher" grenades, he and the others hurled them through every door and window. The sloping fields beyond were suddenly alive with running men in shabby grey, struggling to get away. Bemusedly, Burgett learned from his buddy, Private Phillips, a Pennsylvania Dutchman who spoke some German, that they had taken seventy-five prisoners. Thirty more Germans were dead; the remaining hundred, never dreaming they faced only twenty men, had pulled out.

After that they had sown all the roads out of Ravenoville with Hawkins mines camouflaged under cowpats, breakfasted off K rations of chopped pork and egg yolks and smoked contentedly in the sunshine. Then, as the Germans began filtering back, there was another pitched battle across a blacktop road, so intense that the smell of cordite seeped into their nostrils and lay thick at the backs of their throats.

They were now so close to the shore that they could see the battleships off Utah Beach, and suddenly huge shells "like boxcars twisting slowly through the air" were landing so close that shockwaves of sound were uprooting whole apple trees, spinning them like cabers across the orchard. Hastily the troopers lobbed orange smoke grenades to denote friendly troops, and

Man has walked by the light of conflagrations, and amid the sound of falling cities, and now there is darkness and long watching until it be morning.

(from 'Characteristics' Essays, III, 32, by Thomas Carlyle)

You could write for a week and not give everyone credit for what he did on a front of 1135 yards.

(from Voyage To Victory by Ernest Hemingway, Collier's magazine, July 22, 1944)

the battleship, responding with an orange smoke pot, ceased fire. All of them heaved a sigh of relief.

The rest of the day "passed easily" while they consolidated, chatting about the beach landings and wondering how long it would take to meet up with friendly troops. All told, Burgett supposed, they had not done badly. They had captured a fortified town, taken seventy-five prisoners, and killed as many more. And now they commanded the high ground overlooking one small portion of Utah. After shooting so many men, he had imagined he might feel different, but so far he felt just as usual. Killing Germans was only a job, after all.

Some Germans, as D-Day ended, were coming to feel that death was the better bargain.

Kanonier Friedrich Wurster, a 21-year-old veteran of the Moscow front, was one of 100 gunners taken prisoner by the Westminster Dragoons in a battery behind Gold Beach. Now Wurster was contrasting the quiet courtesy of his captors with Hitler's shrill denunciation of all those taken prisoner as "traitors to the Third Reich." For the first time Wurster thought of the hollow sham that had been the Atlantic Wall, the strange absence of the Luftwaffe, and wondered, "Who had been the betrayed—and who the betrayers?" Thoughts like this were in the mind of *Oberst* Oppeln-Bronikowski, dug in with his tanks at Biéville, watching German officers and their men retreating unscathed from the front towards Caen, a sergeant and two reeling German WACs forming their rearguard —"drunk as pigs, swaying from side to side, singing *Deutschland über Alles*." "The war is lost," Bronikowski decided then.

The history of war does not show any such undertaking so broad in concept, so grandiose in scale, so masterly in execution.

((Josef Stalin to Winston Churchill, June 11, 1944)

Dawn over Sword beach, Ouistreham, Normandy.

For while the tired waves, vainly breaking,/Seem here no painful inch to gain,/Far back, though creeks and inlets making,/Comes silent, flooding in, the main.

And not by eastern windows only,/When daylight comes, comes in the light,/In front, the sun climbs slow, how slowly,/But westward, look, the land is bright.

(from *Say Not the Struggle Naught Availeth* by Arthur Hugh Clough, as quoted in a wartime broadcast by Winston Churchill)

The American Beaches: the late afternoon move inland. (US Army)

204

At the Château de la Roche-Guyon, it was not a truth that Rommel could quite accept as yet. "I hope we can drive them back," he told *Hauptmann* Lang. "I've nearly always succeeded up to now," but he shrugged and spread his hands as he said it. It was as if the old compulsion remained with him to the end: think Victory.

In the twilight along the Bay of the Seine, a thin line like a high watermark now stretched for fully sixty-five miles, and the war correspondent Ernie Pyle surveyed the aftermath of a battle that had cost 10,000 Allied casualties: soldiers' packs and shoe polish, diaries, socks, hand-grenades and Bibles, many Bibles. All these he noted, along with snapshots of families who would never grow older, and the last letters from home, each address razored out for reasons of security — together with torn pistol belts, bloody abandoned shoes, metal mirrors and thousands of waterlogged cigarettes.

Other war correspondents were puzzled by the strange weakness of the opposition — among them Charles Christian Wertenbaker, of *Time* magazine. Granted that the timing of D-Day had been impeccable, with Rommel, as at El Alamein, once more absent from the front — still the first German prisoners seemed to have little heart for fighting. Near Cherbourg, which was to fall on June 26, Wertenbaker put it to one prisoner man-to-man: "Were he and his fellows the best the German Army could offer?" The reply was an epitaph for Adolf Hitler's dreams in the east: "The best of the German Army is dead in Russia."

As darkness fell, Flight Lieutenant Pierre Clostermann, a Free French pilot with the RAF, was patrolling in a Spitfire Mark IX above the land that he had quit four years earlier to join De Gaulle. "On the German side, to all intents and purposes, nothing," he noted later in his log-book, though Omaha Beach was still "a nightmare . . . fires raging from Vierville to Isigny." Then, far below in the Channel, Clostermann saw the most heartening sight of all: half a dozen tugs "sweating and puffing away, dragging a kind of enormous concrete tower sitting on a frame as big as a floating dock." The first Mulberries were on their way to Arromanches and St Laurent, a warrant that the Allies had come to stay.

In his cabin aboard HMS *Goathland*, off Sword, Captain Eric Bush, RN, was pondering his report to the Admiralty as commander of the Naval Assault Group, Force S: a fitting climax to a day that marked the beginning of the end for the Third Reich. At first the preamble was slow to come, but suddenly Bush hit upon it — Admiralty report or no, only lines from Swinburne's *The Armada* would do justice to the day just past:

Never earth nor sea beheld so great a stake before them set,
Save when Athens hurled back Asia from the lists wherein they met.

BUZZ WORDS

The vernacular of the Allied Forces and front-line civilians on the eve of D-Day

ACE Air Force pilot claiming five-plus enemy planes (RAF and USAAF)

ACHING BACK, OH MY Heart-cry of homeward-bound GIs after a night on the town

ACK-ACK Anti-aircraft fire

ADJ Adjutant

AID OF, WHAT'S THIS IN? What does this signify?

ALARM AND DESPONDENCY Wartime depression, deplored by Winston Churchill

ALL RIGHT FOR YOU, IT'S Ironic gibe to those in more agreeable jobs or billets

AMMO Ammunition

ANTS IN HIS/HER PANTS Nervy excess of energy

APPLE KNOCKER Backwoods soldier (US Army)

ARMCHAIR GENERAL Amateur strategist, often ill-informed

AWOL Absent without leave (all services)

BACK-ROOM BOY Civilian technician attached to Armed Forces

BAG, IN THE Made a prisoner of war

BAGS OF Plenty of

BALL, ON THE Alert, lively

BANDIT Any enemy aircraft

BASHER Any mechanic—e.g. instrument basher (RAF)

BASINFUL More than enough hardship

BAT OUT OF HELL, LIKE A Flying fast

BEAM, ON THE; OFF THE On the right track; failing to understand

BIND A tedious person or task; to bore someone

BINT A woman

BLACK, PUT UP A A serious error (RAF officers)

BLINK, ON THE Malfunctioning

BLITZ A lightning war; an air-raid; cleaning a barracks under pressure

BLOCK-BUSTER A huge bomb capable of destroying a city block

BLOW ONE'S TOP An uncontrollable rage

BODS Personnel

BOFFIN Inventor working for the aircraft industry (RAF)

BOG Services latrine

BOMB-HAPPY Shell-shocked

BOOB A serious error (RAF other ranks)

BOUGHT IT Became a casualty, usually fatal

BRASS High-ranking military officers (all services)

BROTHEL CREEPERS Suede shoes

BROWN JOBS The Army (Royal Navy and RAF)

BROWNED OFF Fed up

BRYLCREEM BOYS The RAF (Army and Royal Navy)

BUDDY-BUDDY Close friend (US Army and Navy)

BULL SESSION Lengthy male gossip (all US services)

BULLHORN Public address system relaying orders to lower deck (US Navy)

BUMF Routine services memoranda

BURP GUN Small automatic gun (US Army)

BURTON, GONE FOR A Missing in action (RAF)

BUTTON UP To accomplish a task successfully; to keep a secret (all US services)

CARPET, ON THE To undergo a reprimand

CARRY A TORCH To nourish a passion, often hopeless

CARRY THE CAN To act as a scapegoat

CHAIRBORNE DIVISIONS Office-bound personnel

CHARACTER Eccentric or unusual person (all US services)

CHATTERBOX Anti-aircraft machine-gun (US Navy)

CHEESE-CAKE Girlie photos emphasizing sex-appeal

CHEESED OFF Fed up

CHEW OUT Reprimand severely (US services)

CHIEFIE An RAF Flight Sergeant

CHOCKER Disgruntled (Royal Navy)

CHOW Food; mealtime (US services)

CIVVIES Civilian clothes

CIVVY STREET Civilian life

CLAPPERS, GO LIKE THE In a great hurry

COMBO Small jazz-band of 3/4 players

CONCHIE Conscientious objector to military service

COOKING, WHAT'S? What is happening? (RAF, originally USAF)

COOTIE Body louse (US services)

COULDN'T CARE LESS, I I'm totally indifferent (all UK services)

CRAFTY Well-organized, with an eye to the main chance (RAF)

CREW CUT Close haircut, favoured by American college boat-crews (later by USAF)

CUT A RUG Dance-hall jiving or jitterbugging (US services)

DEAD Very—e.g. dead chocker

DEAD LOSS Total failure; RAF: an unserviceable plane

DEAR JOHN Soldier's farewell letter from wife or girl friend (US services)

DECK, HIT THE Get out of bed (US Army); to crash-land (RAF)

DICEY Hazardous

DIM TYPE Stupid airman or WAAF

DITCH, TO Land an aircraft in the sea

DOG TAGS Identity discs (US services)

DOPE Essential information (US services)

DOWN IN THE DRINK Crash-landing in the Channel or the Atlantic (RAF)

DRAG, SPIT AND A A crafty cigarette (Royal Navy)

DRILL, THE Correct procedure

DUCK Any amphibious vehicle (US services)

DUFF GEN Unreliable report (RAF)

DUTY STOOGE A duty airman or NCO (RAF)

EASY, I'M Amenable (RAF)

EGG Bomb, hand grenade or naval mine (US services)

ERK An aircraftsman (RAF)

EYETIES Italians

FIGHTIN' TOOLS Eating utensils: knife, fork and spoon (US services)

FIRECRACKER Bomb or torpedo (US services)

FISH Torpedo (US Navy)

FIT, ARE YOU? Are you ready? (RAF)

FIZZER British Army/charge sheet/disciplinary

FLAK Lethal fragments of artillery shells; trenchant criticism

FLANNEL To bluff or flatter

FLAP An alarm or panic; an air-raid

FLAPS Ailerons (RAF)

FLAT SPIN, IN A Flustered or confused (RAF)

FLATTOP Aircraft carrier (US Navy)

FLYING COFFIN Glider (USAF)

FORTY-EIGHT Week-end liberty pass (US Navy)

FOUL-UP A blunder (US services)

FOXHOLE Soldier's trench or hole, dug for concealment (US Army)

FROGMAN Navy underwater swimmer using oxygen tank and rubber flippers

FUTURE IN IT, NO Said of a thankless or dangerous mission (RAF)

GEN Information (RAF)

GEORGE DO IT, LET Let someone else do it

GET A LOAD OF THIS! Just listen to this!

GET CRACKING, GET WEAVING Peremptory order to move

GLASSHOUSE Military prison

GOD'S DOG, AS OLD AS Ancient (Royal Navy)

GOOF A congenitally stupid man; to blunder

GOOF OFF To idle or evade work (US services)

GRAVEYARD SHIFT Midnight to 8 a.m. shift for munitions and factory workers

GREASE-GUN The M-3 sub-machine gun (US Army and Navy)

GREASE IT IN Smooth landing of an aeroplane (USAF)

GREMLIN Invisible imp causing problems and malfunctions (USAF and RAF)

GRIFF Information

GROOVE, IN THE In the right mood

GROUPIE RAF Group Captain

HABA HABA, HUBBA HUBBA US Armed Forces command to speed it up

HAB DABS The jitters

HAD IT, HE'S He's too late

HANG OUT THE LAUNDRY Parachute drop (USAAF)

HAPPY IN YOUR WORK, ARE YOU? Mocking query to workers on difficult or dusty job

HARDWARE Weapons (US services)

HARRY FRAUGHTERS A tense or fraught situation (Royal Navy)

HASH MARK Military service stripe (US services)

HAVEN'T A CLUE, I I have no information

HEAD Naval latrine

HEEBIE-JEEBIES Fright or worry

HERSHEY BAR Chocolate bar (US services)

HILL, OVER THE Desertion from the forces (US services)

206

HOLY JOE Chaplain (US Navy)
HOMEWORK, NICE BIT OF Comely girl
HOP Local dance
HOW COME? Why is that? (US services)
HUFF-DUFF High-frequency direction finder (USAAF)

I/C In charge of
IRONS Eating utensils (RAF and Army)

JANKERS Defaulters
JEEP-JOCKEY Truck driver (US Army)
JERRIES Germans
JIFFY BAG Canvas or leather toilet case
JOE Any American soldier
JOKER A wiseacre (US Army)
JOY Luck or satisfaction — e.g. 'No joy?' (Royal Navy and RAF)

KAPUT Broken; out of order
KERFUFFLE A fuss about nothing
KITE An aeroplane (USAAF and RAF)
KNEES, ON MY Overtired
KNOCK IT OFF! Stop it immediately (US Army)
KNOTTED, GET Get lost
KP Kitchen Police: US Army punishment fatigue
KRs King's Regulations
KRAUTS Germans
KRIEGIES American prisoners of war in German camps

LEAD OUT, GET THE Make haste (US services)
LIBERATE To loot (US Army)
LIBERTY SHIP Cargo vessel carrying US military personnel
LMF Lack of moral fibre (RAF)
LOADED Drunk (US services)
LOOEY US Lieutenant
LOVELY GRUB! Just what I wanted!

MAE WEST Inflatable life-preserver worn by aircrew
MAKE IT, I COULDN'T Blanket excuse for failing to keep an appointment or fulfil a task

MEATBALL Dull obnoxious person (US services)
MESS UP To get into trouble (US services)
MG Machine gunner
MILK RUN Easy aerial mission (USAAF)

NAAFI The Navy, Army, and Air Force Institute: canteens for British servicemen
NATTER Idle chatter
NEEDLE To provoke
NO-CLAP MEDAL The Good Conduct Medal (US Army)
NONCOM US non-commissioned officer
NUMBER NINE Laxative pill

ODDS AND SODS Miscellaneous Headquarters personnel
ON A PARTY On a drinking spree
OPPO A close friend (Royal Navy)
ORGANIZE To obtain deviously (RAF)

PADRE Any chaplain
PARTY Commando raid; naval operation or bombing mission (British services)
PASS THE BUCK To shift responsibility
PASSION WAGGON Three-ton truck taking servicemen to a dance
PEGS, ON THE Under military arrest
PICNIC Enjoyable, easy task
PIECE OF CAKE The RAF equivalent of 'picnic'
PINEAPPLE Hand grenade (US Army)
PIN-UP Pretty girl's photograph pinned up in barracks
PISSED Drunk
PLASTERED Drunk
POLICE UP To clean and make tidy a barracks or parade ground
PONGO A soldier (Royal Navy and RAF)
POOPED Exhausted
POPSY Girl-friend
POW Prisoner of war
PRANG To crash or damage an aircraft (RAF and USAAF)

PRESS ON, REGARDLESS Finish the job, whatever the cost
PRO-PACK Prophylactic package against venereal disease
PX Post Exchange: government-owned store on base, selling goods at controlled prices (US services)

QUARTER BLOKE British Army quartermaster
QUEEN MARY Articulated vehicle for transporting aircraft by road (RAF)

R AND R Rest and Rotation: short leave from front line
RANK, PULL To exact hard work in dictatorial fashion (US Army)
RATTLE, THE Royal Navy's report of defaulters
READ, DO YOU? Controller's query to pilot seeking bearings
REDCAP British military policeman
REPPLE DEPPLE Replacement depot (US Army)
RHUBARB Low-flying strafing mission (RAF and USAAF)
ROGER Yes, OK: pilot's acknowledgment of radio instructions (RAF and USAAF)
ROLL IN THE HAY Amorous encounter
ROLL OUT! Get out of bed! (US Army)
ROPEY Inferior, scruffy (RAF)
RUGGED Dangerous or difficult (US Army)
RUST BUCKET Ageing destroyer (US Navy)

SACK Bed or bunk — e.g. Hit the sack (US services)
SAD SACK Maladjusted ill-dressed soldier (US Army)
SAM BROWNE Officer's leather belt
SCATTERGUN Machine gun (US Army)
SCRAMBLED EGGS Gold oak-leaves on senior RAF officer's cap peak

SCREAMING MEEMIES Delirium
SCREW Fornicate
SCUTTLEBUTT Rumours traded round ship's drinking fountain (US Navy and Royal Navy)
SEA LAWYER Naval equivalent of armchair general
SEAT OF THE PANTS Flying by instinct (RAF and USAAF)
SEE THE CHAPLAIN Stop complaining (US Army)
SEEP Amphibious watertight jeep (US Navy)
SHACK UP Unmarried sexual relationship off base
SHAGGED Worn out
SHAKEN RIGID Astonished, flabbergasted (RAF)
SHAKY DO A risky near-fatal affair (RAF)
SHAMBOLIC Totally disorganized (British Army)
SHAVE-TAIL Any second lieutenant (US Army)
SHOOT DOWN IN FLAMES To worst in argument (RAF)
SHOOTING A LINE Boastful exaggeration (RAF)
SHOOTING THE BREEZE Casual gossip: the US services' equivalent of natter
SHORT ARM INSPECTION Medical inspection for venereal disease
SILK, HIT THE To make a parachute jump (USAAF)
SITREP Situation report (British Army)
SKIRT Woman
SKIVER Work-shy serviceman
SKY PILOT Any Armed Forces chaplain (US services)
SLAP-HAPPY Dizzy with joy
SLITTIE Slit trench: the British Army's foxhole
SLOSHED Drunk
SMOOCH To kiss and caress (all services)
SNAZZY Stylish, up-to-date
SNOGGING Love-making (RAF)
SNOOD Women's hair-net
SNOWDROP US Army Military Policeman

SNOW JOB Insincere talk, designed to flatter or impress (US services)
SOLO, GO Trainee pilot's first flight without instructor (RAF)
SOP Sleeping Out Pass
SOUND OFF To count in unison while drilling; to complain at length (US Army)
SPROG New RAF recruit
SQUADDIE British Army private soldier
SQUAWK BOX Public address system loudspeaker (US Navy)
STARKERS Naked (Royal Navy)
STUFFED, GET Earthier version of 'Get lost'
SUIT, THE Any American Armed Forces uniform
SWEATER GIRL Curvaceous pin-up model

TAKE A DIM VIEW To disapprove totally (British services)
TAKE THE MICKEY To taunt
TEAR A STRIP OFF To reproach vigorously
TICKET, GET ONE'S Discharge on medical grounds (British services)
TOP KICK US Army first sergeant
TWERP Obnoxious male
252 Military charge sheet
295 Military leave pass
TYPE A person (RAF)

UNDER THE COUNTER Black Market produce
U/S Unserviceable

V-GIRL Girl offering favours to servicemen

WASH-OUT Student pilot who fails flight training (USAAF)
WHACKO! Splendid!
WINGCO RAF Wing Commander
WIZZO Excellent, from 'wizard' (RAF)

YANK BASHER Mercenary girl pursuing US servicemen

ZAP To shoot someone (US Army)
ZERO HOUR Precise hour of a military operation

15 OPERATIONAL SUMMARY

THE FOLLOWING OPERATIONAL summary gives details of Allied and German forces in action throughout D-Day, listed in terms of orders of battle, strengths and availability.

OPERATION OVERLORD

SUPREME HEADQUARTERS ALLIED EXPEDITIONARY FORCE

Supreme Allied Commander
Gen. Dwight D. Eisenhower

Chief of Staff
Gen. Walter Bedell Smith

TWENTY-FIRST ARMY GROUP

Gen. Sir Bernard L. Montgomery

Commander-in-Chief
Maj.-Gen. Sir Francis W. de Guingand

First Army
Lt. Gen. Omar N. Bradley
VII Corps
Maj. Gen. J. Lawton Collins
V Corps
Maj. Gen. Leonard T. Gerow

US ASSAULT DIVISIONS

OMAHA BEACH

1st US Division
Maj. Gen. Clarence R. Huebner

116 Infantry	5th Rangers
16 Infantry	741 Tank Bn.
18 Infantry	111 Field Artillery Bn.
26 Infantry	7 Field Artillery Bn.
115 Infantry	81 Chemical Bn.
2nd Rangers	

UTAH BEACH

4th US Division
Maj. Gen. Raymond O. Barton

8 Infantry	359 Infantry
22 Infantry	(attached from 90th Div.)
12 Infantry	70 Tank Bn.

US AIRBORNE FORCES

82nd Airborne Division
Maj. Gen Matthew B. Ridgway

505th Parachute Infantry	508th Parachute Infantry
507th Parachute Infantry	325th Glider Infantry

101st Airborne Division
Maj. Gen. Maxwell D. Taylor

501st Parachute Infantry	506th Parachute Infantry
502d Parachute Infantry	327th Glider Infantry

Second Army

General Officer Commanding-in-Chief
Lt-Gen. Sir Miles C. Dempsey

Chief of Staff
Brigadier Maurice Chilton

First Canadian Army

General Officer Commanding-in-Chief
Lt-Gen. Henry Crerar

Chief of Staff
Brigadier Churchill Mann

SWORD BEACH

3rd British Division
Maj.-Gen. Thomas Rennie

8th Brigade.
1st Bn. The Suffolk Regt.
2nd Bn. The East Yorkshire Regt.
1st. Bn. The South Lancashire Regt.
9th Brigade.
2nd Bn. The Lincolnshire Regt.
1st Bn. The King's Own Scottish Borderers
2nd Bn. The Royal Ulster Rifles
185th Brigade.
2nd Bn. The Royal Warwickshire Regt.
1st Bn. The Royal Norfolk Regt.
2nd Bn. The King's Shropshire Light Infantry

Divisional Troops
3rd Reconnaissance Regt. RAC
3rd Divisional Engineers
3rd Divisional Signals
7th, 33rd and 76th Field, 20th Anti-Tank and 92nd
  Light Anti-Aircraft Regts. RA
2nd Bn. The Middlesex Regt. (Machine-Gun)

51st (Highland) Division
Maj. Gen. D. C. Bullen-Smith

152nd Brigade
2nd and 5th Battalions The Seaforth Highlanders
5th Battalion The Queen's Own Cameron Highlanders

153rd Brigade
5th Battalion The Black Watch
1st and 5th/7th Battalions The Gordon Highlanders

154th Brigade
1st and 7th Battalions The Black Watch
7th Battalion The Argyll and Sutherland Highlanders

Divisional Troops
2nd Derbyshire Yeomanry RAC
51st Divisional Engineers
51st Divisional Signals

126th, 127th and 128th Field
61st Anti-Tank and 40th Light Anti-Aircraft Regiments
  RA
1/7th Battalion The Middlesex Regiment (Machine-
  Gun)

JUNO BEACH

3rd Canadian Division
Maj. Gen. Rodney Keller

7th Brigade.
The Royal Winnipeg Rifles
The Regina Rifle Regt.
1st Bn. The Canadian Scottish Regt.
8th Brigade.
The Queen's Own Rifles of Canada
Le Regiment de la Chaudière
The North Shore (New Brunswick) Regt.
9th Brigade.
The Highland Light Infantry of Canada
The Stormont, Dundas and Glengarry Highlanders
The North Nova Scotia Highlanders

Divisional Troops

7th Reconnaissance Regt. (17th Duke of York's Royal
   Canadian Hussars)

3rd Canadian Divisional Engineers

3rd Canadian Divisional Signals

12th, 13th and 14th Field, 3rd Anti-Tank and 4th
   Light Anti-Aircraft Regt. RCA

The Cameron Highlanders of Ottawa (Machine-Gun)

GOLD BEACH

50th British (Northumbrian) Division
Maj.-Gen. Douglas Graham

69th Brigade.

5th Bn. The East Yorkshire Regt.

6th and 7th Bn. The Green Howards

151st Brigade.

6th, 8th and 9th Bns. The Durham Light Infantry

231st Brigade.

2 Bn. The Devonshire Regt.

1st Bn. The Hampshire Regt.

1st Bn. The Dorsetshire Regt.

Divisional Troops

61st Reconnaissance Regt. RAC

50th Divisional Engineers

50th Divisional Signals

74th, 90th and 124th Field, 102nd Anti-Tank and
   25th Light Anti-Aircraft Regts. RA

2nd Bn. The Cheshire Regt. (Machine-Gun)

49th (West Riding) Division
Maj. Gen. Evelyn Barker

70th Brigade (to 20.8.44)

10th and 11th Battalions The Durham Light Infantry

1st Battalion The Tyneside Scottish

146th Brigade

4th Battalion The Lincolnshire Regiment

1/4th Battalion The King's Own Yorkshire Light
   Infantry

Hallamshire Battalion The York and Lancashire
   Regiment

147th Brigade

11th Battalion The Royal Scots Fusiliers

6th Battalion The Duke of Wellington's Regiment
   (to 6.7.44)

7th Battalion The Duke of Wellington's Regiment

Divisional Troops

49th Reconnaissance Regiment RAC

49th Divisional Engineers

49th Divisional Signals

69th, 143rd and 185th Field, 55th Anti-Tank and
   89th Light Anti-Aircraft Regiments RA

2nd Princess Louise's Kensington Regiment (Machine-
   Gun)

OTHER FORMATIONS

79th Armoured Division
Maj.-Gen. Sir Percy Hobart

30th Armoured Brigade.

22nd Dragoons

1st Lothians and Border Horse

2nd County of London Yeomanry (Westminster
   Dragoons)

141st Regt. RAC

1st Tank Brigade.

11th, 42nd and 49th Bns. RTR

1st Assault Brigade. RE

5th, 6th and 42nd Assault Regts. RE

79th Armoured Divisional Signals

1st Canadian Armoured Personnel Carrier Regt.

1st Special Service Brigade.

Nos. 3, 4 and 6 Commandos

No. 45 (Royal Marine) Commando

4th Special Service Brigade

Nos. 41, 46, 47 and 48 (Royal Marine) Commandos

Royal Marine Armoured Support Group: 1st and 2nd
   Royal Marine Armoured Support Regts.

Units of the Royal Artillery and Royal Engineers

6th Airborne Division
Maj.-Gen. Richard Gale

3rd Parachute Brigade.
8th and 9th Bns. The Parachute Regt.
1st Canadian Parachute Bn.
5th Parachute Brigade.
7th, 12th and 13th Bns. The Parachute Regt.
6th Airlanding Brigade
12th Bn. The Devonshire Regt.
2nd Bn. The Oxfordshire and Buckinghamshire Light
    Infantry
1st Bn. The Royal Ulster Rifles

Divisional Troops
6th Airborne Armoured Reconnaissance Regt. RAC
6th Airborne Divisional Engineers
53rd Airlanding Light Regt. RA
6th Airborne Divisional Signals

GERMAN ORDER OF BATTLE ON D-DAY

Supreme Command West
Generalfeldmarschall Gerd von Rundstedt

Army Group B
Generalfeldmarschall Erwin Rommel

Seventh Army
Generaloberst Friedrich Dollman

LXXXIV Corps
General der Artillerie Erich Marcks
General der Artillerie Wilhelm Fahrmbacher
General der Infanterie Dietrich von Choltitz

Units of LXXXIV Corps identified on VII Corps

front:

17th SS–Panzer Grenadier Division
    (Goetz von Berlichingen)
    Genlt. Werner Ostendorf, CG
    37th Panzer Grenadier Regiment
    38th Panzer Grenadier Regiment
77th Division
    Genlt. Rudolf Stegmann, CG
    Obst. Rudolf Bacherer
91st Luftlande (Airborne) Division
    Genmaj. Wilhelm Falley, CG
    Obst. Eugen Koenig, CO
    1057th Grenadier Regiment
    1058th Grenadier Regiment
243rd Division
    Genlt. Heinz Hellmich, CG
    (KIA 17 June)
    Obst. Bernard Klosterkemper, CO
    920th Grenadier Regiment
    921st Grenadier Regiment
    922nd Grenadier Regiment
265th Division
    Genlt. Walter Duevert, CG
    894th Grenadier Regiment
    895th Grenadier Regiment
    896th Grenadier Regiment
352nd Division
    Genlt. Dietrich Kraiss
    914th Grenadier Regiment
709th Division
    Genlt. Karl W. von Schlieben, CG
    919th Grenadier Regiment
    729th Grenadier Regiment
    739th Grenadier Regiment
    649th Ost Battalion, attached
    795th Georgian Battalion, attached
Sturm Battalion AOK 7 (attached to 709th Division)
    Maj. Hugo Messerschmidt, CO
    6th Parachute Regiment (attached to the 91st
      Division)
    Maj. Freiherr Friedrich von der Heydte

FORCES AVAILABLE IN EUROPEAN THEATRE OF OPERATIONS FOR OPERATION OVERLORD

LAND FORCES

	Infantry	Armoured	Airborne	Total
United States	13	5	2	20
British	8	4	2	14
Canadian	2	1	—	3
French	—	1	—	1
Polish	—	1	—	1
TOTAL	23	12	4	39

AIR FORCES

ALLIED EXPEDITIONARY AIR FORCE

Royal Air Force, Second Tactical Air Force
Royal Air Force, Air Defence of Great Britain
Royal Air Force, Airborne and Transport Forces
United States Ninth Air Force

ALLIED STRATEGIC AIR FORCE

Royal Air Force, Bomber Command
United States Eighth Air Force

ROYAL AIR FORCE COASTAL COMMAND

AIRCRAFT ON OPERATIONAL STATIONS JUNE 6 1944

A. Summary by Types:

	Operational & non operational	Operational	Effective Strength
Heavy bombers	3958	3455	3130
Medium and light bombers	1234	989	933
Fighters and fighter bombers	4709	3824	3711
TOTAL	9901	8268	7774

B. Summary by Command:

	Operational & non operational	Operational	Effective Strength
VIII A/F			
Heavy bombers	2578	2243	1947
Fighters	1144	961	961
IX A/F			
Medium bombers	624	513	467
Light bombers	228	165	156
Fighters	1487	1132	1123

	Operational & non operational	Operational	Effective Strength
BOMB CMD			
Heavy bombers	1380	1212	1183
Light bombers	134	98	97
2ND TAF			
Medium bombers	88	67	67
Light bombers	160	146	146
Fighters	1006	856	831
ADGB			
Fighters	1072	875	796
TOTAL	9901	8268	7774

*Operational aircraft with crews available.

OPERATION NEPTUNE

NAVAL ORGANIZATION

Allied Naval Commander-in-Chief Expeditionary
Force (ANCXF)
Admiral Sir Bertram H. Ramsay

Chief of Staff
Rear-Admiral George Creasy

Chief Naval Administrative Officer
and Flag Officer British Assault Area (designate)
Rear-Admiral James Rivett-Carnac

Rear-Admiral Mulberry/Pluto
Rear-Admiral William Tennant

WESTERN NAVAL TASK FORCE

Rear-Admiral Alan G. Kirk USN
USS *Augusta* (Cruiser)

EASTERN NAVAL TASK FORCE

Rear-Admiral Sir Philip Vian
HMS *Scylla* (Cruiser)

ASSAULT FORCES

FORCE U
Rear-Admiral Don P. Moon
USS *Bayfield* (HQ Ship)

FORCE O
Rear-Admiral John L. Hall Jr, USN
USS *Ancon* (HQ Ship)

FORCE G
**Commodore (1st Class)
Cyril Douglas-Pennent RN**
HMS *Bulolo* (HQ Ship)

FORCE J
**Commodore (1st Class)
George Oliver RN**
HMS *Hilary* (HQ Ship)

FORCE S
Rear-Admiral Arthur Talbot
HMS *Largs* (HQ Ship)

BOMBARDING FORCES

FORCE A (Supporting FORCE U)
Rear-Admiral Morton L. Deyo, USN,
USS *Tuscaloosa* (Cruiser)

FORCE C (Supporting FORCE O)
Rear-Admiral Carleton F. Bryant USN
USS *Texas* (Battleship)

FORCE K (Supporting FORCE G)

FORCE E (Supporting FORCE J)
Rear-Admiral Frederick Dalrymple-Hamilton
HMS Belfast (Cruiser)

FORCE D (Supporting FORCE S)
Rear-Admiral Wilfrid Patterson,
HMS *Mauritius* (Cruiser)

FOLLOW-UP FORCES

FORCE B
Commodore C. D. Edgar, USN

FORCE L
Rear-Admiral William Parry
USS *Maloy* (Destroyer)

ADMINISTRATION

Flag Officer West
Rear-Admiral J. Wilkes, USN

Commodore Depot Ships
Commodore (2nd Class) Hugh England, RN
HMS *Hawkins* (Cruiser)

Naval Officer-in-Charge (ashore)

Utah Area
Captain J. E Arnold, USNR

Omaha Area
Captain Camp, USN

Gold Area
Captain George Dolphin, RN

Juno Area
Captain Colin Maud, RN

Sword Area
Captain W. R. C. Leggatt, RN

ALLIED NAVAL FORCES

USA

Battleships

ARKANSAS	NEVADA	TEXAS

Cruisers

AUGUSTA	QUINCY	TUSCALOOSA

Destroyers

BALDWIN	BARTON	BUTLER
CARNICK	CHERARDI	CORRY
DOYLE	ELLYSON	ENDICOTT
FITCH	FORREST	FRANKFORD
GLENNON	HAMBLETON	HARDING
HERNDON	HOBSON	JEFFERS
LAFFEY	MCCOOK	MEREDITH
MURPHY	NELSON	O'BRIEN
PLUNKETT	RODMAN	SATTERLEE
SHUBRICK	THOMPSON	WALKER

HQ Ships

ANCON	BAYFIELD

Frigates

BORUM	MALOY

Patrol Craft

484	617	1233
552	618	1252
564	619	1261
565	1176	1262
567	1225	1263
568	1232	

Minesweepers

AUK	BROADBILL	CHICKADEE
NUTHATCH	PHEASANT	STAFF
SWIFT	THREAT	TIDE

FRENCH

Cruisers

GEORGES LEYGUES	MONTCALM

Destroyer
LA COMBATTANTE

Corvettes

ACONIT	RENONCULE

Frigates

LA DECOUVERTE	L'AVENTURE	LA SURPRISE
L'ESCARAMOUCHE		

POLISH

Cruiser
DRAGON

Destroyers

KRAKOWIAK	SLAZAK

NORWEGIAN

Destroyers

GLAISDALE	STORD	SVENNER

GREEK

Corvettes

KRIEZIS	TOMPAZIS

NETHERLANDS

Sloops

FLORES	SOEMBA

BRITISH

Battleships

RAMILLIES	RODNEY	WARSPITE

Cruisers

AJAX	ARETHUSA	ARGONAUT
BELFAST	BELLONA	BLACK PRINCE
DANAE	DIADEM	EMERALD
ENTERPRISE	FROBISHER	GLASGOW

Cruisers

HAWKINS	MAURITIUS	ORION
SCYLLA	SIRIUS	

Monitors

EREBUS	ROBERTS

HQ Ships

BULOLO	HILARY	LARGS

Destroyers

ALGONQUIN	ASHANTI	BEAGLE
BLANKNEY	BLEASDALE	BRISSENDEN
CAMPBELL	CATTISTOCK	COTSWOLD
COTTESMORE	DUFF	EGLINTON
FAULKNER	FURY	GRENVILLE
HAIDA	HAMBLEDON	HOTHAM
HURON	IMPULSIVE	ISIS
JERVIS	KELVIN	KEMPENFELT
MELBREAK	MIDDLETON	OBEDIENT
OFFA	ONSLAUGHT	ONSLOW
OPPORTUNE	ORIBI	ORWELL
PYTCHLEY	SAUMAREZ	SAVAGE
SCORPION	SCOURGE	SERAPIS
SIOUX	STEVENSTONE	SWIFT
TAYLBONT	TANATSIDE	TARTAR
ULSTER	ULYSSES	UNDAUNTED
UNDINE	URANIA	URCHIN
URSA	VENUS	VERSATILE
VERULAM	VESPER	VIDETTE
VIGILANT	VIMY	VIRAGO
VIVACIOUS	VOLUNTEER	WENSLEYDALE
WESTCOTT	WRESTLER	

Frigates

CHELMER	HALSTED	HOLMES
RETALICK	RIOU	ROWLEY
STAYNER	THORNBOROUGH	TORRINGTON
TROLLOPE	NITH	

Corvettes

ALBERNI	ARMERIA	AZALEA
CAMPANULA	CLARKIA	CLEMATIS
CLOVER	GODETIA	KITCHENER
LAVENDER	MIGNONETTE	MIMICO
NARCISSUS	OXLIP	PENNYWORT
PETUNIA	PINK	

Sloops

HIND	MAGPIE	REDPOLE
STORK		

Asdic Trawlers

BOMBARDIER	BRESSAY	COLL
DAMSAY	FIARAY	FLINT
FOULNESS	FUSILLIER	GAIRSAY
GATESHEAD	GRENADIER	HUGH WALPOLE
LANCER	LINDISFARNE	LORD AUSTIN
NORTHERN FOAM	NORTHERN GEM	NORTHERN GIFT
NORTHERN PRIDE	NORTHERN REWARD	NORTHERN SKY
NORTHERN SPRAY	NORTHERN SUN	NORTHERN WAVE
OLIVINA	SAPPER	SKYE
TEXADA	VELETA	VICTRIX

Fleet Minesweepers

ARDROSSAN	BANGOR	BEAUMARIS
BLACKPOOL	BLAIRMORE	BOOTLE
BOSTON	BRIDLINGTON	BRIDPORT
BRITOMART	CARAQUET	CATHERINE
CATO	COCKATRICE	COWICHAN
DORNOCK	DUNBAR	EASTBOURNE
ELGIN	FANCY	FORT WILLIAM
FORT YORK	FRASERBURGH	FRIENDSHIP
GAZELLE	GEORGIAN	GLEANER
GORGON	GOZO	GRECIAN
GUYSBOROUGH	HALCYON	HARRIER
HOUND	HUSSAR	HYDRA
ILFRACOMBE	JASON	KELLET
KENORA	LARNE	LENNOX
LIGHTFOOT	LLANDUDNO	LOYALTY
LYDD	LYME REGIS	MALPEQUE
MELITA	MILLTOWN	MINAS
ONYX	ORESTES	PANGBOURNE
PARRSBORO	PELORUS	PERSIAN
PICKLE	PINCHER	PIQUE
PLUCKY	POOLE	POSTILLION
QUALICUM	RATTLESNAKE	READY
RECRUIT	RIFLEMAN	ROMNEY
ROSS	RYE	SALAMANDER
SALTASH	SEAGULL	SEAHAM
SELKIRK	SHIPPIGAN	SIDMOUTH
SPEEDWELL	STEADFAST	SUTTON
TADOUSSAC	TENBY	VESTAL
WASAGA	WEDGEPORT	WHITEHAVEN
WORTHING		

Principal Vessels	324
Landing Ships and Craft	4126
Ancillary Ships and Craft	736
Merchant Ships	864
	6050

TOTAL STRENGTHS— OFFICERS AND MEN

Air	659,554
Land	1,931.885
Sea	285,000
TOTAL	2,876,439

BIBLIOGRAPHY

Ambrose, Stephen E. *The Supreme Commander: The War Years of General Dwight D. Eisenhower*. New York: Doubleday, 1970. *Pegasus Bridge*. London: Allen and Unwin, 1984.

'Anti-Invasion', in *The Royal Armoured Corps Journal, Vol. IV*, 1950.

Arnold, Gen. H. H. *Global Mission*. London: Hutchinson, 1951.

Aron, Robert. *De Gaulle Before Paris*. London: Putnam, 1962.

Austin, A. B. *We Landed at Dawn*. London: Victor Gollancz, 1943.

Babington Smith, Constance. *Evidence in Camera*. London: Chatto and Windus, 1958.

Baker, Carlos. *Ernest Hemingway: A Life Story*. London: William Collins, 1969.

Baldwin, Hanson W. *Battles Lost and Won*. London: Hodder and Stoughton, 1967.

Balfour, Michael. *Propaganda in War, 1939–45*. London: Routledge Kegan Paul, 1979.

Bedell-Smith, Gen. Walter. *Eisenhower's Six Great Decisions*. New York: Longmans Green, 1956.

Bekker, Cajus. *The Luftwaffe War Diaries*. New York: Doubleday, 1970.

Belfield, Eversley (with Hubert Essame). *The Battle for Normandy*. London: Batsford, 1965.

Bendiner, Elmer. *The Fall of Fortresses*. London: Souvenir Press, 1981.

Bennett, Ralph. *Ultra in the West*. London: Hutchinson, 1979.

Bird, Will R. *No Retreating Footsteps*. Halifax, N.S: Kentville Publishing Co., 1947.

Birdsall, Steve. *Log of the Liberators*. New York: Doubleday, 1973.

Blond, Georges. *Le Débarquement, 6 Juin, 1944*. Paris: Arthème Fayard, 1951.

Blue, Allan G. *B-24 Liberator*. New York: Scribner, 1977.

Blumenson, Martin. *Eisenhower*. New York: Ballantine Books, 1972.

Blumentritt, Gen. Günther. *Rundstedt, the Soldier and the Man*. (trans. Cuthbert Reavely). London: Odhams Press, 1952.

Boussel, Patrice. *The D-Day Beaches Pocket Guide*. London: Macdonald, 1965.

Bowyer, Michael A. F. *2 Group, RAF, 1936–45*. London: Faber and Faber, 1974.

Bradley, Gen. Omar N. *A Soldier's Story*. London: Eyre and Spottiswoode, 1952.

Bradley, Gen. Omar N. *A General's Life*. London: Sidgwick and Jackson, 1982.

Bramwell, James (with Hugh Mount). *Red (Cross) Devils*. Aldershot: privately printed, 1945.

Brendon, Piers. *Ike: The Life and Times of Dwight D. Eisenhower*. London: Secker and Warburg, 1987.

Brereton, Lt-Gen. Lewis H. *The Brereton Diaries*. New York: William Morrow, 1946.

Brown, John Mason. *Many a Watchful Night*. London: Hamish Hamilton, 1944.

Bruce, George. *Second Front Now!* London: Macdonald and Janes, 1979.

Bryant, Sir Arthur. *Triumph in the West, 1943–46*. London: William Collins, 1959.

Buckley, Christopher. *Norway–Commandos–Dieppe*. London: HMSO, 1951.

Bullock, Alan. *The Life and Times of Ernest Bevin*. Vols 1 and 2. London: William Heinemann, 1960, 1967.

Burgett, Donald R. *As Eagles Screamed*. New York: Bantam Books, 1979.

Burn, Lambton. *'Down Ramps!'* London: Carroll and Nicholson, 1947.

Burns, James McGregor. *Roosevelt: The Soldier of Freedom*. London: Weidenfeld and Nicolson, 1971.

Busch, Noel. 'Montgomery', in *Life* Magazine, New York, May 15, 1944.

Bush, Capt. Eric, RN *Bless Our Ship*. London: George Allen and Unwin, 1958.

Bushell, Thomas. *Eight Bells*. London: Trade and Travel Publications, 1950.

Butcher, Capt. Harry C., USNR. *Three Years With Eisenhower*. London: William Heinemann, 1946.

By Air to Battle: The Official Account of the British First and Sixth Airborne Divisions. London: HMSO, 1945.

Calder, Angus. *The People's War*. London: Jonathan Cape, 1969.

Canada's Battle in Normandy. Ottawa: King's Printer, 1946.

Capa, Robert. *Slightly Out of Focus*. New York: Henry Holt, 1947.

Carell, Paul. *Invasion–They're Coming!* London: George Harrap, 1962.

Carpenter, Iris. *No Woman's World*. Boston: Houghton Mifflin, 1946.

Chalfont, Alun. *Montgomery of Alamein*. London: Weidenfeld and Nicolson, 1976.

Chalmers, Rear-Admiral W. S. *Full Cycle: The Biography of Admiral Sir Bertram Home Ramsay*. London: Hodder and Stoughton, 1959.

Chaplin, W. W. *The Fifty-Three Days*. Indianapolis: Bobbs-Merrill, 1944.

Chatterton, Brig. George. *The Wings of Pegasus*. London: Macdonald, 1962.

Churchill, Rt Hon. Winston S. *The Second World War*. (6 vols). London: Cassell, 1948–54.

Clay, Maj. Ewart W. *The Path of the 50th*. Aldershot: Gale and Polden, 1950.

Clifton-James, M. E. *I Was Monty's Double*. London: Rider, 1954.

Clostermann, Pierre. *The Big Show*. London: Chatto and Windus, 1951.

Cole, Lt-Col. Howard N. *On Wings of Healing*. Edinburgh: William Blackwood, 1963.

Collier, Richard. *Ten Thousand Eyes*. London: William Collins, 1958.

Collier, Richard. *The War That Stalin Won*. London: Hamish Hamilton, 1983.

Collier Richard. *The Warcos*. London: Weidenfeld and Nicolson, 1989.

Collins, Gen. J. Lawton, *Lightning Joe*. Baton Rouge: Louisiana State University Press, 1979.

Colville, Sir John. *The Churchillians*. London: William Collins, 1981.

Cooper, John P. Jr. *The History of the 110th Field Artillery*. Baltimore: War Records Division, Maryland Historical Society, 1953.

Cooper, John St John. *Invasion! The D-Day Story*. London: Beaverbrook Newspapers, 1954.

Craven, Wesley F. and Cate, James L. *The Army Air Force in World War Two: Europe–Torch to Point Blank*. Chicago: University of Chicago Press, 1949.

Craven, Wesley F. and Cate, James L. *The Army Air Force in World War Two: Men and Planes*. Chicago: University of Chicago Press, 1955.

Crookenden, Napier. *Dropzone Normandy*. London: Ian Allan, 1976.

Cruickshank, Charles. *Deception in World War Two*. Oxford: Oxford University Press, 1979.

D-Day–the Normandy Invasion in Retrospect. Lawrence, Kansas: University Press of Kansas, 1971.

Danckwerts, P. V., 'King Red and Co.,' in *The Royal Armoured Corps Journal*, Vol. 1, July, 1946.

Danger Forward. Atlanta, Ga: Albert Love Enterprises, 1947.

Dank, Milton. *The Glider Gang*. London: Cassell, 1978.

Davis, Brian L. *US Airborne Forces Europe, 1942–45*. London: Arms and Armour Press, 1974.

Davis, Kenneth S. *The American Experience of War*. London: Secker and Warburg, 1967.

Dawson, W. Forrest. *Saga of the All-American (82nd Airborne Div.)* Atlanta, Ga: Albert Love Enterprises, 1946.

Deane, John R. *The Strange Alliance*. New York: Viking, 1947.

De Guingand, Maj.-Gen. Sir Francis. *Operation Victory*. London: Hodder and Stoughton, 1960.

Deighton, Len. *Goodbye, Mickey Mouse*. London: Hutchinson, 1982.

Dempsey, Lt-Gen. Miles. *Operations of the 2nd Army in Europe*. London: War Office, 1957.

Devlin, Gerard M. *Paratrooper*. London: Robson Books, 1979.

Devlin, Gerard M. *Silent Wings: The Story of The Glider Pilots of World War Two*. W. H. Allen, 1985.

Dunn, Walter Scott. *Second Front Now–1943*. Alabama: University of Alabama Press, 1980.

Dupuy, Colonel Trevor N. *A Genius For War*. London: Macdonald and Jane's, 1977.

Durnford-Slater, John. *Commando*. London: William Kimber, 1953.

Eden, Rt Hon. Anthony (Lord Avon). *Memoirs, Vol. II: The Reckoning*. London: Cassell, 1965.

Edwards, Commander Kenneth, RN. *Operation Neptune*. London: William Collins, 1946.

Ehrman, John. *Grand Strategy*. Vol. V. London: HMSO, 1956.

Eisenhower, Dwight D. *Crusade in Europe*. London: William Heinemann, 1949.

Eisenhower, Dwight D. *The Papers of Dwight David Eisenhower: The War Years*. (ed. Alfred D. Chandler Jr). (5 vols). Baltimore: Johns Hopkins Press, 1970.

Ellis, Maj. L. F. *Victory in the West*. Vol. I. London: HMSO, 1962.

Ellsberg, Rear-Admiral Edward. *The Far Shore*. London: Anthony Gibbs & Phillips, 1961.

Farago, Ladislas. *The Game of the Foxes*. New York: David McKay, 1971.

Fergusson, Sir Bernard. *The Black Watch and the King's Enemies*. London: William Collins, 1950.

Fergusson, Sir Bernard. *The Watery Maze*. London: William Collins, 1961.

Foot, M. R. D. *Resistance*. London: Eyre Methuen, 1976.

Fourth Infantry Division. Baton Rouge, La: Army and Navy Publishing Co., 1946.

Frankland, Noble. *The Bombing Offensive Against Germany*. London: Faber and Faber, 1965.

Fraser, Sir David. *Alanbrooke*. London: William Collins, 1982.

Fraser, Sir David. *And We Shall Shock Them*. London: Hodder and Stoughton, 1983.

Freeman, Roger A. *The Mighty Eighth*. London: MacDonald & Co., 1970.

Freidin, Seymour, and Richardson, William (ed). *The Fatal Decisions*. New York: William Sloane Associates, 1956.

From Texas to Teismach, the 457 AAA AW Battalion. Nancy, France: Imprimerie A. Humblot, 1945.

Gale, Lt-Gen. Sir Richard. *With the Sixth Airborne Division in Normandy*. London: Sampson Low, Marston, 1948.

Gale, Lt-Gen. Sir Richard. *Call To Arms*. London: Hutchinson, 1968.

Gant, Roland. *How Like a Wilderness*. London: Victor Gollancz, 1946.

Gavin, Lt-Gen. James M. *Airborne Warfare*. Washington, DC: Infantry Journal Press, 1947.

Gavin, Lt-Gen. James M. *On To Berlin*. New York: Viking, 1978.

Gellhorn, Martha. *The Face of War*. London: Rupert Hart-Davis, 1959.

Gilchrist, Donald. *Castle Commando*. Edinburgh: Oliver and Boyd, 1960.

Gilchrist, Donald. *Don't Cry For Me*. London: Robert Hale, 1982.

Gleeson, James and Waldron, Tom. *Now It Can Be Told*. London: Paul Elek, 1952.

Gleeson, James and Waldron, Tom. *The Frogmen*. London: Evans Bros. 1950.

Glover, Denis. *It Was D-Day*, in Penguin New Writing. London, No. 23, 1945.

Golding, William. *The Hot Gates*. London: Faber and Faber, 1965.

Goldsmith, Maurice. *Sage: a life of J. D. Bernal*. London: Hutchinson, 1980.

Golley, John. *The Big Drop: The Guns of Merville*. New York: Jane's, 1982.

Gunning, Hugh. *Borderers in Battle*. Berwick-on-Tweed: Martin and Co., 1948.

Hall, Grover C. Jr. *1000 Destroyed*. London: Putnam, 1962 edn.

Hamilton, Nigel. *Monty: Master of the Battlefield, 1942–1944*. London: Hamish Hamilton, 1983.

Hansen, Harold A. and others. *Fighting For Freedom*. Philadelphia: John C. Winston, 1947.

Harris, L. H. *Signal Venture*. Aldershot: Gale and Polden, 1951.

Harrison, Gordon A. *Cross-Channel Attack*. Washington, DC: Office of the Chief of Military History, Department of the Army, 1951.

Harrison, Michael. *Mulberry: The Return in Triumph*. London: W. H. Allen, 1965.

Hart, Capt. B. H. Liddell. *The Other Side of the Hill*. London: Cassell, 1951 edn.

Hartcup, Guy. *Code-Name Mulberry*. Newton Abbot, Devon: David and Charles, 1977.

Hartcup, Guy. *The Challenge of War*. Newton Abbot, Devon: David and Charles, 1970.

Harzstein, Robert E. *The War That Hitler Won*. London: Hamish Hamilton, 1979.

Hastings, Max. *Overlord*. London: Michael Joseph, 1984.

Haswell, Jock. *The Intelligence and Deception of the D-Day Landings*. London: B. T. Batsford, 1979.

Hawkins, Desmond. (with Donald Boyd) (ed). *BBC War Report*. London: Oxford University Press, 1946.

Hayn, Friedrich. *Die Invasion*. Heidelberg: Kurt Vowinckel Verlag, 1954.

Heavey, Brig.-Gen. William. *Down Ramp*. Washington, DC: Infantry Journal Press, 1947.

Hemingway, Ernest. *By-Line: Ernest Hemingway*. (ed. William White). New York: Bantam Books, 1968.

Herval, René. *Bataille de Normandie*. Paris: Editions de Notre-Dame, 1946.

Hess, William T. *P-47–Thunderbolt*. London: Ian Allan, 1976.

Hickey, Rev. R. M. *The Scarlet Dawn*. Campbellton, NB: Tribune Publishers, 1949.

Hickling, Vice-Admiral Harold. *Sailor at Sea*. London: William Kimber, 1965.

Hinsley, Professor F. H. and others. *British Intelligence in the Second World War, Vol. II*. London: HMSO, 1981.

POPULAR SONGS AND FILMS ON THE EVE OF D-DAY

SOME OF THE SONGS

I Couldn't Sleep a Wink Last Night
Mairzy Doats (and Dozy Doats)
Besame Mucho
A Lovely Way to Spend an Evening
Shoo Shoo, Baby
No Love, No Nothin'
My Heart Tells Me
I Love You
I'll Get By
Long Ago and Far Away
Do Nothing Till You Hear from Me
San Fernando Valley

SOME OF THE FILMS

Gung Ho
Song of Russia
The Heavenly Body
The Desert Song
Charlie Chan in the Secret Service
A Guy Named Joe
Buffalo Bill
Tender Comrade
Four Jills and a Jeep
Calling Dr Death
Hi Ya Sailor
The Purple Heart
Andy Hardy's Blonde Trouble
Fanny By Gaslight
Destination Tokyo
Demobbed

History in the Writing. New York: Duell, Sloane and Pearce, 1945.

Hobbs, J.P. *Dear General: General Eisenhower's Wartime Letters to Marshall*. Baltimore, Md: Johns Hopkins Press, 1971.

Hollis, Lt-Gen. Sir Leslie, with James Leasor. *War at the Top*. London: Michael Joseph, 1959.

Hollister, Paul, and Robert Strunsky. (ed) *D-Day Through Victory in Europe*. New York: Columbia Broadcasting System, 1945.

Holman, Gordon. *Stand By To Beach!* London: Hodder and Stoughton, 1944.

Howard, Michael. *British Intelligence in the Second World War*, Vol. V. London: HMSO, 1990.

Howarth, David. *The Dawn of D-Day*. London: William Collins, 1959.

Hoyt, Edwin P. *The Invasion Before Normandy: The Secret Battle of Slapton Sands*. London: Robert Hale, 1987.

Huston, James H. *Out of the Blue*. West Lafayette, Ind: Purdue University Press, 1972.

Infield, Glenn. *Big Week*. London: NEL, 1976.

Ingersoll, Ralph. *Top Secret*. New York: Harcourt Brace, 1946.

Irving, David. *The Rise and Fall of the Luftwaffe*. London: Weidenfeld and Nicolson, 1974.

Irving, David. *The Trail of the Fox*. London: Weidenfeld and Nicolson, 1977.

Irving, David. *The War Between the Generals*. London: Allen Lane, 1981.

Jablonski, Edward. *Flying Fortress*. New York: Doubleday, 1965.

Jablonski, Edward (with Lowell Thomas). *Doolittle*. New York: Doubleday, 1969.

Jackson, Lt-Col. G.S. *Operations of Eighth Corps*. London: St. Clement's Press, 1948.

Johnson, Franklyn A. *One More Hill*. New York: Funk and Wagnalls, 1949.

Jefferson, Alan. *Assault on the Guns of Merville*. London: John Murray, 1987.

Johnson, Garry (with Christopher Dunphie). *Brightly Shone the Dawn*. London: Frederick Warne, 1980.

Johnson, Group Captain J.E. *Wing Leader*. New York: Ballantine Books, 1957.

Johnson, Robert S. (with Martin Caidin). *Thunderbolt*. New York: Ballantine Books, 1958.

Jones, Prof. R.V. *Most Secret War*. London: Hamish Hamilton, 1978.

Kahn, David. *Hitler's Spies*. London: Hodder and Stoughton, 1978.

Kaplan, Philip (with Rex Oliver Smith). *One Last Look*. New York: Abbeville Press, 1983.

Keegan, John. *Six Armies in Normandy*. London: Jonathan Cape, 1982.

Kennedy, Maj.-Gen. Sir John. *The Business of War*. London: Hutchinson, 1957.

Kieffer, Cdt Philippe. *Beret Vert*. Paris: Editions France-Empire, 1962.

Koskimaki, George E. *D-Day with the Screaming Eagles*. New York: Vantage Press, 1970.

Ladd, James. *Commandos and Rangers of World War II*. New York: St Martin's Press, 1978.

Ladd, James. *Assault From The Sea*. 1939–45. Newton Abbot, Devon: David and Charles, 1976.

Lamb, Richard. *Montgomery in Europe*. London: Buchan and Enright, 1983.

Lambermont, Paul. *Lorraine Squadron*. London: Cassell 1956.

Lane, Ronald L. *Rudder's Rangers*. Manassas, Va: Ranger Association, 1979.

LeMay, Gen. Curtis E. (with Mackinlay Kantor). *Mission with LeMay*. New York: Doubleday, 1965.

Lemonnier-Gruhier, François. *La Brèche de Sainte-Marie-du-Mont*. Paris: Editions Spes, 1949.

Lipscomb, Frank. *The D-Day Story*. Southsea, Hants: R. Matthews and S.W.P. Barrell, 1966.

Lockhart, Robert Bruce. *Comes The Reckoning*. London: Putnam, 1947.

Lockhart, Robert Bruce. *The Marines Were There*. London: Putnam, 1950.

Longmate, Norman. *How We Lived Then*. London: Hutchinson, 1971.

Longmate, Norman. *The GIs: The Americans in Britain, 1942–45*. London: Hutchinson, 1975.

Lovat, Lord. *March Past*. London: Weidenfeld and Nicolson, 1978.

Lowman, Major F.H. 'Dropping into Normandy' in *The Oxfordshire and Bucks Light Infantry Journal*, January, 1951.

McBryde, Brenda. *A Nurse's War*. London: Chatto and Windus, 1979.

McDougall, Murdoch C. *Swiftly They Struck: The Story of No. 4 Commando*. London: Odhams Press, 1954.

McGivern, Cecil. *The Harbour Called Mulberry*. London: Pendulum Publications, 1945.

McLachlan, Donald. *Room 39*. London: Weidenfeld and Nicolson, 1968.

Mackesy, Kenneth. *Armoured Crusader: General Sir Percy Hobart*. London: Hutchinson, 1967.

Madden, Capt. J.R. 'Ex Coelis', in *The Canadian Army Journal*, Vol. XI, No. 1.

Maisky, Ivan. *Memoirs of a Soviet Ambassador, 1939–43*. London: Hutchinson, 1967.

Majdalany, Fred. *The Fall of Fortress Europe*. London: Hodder and Stoughton, 1969.

Manchester, William. *The Glory and the Dream*. London: Michael Joseph, 1975.

Marshall, S.L.A. *Men Against Fire*. New York: William Morrow, 1947.

Marshall, S.L.A. *Night Drop*. London: Macmillan, 1962.

Melville, Alan. *First Tide*. London: Skeffington, 1945.

Messenger, Charles. *The Commandos, 1940–1946*. London: William Kimber, 1985.

Michie, Allan A. *Honour For All*. London: George Allen and Unwin, 1946.

Michie, Allan A. *The Invasion of Europe*. London: George Allen and Unwin, 1965.

Mills-Roberts, Derek. *Clash By Night*. London: William Kimber, 1956.

Monks, Noel. *Eye-Witness*. London: Frederick Muller, 1955.

Montgomery, Field-Marshal The Viscount. *The Memoirs of Field-Marshal Montgomery of Alamein*. London: William Collins, 1958.

Moorehead, Alan. *Eclipse*. London: Hamish Hamilton, 1945.

Morgan, Lt-Gen. Sir Frederick. *Overture To Overlord*. London: Hodder and Stoughton, 1950.

Morgan, Lt-Gen. Sir Frederick. *Peace and War*. London: Hodder and Stoughton, 1961.

Morison, Samuel Eliot. *United States Naval Operations in World War Two*, Vol. XI. Boston: Little, Brown, 1957.

Mosley, Leonard. *Backs To The Wall*. London: Weidenfeld and Nicolson, 1971.

Mosley, Leonard. *The Reich Marshal*. London: Weidenfeld and Nicolson, 1974.

Mrazak, Col. James E. *The Glider War*. New York: St Martin's Press, 1975.

Munro, Ross. *Gauntlet To Overlord*. Toronto: The Macmillan Company of Canada, 1945.

Newnham, Group Captain Maurice. *Prelude to Glory*. London: Sampson Low, Marston, 1947.

Nightingale, Lt-Col. P. R. *A History of the East Yorkshire Regiment*. London: William Sessions, 1952.

Norman, Albert. *Operation Overlord*. Harrisburg, Penna: The Military Service Co., 1952.

'Normandy's Made-in-England Harbours,' in *The National Geographic Magazine*, Washington, DC, May, 1945.

North, John. *North-West Europe, 1944–45*. London: HMSO 1953.

Norton, G. G. *The Red Devils*. London: Leo Cooper, 1971.

Oldfield, Barney. *Never a Shot in Anger*. New York: Duell, Sloan and Pearce, 1956.

Otway, Col. Terence. *The Second World War, 1939–45—Airborne Forces*. London: War Office, 1946.

Palmer, Robert R. and Keast, William R. *The US Army in World War Two: The Procurement and Training of Ground Combat Troops*. Washington, DC: Office of the Chief of Military History, 1948.

Panter-Downes, Mollie. *London War Notes, 1939–45*. London: Longmans, 1972.

Parkinson, Roger. *A Day's March Nearer Home*. London: Hart-Davis, MacGibbon, 1974.

Pawle, Gerald. *The Secret War*. London: George Harrap, 1956.

Pawle, Gerald. *The War and Colonel Warden*. London: George Harrap, 1963.

Peis, Gunther. *The Mirror of Deception*. London: Weidenfeld and Nicolson, 1977.

Perrault, Gilles. *The Secrets of D-Day*. London: Arthur Barker, 1965.

Pogue, Forrest C. *The Supreme Command*. Washington, DC: Office of the Chief of Military History, Department of the Army, 1946.

Pogue, Forrest C. *George C. Marshall*, Vols. II and III. New York: Viking, 1965, 1973.

Popov, Dusko. *Spy/Counterspy*. London: Weidenfeld and Nicolson, 1974.

Priller, Josef. *Geschichte eines Jagdgeschwaders*. Heidelberg: Vowinckel Verlag, 1962.

Pyle, Ernie. *Brave Men*. New York: Henry Holt, 1944.

Ranger—a short history. Fort Benning, Ga: US Army Infantry School, 1962.

Rapport, Leonard, and Northwood, Arthur, Jr. *Rendezvous with Destiny*. Washington, DC: Infantry Journal Press, 1948.

Reit, Seymour. *Masquerade*. London: Robert Hale, 1979.

Reyburn, Wallace. *Rehearsal for Invasion*. London: George G. Harrap, 1943.

Reynolds, Quentin. *The Amazing Mr Doolittle*. London: Cassell, 1954.

Reynolds, Quentin. *Dress Rehearsal*. London: Angus and Robertson, 1943.

Ridgway, Gen. Matthew B. *Soldier: The Memoirs of Matthew B. Ridgway*. New York: Harper & Bros., 1956.

Robertson, Terence. *Dieppe: The Shame and the Glory*. London: Hutchinson, 1963.

Rommel Papers, The. (ed. B. H. Liddell Hart). London: William Collins, 1953.

Rooney, Andrew A. *The Fortunes of War*. Boston: Little, Brown, 1962.

Ruge, Rear-Admiral Friedrich. *Rommel in Normandy*. London: Macdonald, 1979.

Ruppenthal, Major Roland G. *Utah to Cherbourg*. Washington, DC: Office of the Chief of Military History, Department of the Army, 1946.

Ryan, Cornelius. *The Longest Day*. London: Victor Gollancz, 1960.

Salmond, J. B. *The History of the 51st Highland Division, 1939–45*. Edinburgh: William Blackwood, 1953.

Samain, Bryan. *Commando Men*. London: Stevens & Sons, 1948.

Sampson, Brig.-Gen. Francis L. *Paratrooper Padre*. Washington, DC: Catholic University of America Press, 1948.

Saunders, Hilary St George. *The Green Beret*. London: Michael Joseph, 1949.

Saunders, Hilary St George. *The Red Beret*. London: Michael Joseph, 1950.

Scarfe, Norman. *Assault Division*. London: William Collins, 1947.

von Schweppenburg, Gen. Baron Leo Geyr, 'Invasion without Laurels', in *An Cosantoir*, Vol. IX, No. 12 and Vol. X, No. 1, Dublin, 1949–50.

Scott, Desmond. *Typhoon Pilot*. London: Secker and Warburg, 1982.

Sergueiev, Lily. *For Secret Service Rendered*. London: William Kimber, 1968.

Shapiro, Lionel. *The Sixth of June*. London: William Collins, 1956.

Shulman, Milton. *Defeat in the West*. London: Secker & Warburg, 1947.

Smith, Norman. *Tank Soldier*. Lewes, Sussex: The Book Guild, 1989.

Snyder, Louis Lee (ed.). *Masterpieces of War Reporting*. New York: Messner, 1962.

Speer, Albert. *Inside the Third Reich*. (trans. Richard and Clara Winston). London: Weidenfeld and Nicolson, 1970.

Speidel, Lt-Gen. Dr Hans. *We Defended Normandy*. London: Michael Jenkins, 1951.

Stacey, Col. C. P. *The Canadian Army, 1939–45*, Vol. III. Ottawa: King's Printers, 1960.

Stafford, David. *Britain and European Resistance*. London: Macmillan, 1980.

Stagg, James M. *Forecast for Overlord*. New York: W. W. Norton, 1972.

Stanford, Cdr Alfred, USNR. *Force Mulberry*. New York: William Morrow, 1951.

Strong, Maj.-Gen. Sir Kenneth. *Intelligence at the Top*. New York: Doubleday, 1969.

Strutton, Bill, and Pearson, Michael. *The Secret Invaders*. London: Hodder and Stoughton, 1958.

Synge, Capt. W. A. T. *The Story of the Green Howards*. Richmond, Yorks: The Green Howards, 1952.

Taylor, Charles H. *Omaha Beachhead*. Washington, DC: Office of the Chief of Military History, Department of the Army, 1946.

Taylor, J. E. *The Last Passage*. London: George Allen and Unwin, 1946.

Taylor, Gen. Maxwell D. *Swords and Ploughshares*. New York: W. W. Norton, 1972.

Tedder, Marshal of the RAF Lord. *With Prejudice*. London: Cassell, 1966.

Terkel, Studs. *The Good War*. London: Hamish Hamilton, 1984.

Thompson, Leroy. *The All Americans: the 82nd Airborne*. Newton Abbot, Devon: David and Charles, 1988.

Toland, John. *Adolf Hitler*. New York: Doubleday, 1976.

Trevor, Elleston. *The Killing Ground*. London: William Heinemann, 1956.

Tugwell, Maurice. *Airborne to Battle*. London: William Kimber, 1971.

Turner, John Frayn. *Invasion 1944*. London: George Harrap, 1959.

Turner, Lt-Col. Richard E. *Mustang Pilot*. London: William Kimber, 1970.

Tute, Warren (with John Costello and Terry Hughes). *D-Day*. London: Sidgwick and Jackson, 1974.

Verney, Maj.-Gen. G. L. *The Desert Rats*. London: Hutchinson, 1955.

Vian, Admiral Sir Philip. *Action this Day*. London: Frederick Muller, 1960.

Walker, David. *Lunch with a Stranger*. London: Allan Wingate, 1957.

Warlimont, Gen. Walter. *Inside Hitler's Headquarters*. (trans. R. H. Barry). New York: Frederick Praeger, 1966.

Warner, Philip. *The D-Day Landings*. London: William Kimber, 1980.

Watney, John. *The Enemy Within*. London: Hodder and Stoughton, 1946.

Watts, James Cadman. *Surgeon at War*. London: George Allen and Unwin, 1955.

Watts, Stephen. *Moonlight on a Lake in Bond Street*. London: The Bodley Head, 1961.

Weigley, Russell F. *Eisenhower's Lieutenants*. London: Sidgwick and Jackson, 1981.

Weller, George. *The Story of the Paratroops*. New York: Random House, 1958.

Wernher, Maj.-Gen. Sir Harold. *World War Two: Personal Experiences*. London: privately printed, 1950.

Wertenbaker, Charles Christian. *Invasion!* New York: D. Appleton-Century, 1944.

West, Nigel. *MI5*. London: Weidenfeld and Nicolson, 1981.

Westphal, Gen. Siegfried. *The German Army in the West*. London: Cassell, 1951.

Wilson, Andrew. *Flame Thrower*. London: William Kimber, 1956.

Winfield, Rex. *The Sky Belongs To Them*. London: William Kimber, 1976.

Woollcombe, Robert. *Lion Rampant*. London: Leo Cooper, 1970.

Wright, Laurence. *The Wooden Sword*. London: Elek Books, 1967.

Wykeham, Peter. *Fighter Command*. London: Putnam, 1960.

Young, Peter. *Storm From The Sea*. London: William Kimber, 1956.

Ziegler, Philip. *Mountbatten*. London: William Collins, 1985.

MARGIN CREDITS

The author and publisher would like to thank all the writers, publishers and literary representatives who have given permission to quote material. The writers are listed in alphabetical order below:

Alexander Baron: extract from *From the City, From the Plough*, Jonathan Cape, 1948, reprinted by permission of Lemon, Unna Durbridge, Ltd. Piers Brendon: extract from *Ike: The Life and Times of Dwight D. Eisenhower*, reprinted by permission of Martin Secker and Warburg Ltd. Norman Cameron: extract from 'The Verdict', from *Collected Poems*, The Hogarth Press, 1957, reprinted by permission of Random Century Group Ltd. Robert A. Chaloner: extract from 'Home Front—1942', from *More Poems From the Forces*, ed. K. Rhys, Routledge, 1943, reprinted by permission of Curtis Brown Ltd. Timothy Corsellis: extract from 'News Reel of Embarkation', from *Poems From the Forces*, ed. K. Rhys, Routledge, 1941; R. N. Currey: extract from 'Training Depot', from *This Other Planet*, Routledge, 1945; Keith Douglas: extracts from 'Actors Waiting in the Wings of Europe' and 'Sportsmen', © Marie J. Douglas, 1978, reprinted from *Complete Poems* (ed. Desmond Graham), 1978, reprinted by permission of the Oxford University Press. F. Scott Fitzgerald: extract from *The Crackup* (ed. Edmund Wilson), New Directions, New York. Francis Gelder: extract from 'A Ballad of 1941', from *Poems of the War by Younger Poets*, ed. Patricia Ledward and Christopher Strang, Cambridge University Press, 1942. Wilfrid W. Gibson: extract from 'Lament', from *Collected Poems*, reprinted by permission of Macmillan London Ltd. Christopher Hassall: extract from 'Night Convoy', from *The Slow Night*, Arthur Barker, 1949. A. P. Herbert: 'The Harbour', from *Light the Lights*, Methuen, 1945, reprinted by permission of A. P. Watt Ltd on behalf of Crystal Hale and Jocelyn Herbert. John Hersey: extract from *The War Lover*, Alfred A. Knopf Inc., 1959. Randall Jarrell: 'The Death of the Ball Turret Gunner' and extract from 'Losses', from *Collected Poems*, 1948,

reprinted by permission of Faber and Faber Ltd. Sidney Keyes: extract from 'Moonlight Night on the Port' from *Complete Poems*, Routledge, 1988. John Manifold: extract from 'Camouflage', from *Poems From the Forces*, ed. K. Rhys, Routledge, 1941. Edna St Vincent Millay: extract from 'Poem and Prayer for and Invading Army', from *Collected Poems*, ed. Norma Millay, Harper Bros, 1956, reprinted by permission of A. M. Heath Ltd. Nicholas Monsarrat: extract from *The Cruel Sea*, Cassell, 1953. Alfred Noyes: extract from 'The Highwayman', from *Collected Poems*, John Murray, 1941. Mollie Panter-Downes: extract from *London War Notes*, Farrar, Straus & Giroux Inc., 1972, reprinted by permission of Laurence Pollinger Ltd. John Pudney: extract from 'Security', from *Ten Summers*, The Bodley Head, 1942, reprinted by permission of David Higham Associates Ltd. Anthony Richardson: extract from 'To You Who Were Not With Us', from *Air Force Poetry*, ed. John Pudney and Henry Treece, The Bodley Head, 1944. Joyce Rowe: 'Dieppe', from *Poems for France* (ed. Nancy Cunard, 'La France Libre', 1944. 'Sagittarius' (Olga Katzin): 'Song Before Sunrise', from *Quiver's Choice*, 1945, reprinted by permission of Jonathan Cape Ltd. Irwin Shaw: extract from *The Young Lions*, © Irwin Shaw, Jonathan Cape, 1950, reprinted by permission of Tessa Sayle Agency. Stevie Smith: 'Not Waving But Drowning', from *The Collected Poems*, Penguin 20th Century Classics, reprinted by permission of James MacGibbon as executor. Sir Stephen Spender: extract from 'I think continually . . .', from *Collected Poems*, 1955, reprinted by permission of Faber and Faber Ltd. Ruthven Todd: extract from 'It Was Easier', from *Poetry in Wartime*, ed. M. J. Tambimuttu, Nicholson and Watson, 1942.

NOTE Although every attempt has been made to clear copyright, in some instances it has been difficult to track down copyright holders. The publishers apologize for any omissions.

INDEX

221

ACKNOWLEDGEMENTS

We have to thank the many D-Day planners and veterans, in some instances their families and widows, whose help over the years has proved invaluable. Without their aid and encouragement, their loans of photographs and personal memorabilia, together with countless hours of interviews, this picture of D-Day as it seemed to those who took part in it would not have been possible. Some of the people cited here are no longer living, but all those listed below contributed enormously to the final outcome:

Field-Marshal Lord Alanbrooke, Hildegard Anderson, Simon Anglim (National Airborne Museum), Albert Augé, Professor John L. Austin, Robert Barr, General Günther Blumentritt, Henry Brown, MBE (Commando Association), Donald R. Burgett, Captain Eric Bush, RN, Jane Carmichael (Imperial War Museum), Pat Collier, Michael Conway (1940 Association), Elsie Couch, Christopher Coughlan, Professor Hervé Cras (Service Historique de la Marine, Paris), Matthew Davies, Lt-Gen. Sir Miles Dempsey, André Dewavrin, Michael Dowdell (Torquay Central Library), Odette Duchez, Léon Dumis, General Dwight D. Eisenhower, Christopher Fagg, André Farine, Monica and Mike Fisher, Dr Michael Fopp (RAF Museum), General Adolf Galland, A.D. Gilbert (D-Day and Normandy Fellowship), John Gilbert, Léonard Gille, Dany and Marcel Girard, Jonathan Grimwood, André Heintz, John J. Honalsey (Chief, Historical Reference Branch, US Army Military History Institute, Carlisle Barracks, Pa), Lt-Col. Asbury H. Jackson (US Army Historical Division), Professor R.V. Jones, Louis F. Lisko (Ranger Battalions Association of World War II), Daniel Lomenech, Jean Marion, Georges Mercader, Professor Henri Michel, Field-Marshal Lord Montgomery of Alamein, Lt-Gen. Sir Frederick Morgan, Elizabeth Murray, Bruce Ogden Smith, MM, Captain H. Ryan Price, Tip Randolph (National Secretary, World War II Glider Pilots Association), Gilbert Renault, Ian G. Robertson (National Army Musuem), Professor Dr Jürgen Rohwer (Bibliothek für Zeitgeschichte, Stuttgart), Mrs Margaret Rudder, General Hans von Salmuth, Dr Eugen Schmalz (Bundesarchiv-Koblenz), Michael Shaw, Ray Shaw, Captain James Stopford, RN, Dr Roderick Suddaby and Simon Robbins (Imperial War Museum), General Maxwell D. Taylor, Admiral Sir William Tennant, RN, Marshal of the RAF Lord Tedder, Jeanne Verinaud, Suzanne and Larry Viner (The Advertising Archives), Stu Voight (101st Airborne Museum, Fort Campbell, Ky), Ann Walker, Brigadier E.T. Williams, Brigadier Peter Young DSO, MC.